Romewalks

This series originated with PARISWALKS by
Alison and Sonia Landes.
Other titles in the series include:

LONDONWALKS by *Anton Powell*
JERUSALEMWALKS by *Nitza Rosovsky*
FLORENCEWALKS by *Anne Holler*
VIENNAWALKS by *J. Sydney Jones*

ANYA M. SHETTERLY

Romewalks

Photographs by Anya M. Shetterly

An Owl Book
A New Republic Book
Henry Holt and Company
New York

To the many friends who were there for me

Published by Henry Holt and Company, Inc.,
115 West 18th Street, New York, New York 10011.
Published in Canada by Fitzhenry & Whiteside Limited,
91 Granton Drive, Richmond Hill, Ontario L4B 2N5.

Library of Congress Cataloging-in-Publication Data
Shetterly, Anya M.
Romewalks.
"A New Republic book."
Includes index.
1. Rome (Italy)—Description—1975—Tours.
I. Title.   II. Title: Romewalks.
DG804.S45   1984   914.5′63204927   83-12938
ISBN 0-8050-0553-6 (An Owl Book: pbk.)

Henry Holt books are available at special discounts
for bulk purchases for sales promotions, premiums,
fund-raising, or educational use. Special editions or
book excerpts can also be created to specification.

For details contact: Special Sales Director,
Henry Holt and Company, Inc., 115 West 18th Street,
New York, New York 10011.

Designed by Jacqueline Schuman
Maps by David Lindroth

Printed in the United States of America
Recognizing the importance of preserving the written word,
Henry Holt and Company, Inc., by policy, prints all of its
first editions on acid-free paper. ∞

5   7   9   10   8   6   4

Grateful acknowledgment is made for use of
portions of "My Rome" by Muriel Spark.
Copyright © 1983 by The New York Times
Company. Reprinted by permission.

Contents

Acknowledgements   xi

Introduction   1

Information and Advice   7
Before You Go 7 / General Information *10* /
Accommodations *16* / Transportation *17* /
Food and Drink *20* / Tipping *23* /
Telephone, Telegraph, Post Office *24* /
Money and Banking *25* /
Shopping *25* / Emergencies *27* /
A Word of Warning *27* /
Glossary of Architectural Terms *28* /
A Brief History of Rome *30* /

Walk 1
The Artisans and the Bourgeoisie:
Around the Piazza Navona
39

Walk 2
The Empire, the Church, and the Jews:
The Jewish Ghetto
85

Walk 3
Streets of the Papacy:
The Neighborhood of the Campo dei Fiori
131

Walk 4
A Village Within the City:
The Island and Southern Trastevere
189

Restaurants and Shops   227
Index   235

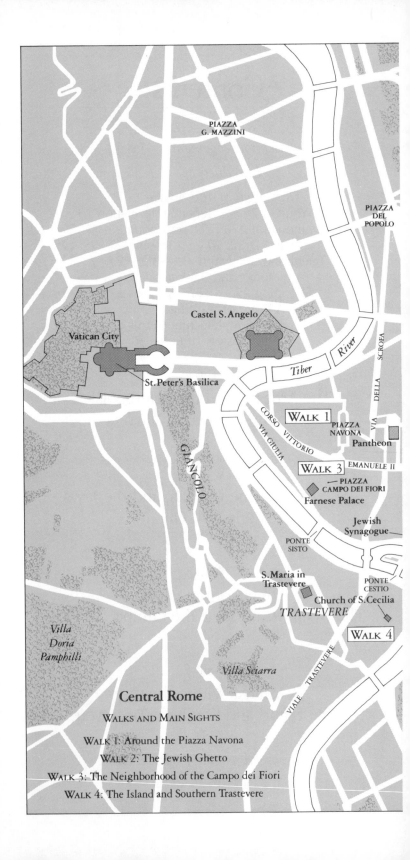

PIAZZA
G. MAZZINI

PIAZZA
DEL
POPOLO

Vatican City

Castel S. Angelo

Tiber River

VIA DELLA SCROFA

St. Peter's Basilica

WALK 1

PIAZZA
NAVONA

Pantheon

CORSO VITTORIO

VIA GIULIA

GIANCOLO

WALK 3 EMANUELE II

PIAZZA
CAMPO DEI FIORI

Farnese Palace

Jewish
Synagogue

PONTE
SISTO

S. Maria in
Trastevere

PONTE
CESTIO

Church of S. Cecilia

TRASTEVERE

WALK 4

*Villa
Doria
Pamphilli*

Villa Sciarra

VIALE TRASTEVERE

Central Rome

WALKS AND MAIN SIGHTS

WALK 1: Around the Piazza Navona

WALK 2: The Jewish Ghetto

WALK 3: The Neighborhood of the Campo dei Fiori

WALK 4: The Island and Southern Trastevere

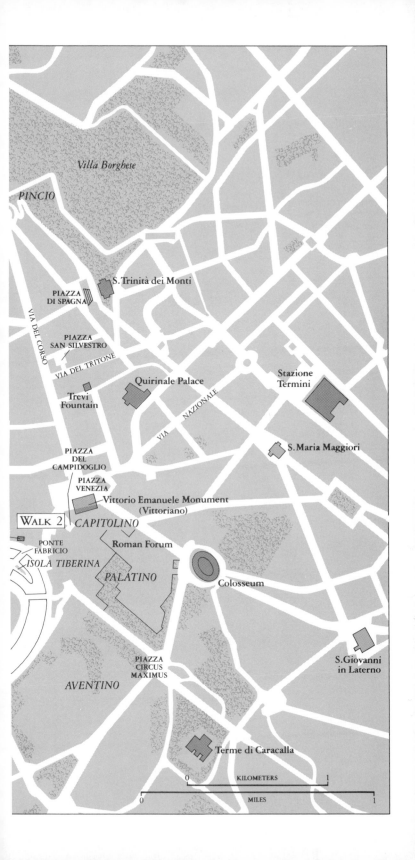

Villa Borghese

PINCIO

S. Trinità dei Monti

PIAZZA
DI SPAGNA

VIA DEL CORSO

PIAZZA
SAN SILVESTRO

VIA DEL TRITONE

Quirinale Palace

Stazione
Termini

Trevi
Fountain

VIA NAZIONALE

S. Maria Maggiori

PIAZZA
DEL
CAMPIDOGLIO

PIAZZA
VENEZIA

Vittorio Emanuele Monument
(Vittoriano)

WALK 2

CAPITOLINO

Roman Forum

PONTE
FABRICIO

ISOLA TIBERINA

PALATINO

Colosseum

S. Giovanni
in Laterno

PIAZZA
CIRCUS
MAXIMUS

AVENTINO

Terme di Caracalla

0   KILOMETERS   1

0   MILES   1

Acknowledgments

This book would not have been written without the enthusiasm, directions, and stories of many Romans: friends, acquaintances, and passersby. I also want to thank the staffs of the American Academy Library, the Ernesto Besso Foundation, the Archives of the City of Rome, and the Jewish Museum.

Most important are the thanks I owe to people who gave me the support and refuge I needed to finish this project: Tita and Steve Ostrow, Henry Berg, Harry Hives, John and Maryon Drenttel, and my parents, Pat and Howard Shetterly.

I am grateful to Marty Peretz for suggesting the idea of *Romewalks*; To Marc Granetz, the editor of this book, for his patience and good humor; and to Pamela Christy, George Watkins, and Kevin Scott for their help.

Before I left for Rome, Kate Costello said, "You should write a book." Little did she realize that she would one day help me type the final draft. Thanks for the hint, the bed, and the typing.

Finally, a warm thanks to Carolyn Ervin, ever the best of friends.

Romewalks

Introduction

Henry James's reaction was: "It beats everything: it leaves the Rome of your fancy—your education—nowhere. . . . I went reeling and moaning through the streets in a fever of enjoyment . . . the effect is something indescribable." Rome has provoked this kind of excitement in many people, myself included. To a large degree this response is due to surprise—there is just so much more here than we ever expect—but it is also caused by confusion. Scattered throughout the city's historic center are layers of images associated with two and a half millennia of history. Even when something appears to belong to a definite period, a second glance often betrays a bewildering span of centuries. Nowhere in central Rome is there a sense of a well-planned city; instead, it is a fragmented and untidy city which has been that way since the days of the Roman republic. While the urban plans of the sixteenth and seventeenth centuries placed a great value on organization, they were ultimately exuberant and far from comprehensive. Especially today, after the spotty additions of the republicans at the turn of the century and the Fascists in the 1920s and 1930s, the effect is one of a careless blend of contrasting plans, styles, and ideas. This collage, so dominant in the visual landscape, is Rome's fascination. It bespeaks the very spirit of the city, for Rome is not just a monument to history, art, architecture, or Western civilization; it is a city of people who have used and reused their monuments and buildings to create pockets of community life.

That these communities have endured makes Rome different from most cities and adds an emotional richness to her already recognized physical drama and beauty. Her neighborhoods are never defined simply by socioeconomic or physical boundaries. Although the city is formally divided into twenty-two quarters, or *riones*, some of which have existed since the Roman Empire, these are artificial distinctions. Instead, neighborhoods are defined more by shared culture

1

and history. And, because it is Rome, by the buildings themselves.

While not a comprehensive guide, this book presents a specific and intimate view of Rome, one that derives from my own experience of the city. The four walks here through neighborhoods of the historic center of Rome are among the most satisfying ways to learn about the city's past and present. They are also a good way to organize the myriad images and to understand the many transitions in the city's growth. Rome has so much to offer, and these walks will satisfy your desire to sightsee, shop, and just wander. The streets themselves are like display cases, inviting your close attention.

I have chosen four neighborhoods to explore: the Piazza Navona, the Jewish Ghetto, the Campo dei Fiori, and the southern end of Trastevere. Each of these neighborhoods shows a different perspective on the life and history of the city. Each is also rich in tradition, culture, architecture, and charm.

The neighborhood of the Piazza Navona forms a semicircle around one of Rome's most important and beautiful landmarks. Located in the heart of the ancient Roman Campus Martius, this neighborhood of baroque churches and intimate, narrow streets packed with small houses reflects the area's status as a prosperous bourgeois and artisan quarter dating from the late sixteenth century. Today it is still considered an artisan district and one of the most elegant sections of central Rome. For the last two centuries this neighborhood has been famous for its antique trade; the main streets are filled with fancy antique shops, and on the smaller side streets are numerous artisan shops specializing in the making or restoring of antique furniture and art. It is an education to pass these studios, which during the summer expand onto the cobblestone streets. One learns to appreciate the painstaking labor involved in refurbishing an old desk encrusted with aged lacquer, dirt, and paint; or that of chiseling away at a block of dark pink marble to form, eventually, a bust of one of the heroes of the Roman Empire. If you're lucky you may even observe a master teaching his apprentice how to wax the back of a canvas painting that is being rematted.

In her book *Rome and a Villa*, Eleanor Clark says of

the old Jewish Ghetto that "nowhere in Rome is one so acutely aware of the ancient city that lies buried beneath." This is a part of town where the ruins of the Roman Empire blend dramatically and unpretentiously with the multifaceted cityscape of modern Rome. During the Roman Empire this area was crowned with important buildings: the Circus of Flaminius, used for horse races and triumphal court; the Portico d'Ottavia, a meeting place that included temples, libraries, and exhibition halls; the Teatro di Marcello, said to be the model for the Colosseum; and the Foro Holitorium, the vegetable market and its adjoining temples. Except for the Circus of Flaminius, the ruins of this period are not only visible, but have been recycled at various points in time for modern use. Their wonder lies in the fact that they do not stand just as museum pieces.

The history of this neighborhood is closely tied to that of the Jewish population in Rome. Though the Ghetto is long gone this remains a predominately Jewish neighborhood. The synagogue dominates the banks of the Tiber, the restaurants specialize in Roman Jewish cuisine, and only three shops in one area are owned by non-Jews. Nowhere else in Rome is the *passeggiata*, the traditional evening walk, taken so seriously. The entire community gathers on one street; they create such a boisterous scene that a Roman friend of mine, unfamiliar with the neighborhood, was sure a demonstration was taking place.

An interesting characteristic of Roman life in the *centro storico*, center-city, is the degree to which the city is shared by the rich and poor alike. When I first moved to Rome I lived on what is considered by many to be the equivalent of Manhattan's Sutton Place, studded as it was with the palazzi of Marchesa so-and-so and Prince whatever. Yet in the same building, and around the corner, my neighbors were working-class people in the hardiest sense of the word—not the servants of Via Giulia, but the bus driver, pastamaker, local bag-lady, mechanic, and on up the social scale to the schoolteacher, lawyer, and Valentino model. Together, these were the clients for early morning *cappuccino* at the local bar. The neighborhood surrounding the Campo dei Fiori is typical of this phenomenon. Although it is an area of sharp contrasts —Renaissance Rome at her secular best mixed with aging medieval streets—architectural distinctions no longer clearly define economic status.

More than other Roman neighborhoods, the Campo dei Fiori has been carefully shaped by the Catholic Church. Located directly across the river from the Vatican, this area always provided primary access for pilgrims. Some roads were built to steer the crowds in certain directions, others to create monumental entrances. Palaces were erected to house the cardinals and relatives of the popes. In fact, Renaissance Rome was created and fully orchestrated by the Catholic Church. Today, though, the Church has little influence in this neighborhood, and instead the well-planned piazza of Inquisition fame accommodates central Rome's largest outdoor market. Here also is the setting for many of the endless demonstrations of the neighborhood's well-established Communist party and feminists.

Trastevere, which means "across the Tiber," refers to a long stretch of the city along the river on the Vatican side. The S. Maria in Trastevere area is well known as the chic counterculture center of Rome. There is also, however, a quieter Trastevere further downriver that has not become popular among visitors and continues to have a rich neighborhood life of its own. The very first time I walked through this area I felt intimidated by its sense of isolation. Everything is hidden down narrow streets or behind high walls, and it is exceptionally quiet unless the schools are letting out. In contrast to other walks, a good half of this one is made up of public institutions; walled-in monasteries and convents with gardens, schools, a home for the aged, and a very large building in restoration. The little remaining space is packed in very closely around winding streets. But once one knows which doors to knock on, the gardens with their cloisters are like no others in Rome and the unassuming little shops give one a very strong sense of community. This is a wonderful walk during which medieval Rome can come alive for you.

At every turn, during these approximately two- to three-hour walks, there is some detail that recalls Rome's varied history and the life of its people, be it the graceful baroque line added to an early Christian church or an ancient Roman ruin used to house the local fish market; the graceful fountains that spurt water from sources originally discovered by the ancient Romans, or a house that once belonged to a famous sixteenth-century courtesan. These are all vivid images typical of Rome's charm, and each has a story.

My purpose in writing *Romewalks* is to recount these stories in the context of a community and lead you to a personal knowledge of Rome's complex and exciting history. I hope that it will encourage you to undertake a protracted exploration of all of Rome's streets and neighborhoods—you may even fall in love with this city as I have!

Information and Advice

Before You Go

Getting to know Rome can be a life's work, or at least one of many years. She has many faces—classical, medieval, Renaissance, baroque, modern, religious—and within each there is a rich collection of history, folklore, and art. The experience can be overwhelming if you don't think about your trip and plan for it before you go.

Well in advance of your departure call or write the Italian Government Travel Office at any of the following locations:

630 Fifth Avenue
New York, N.Y. 10020 (212) 245-4822

500 North Michigan Avenue
Chicago, Ill. 60611
(312) 644-0990

360 Post Street
San Francisco, Calif. 94108
(415) 392-6206

Ask for information about Rome and they will send you brochures on sightseeing, hotels, restaurants, and, most important, a map. As you will be doing a lot of walking your map may be your most precious guide. It will also help you in your choice of hotel.

Book your hotel room as soon as you have decided on your schedule and make sure you receive a confirmation from the hotel. You will need a passport and, if you are planning to stay in Italy for more than three months, a visa—call the Italian Consulate for information and instructions on how to apply for one. You will also need an International Driving Permit if you plan to use a car; this can be obtained from the AAA.

The best time to visit Rome is in late spring and autumn. Winters are moderate but very wet, which means you will primarily see the interiors of the city and miss one of the most important attractions—the street life. July and August are hot, and most Romans flee to the beaches leaving the city half-deserted and many of its restaurants and shops closed. In my experience the very best time to visit Rome is in late September and October. Then the city is in full gear, the weather is dry and still warm, and you can still enjoy the outdoor restaurants and cafés.

When choosing your wardrobe don't underestimate the possibility of extremes. During the summer there are few air conditioners and during the winter it can get very cold, especially behind Rome's thick damp walls. In the spring and fall temperatures change suddenly, so be prepared to dress in layers. The most basic item in your suitcase should be a comfortable pair of walking shoes; most of Rome's streets are cobblestoned and you will be doing a lot of walking. Italians are very style conscious, and, while not formal, they maintain a more conservative approach to dress than we do. Men and women, for instance, do not wear shorts in the city, and these, along with short skirts and bare arms, are not allowed in many of the churches you will want to visit. Remember, too, that Italian electricity is 220 volts with outlets requiring two rounded plugs, so you will need an adapter to use your hair dryer or electric razor.

You can add an exciting dimension to your trip by doing some of your own research. No other city has been contemplated, discussed, and described as much as Rome, and your impressions of the city will be that much more meaningful for the number of perspectives you bring with you—from the documentations of the ancients to the insights of Gibbon and Gregorovius to the awe of Goethe to the incisive observations of Stendhal to the romance of Hawthorne to the enthusiasm of James. You can also look at Rome through the eyes of Piranesi, Lorrain, Franz, and many other artists. Below is a list of books that will help you plan your itinerary and feed your imagination.

GENERAL BOOKS ON ROME

- L. Berarelli, *Roma e Dintorni* (Guide of the Italian Touring Club)
- E. Bowen, *A Time in Rome*
- E. Clark, *Rome and a Villa*
- J. Evelyn, *Diary*

W. Goethe, *Roman Elegies*
A. Hare, *Walks in Rome*
N. Hawthorne, *Notebooks in France and Italy*
P. Hofmann, *Rome: The Sweet Tempestuous Life*
H. James, *Italian Hours*
J. Lees Milne, *Roman Mornings*
E. Lucas, *Wandering in Rome*
A. Lyall, *Rome Sweet Rome*
G. Masson, *A Companion Guide to Rome*
H. V. Morton, *A Traveller in Rome*
W. Murray, *Italy, the Fatal Gift*
R. Rodd, *Rome of the Renaissance and Today*
K. Simon, *Rome, Places and Pleasures*
Stendhal, *Promenades dans Rome*
W. Story, *Roba di Roma*

ROMAN HISTORY

J. Burckhardt, *The Civilization of the Renaissance in Italy*
E. Gibbon, *The History of the Decline and Fall of the Roman Empire*
F. Gregorovius, *History of the City of Rome in the Middle Ages*
E. Hamilton, *The Roman Way*
J. Klaczko, *Rome and the Renaissance*
R. Krauthimer, *Rome, Profile of a City 312–1308*
R. Lanciani, *The Golden Days of the Renaissance in Rome*
R. Lanciani, *Pagan and Christian Rome*
L. von Pastor, *The History of Popes from the Close of the Middle Ages*
W. Pater, *The Renaissance*
Suetonius, *Lives of the Caesars*
J. A. Symonds, *The Renaissance in Italy*

ROMAN ART AND ARCHITECTURE

J. Ackerman, *The Architecture of Michelangelo*
M. Armellini, *Le Chiese di Roma dal Secolo IV al XIX*
B. Berenson, *Italian Painters of the Renaissance*
M. Briggs, *Baroque Architecture*
A. Fabber, *Roman Baroque Art*
W. Friedlander, *Claude Lorrain*
E. Hutton, *The Cosmati*
P. MacKendrick, *The Mute Stone Speaks*
W. Mâle and D. Buxton, *The Early Churches of Rome*
C. Marucchi, *The Roman Forum and Palatine*
G. Masson, *Italian Villas and Palaces*
A. Rinaldi, *L'Arte in Roma dal Seicento al Novecento*

M. Scherer, *Marvels of Ancient Rome*
G. Scott, *The Architecture of Humanism*
A. Strong, *Art in Ancient Rome*
P. Toesca, *Pietro Cavallini*
C. de Tolnay, *Michelangelo*
J. Toynbee and J. Ward Perkins, *The Shrine of St. Peter's*
G. Vasari, *Lives of the Artists*
A. Venturi, *Short History of Italian Art*
R. Wittkower, *Art and Architecture in Italy 1600–1750*
R. Wittkower, *Gian Lorenzo Bernini*

LITERATURE SET IN ROME

R. Browning, "The Bishop Orders His Tomb at St. Praxed's Church"
Byron, "Childe Harold's Pilgrimage"
N. Hawthorne, *The Marble Faun*
H. James, *Roderick Hudson*
M. de Staël, *Corinne*
M. Yourcenar, *Memoirs of Hadrian*

General Information

After your initial flurry of excitement at the sights of Roman pines, the cupolas on the horizon, the jumble of terra-cotta buildings, and the Colosseum, your feelings of Rome may shift to not-so-pleasant frustrations. Rome is a city that has outgrown its narrow streets; the congestion of people, cars, and buses combined with the noise is infamous. At the beginning of the second century Juvenal complained that the noise "could break the sleep of a deaf man," so not all these annoyances are modern. They are a part of the city's culture. It is, however, possible to keep from getting completely overwhelmed by arriving with certain expectations and by learning to cope with the unavoidable. St. Ambrose's advice to St. Augustine still holds, "When you are in Rome, live in the Roman style." Above all, this means coming to Rome with patience, time, and perseverance.

Two things you can do when planning your trip. First, if possible, make a reservation in a hotel away from the train station and major streets. Second, a point that I cannot overemphasize, give yourself plenty of time for everything. It takes almost twice as long to do anything in Italy as it does in America, and you will be the lucky traveler if you don't run into a major strike of some sort. Even if you have come to live in Rome for a while you won't see everything there is to see, so certainly don't try to do so in a week or two. Leave plenty of time just to wander around and make alternative plans in case the museum or church you want to see is closed for restoration (*"Chiuso per restauro"* is a very familiar sign all over Italy).

When you arrive in Rome, slow down. Rome's enchantment is physical and comes from touch, smell, taste, and sight, so you must allow for all these sensations. The best way to explore Rome is by taking a walk, as confusing as the streets may seem. Without those plunges in the wrong direction Rome will never be yours. Don't hesitate to ask directions even with a ten-word Italian vocabulary; in any case, there will always be a bar at the next corner where you can pull out your map over a cup of coffee or a glass of Campari. Sitting in these cafés, especially during the summer, is as important to your experience of Rome as the next church or fountain on your list.

The Roman day begins early, ends late, and includes a three-hour siesta that can be unnerving to nine-to-fivers. Most museums and churches are open only in the morning, so you should get an early start and plan your shopping expeditions for the late afternoon. By the time siesta rolls around you will want to sit back at a café or return to your hotel room. This can be a good time to wander the streets, which are then free of the crowds, but if you do, you will miss the show—iron gates are pulled down to cover the shop windows, courtyards are closed, and street life is almost nonexistent. When four or five o'clock rolls around it is like the start of a new day. After nine o'clock you should again do as the Romans and spend your time eating. This is one of the city's most delightful forms of entertainment, and even at the cheapest *trattoria* you can linger over several courses. As the Romans wisely say, you don't get old at the table, so relax and enjoy.

As far as perseverance goes, you will have a better sense of the need for it once you have been in Rome for a few days. I learned to be aggressive in Rome, not in New York City. If you want something, don't be shy; ask, point, and politely insist. If you are standing in what appears to be a line be forewarned, lines are not respected in Rome. In terms of sightseeing, unless a sign is posted that clearly states you can't get in, keep asking and looking for the guard; he may just be out for his cup of coffee.

Being in a foreign country doesn't mean you have to lose touch with the news or your favorite forms of entertainment. *The International Daily News* is an English-language daily, with local and international news, that is published in Rome. *The International Herald Tribune,* published in Paris, is available the afternoon of the day of issue and is the major English-language newspaper in Europe. The Italian papers include *Il Messaggero* for Roman news, *Il Paese Sera* for business news, and *La Repubblica* for the best cultural coverage. *This Week in Rome* provides the week's listing of cultural events, entertainment, restaurants, and shops. The official opera and ballet season runs from November to June at the Teatro dell'Opera (Piazza Beniamino Giglio 1, tel. 46-36-41) and in July and August performances are given at the Baths of Caracalla. *Aida* in the midst of these huge Roman ruins is an impressive spectacle well worth including in your plans if you are visiting during the summer. Tickets for the summer programs are available only on the day of the performance and may be purchased either at the Teatro dell'Opera during the day or the Baths of Caracalla from 8:00 P.M. to 9:00 P.M. Advanced bookings for the winter season may be made by mail, otherwise tickets are available two days before the performance. While there is not an abundance of tickets for the winter season, you can usually obtain something if you get to the box office early.

Most movies in Italy are dubbed into Italian, but there is one theater in town that shows undubbed English and American movies, Pasquino (Vicolo del Piede, tel. 580-36-22). There are also several film clubs that may show movies in English. These will be listed in the *International Daily News,* and you can join the club on the spot for a nominal fee. During the summer months there is an open-air film festival. In the past it has been held near the Arch of Constantine and in the Circus Maximus, but check the paper for the current location and schedules.

Rome's best entertainment offerings are concerts and chamber music. The official season is from October to June with the Accademia di S. Cecilia sponsoring the most important events. Orchestral concerts are held at the Auditorio di Via della Conciliazione (Via della Conciliazione 4, tel. 654-10-44), and chamber recitals at the Sala Accademia di Via dei Greci (Via dei Greci 18, box office Via Vittorio 6, tel. 679-36-17). Recitals are also held almost every night of the week during the winter in various churches and palazzi, and they provide the opportunity to see the interiors of these marvelous buildings flooded in light. During the summer, concerts are held on Michelangelo's piazza (the Campidoglio) at the top of the Capitoline Hill, Bramante's cloister of S. Maria della Pace, Villa Borghese Park and Villa Ada Park, and on the Tiber Island.

Rome has many fairs and festivals throughout the year, but the most important are: the Christmas fair in the Piazza Navona from Advent to Epiphany, on January 6; the International Horse Show at the Piazza di Siena in the Villa Borghese Park in late April; the Roseto di Roma (a rose show) on Via di Valle Murcia from May to the beginning of June; the Noantri Festival in Trastevere during July; and the Summer Festival, with events of all kinds scattered about the city.

On hot summer days, if you are not staying in one of the hotels on the outskirts of the city that has a swimming pool, you may want to go to the beach. Ostia is but a forty-five-minute ride and can be reached by train from the Stazione Termini. For the cleaner beaches stay on the train until the last stop. You then pay to use the facilities of a beach club where you may rent an umbrella and a beach chair. By far the nicest beach near Rome is Fregene, which can be reached only by car.

For tours of the city and its environs there are several possibilities. American Express (Piazza di Spagna 38, tel. 67-64) is one of the best. There are also the Appian Line (Via Vittorio Veneto 84, tel. 474-16-41) and CIT (Piazza della Repubblica 68, tel. 47-98-21). Your hotel will probably have more information and can help make the arrangements you want.

You may be visiting the Vatican and its museum, but if you also want to attend a papal audience you must make a request in advance. During the winter general audiences are held at 11:00 A.M. every Wednesday in the Audience Hall. During the summer they are held at 5:00 P.M. in the piazza designed by Bernini in front of St. Peter's. For tickets apply to the Prefettura della Cassa Pontificia, Città del Vaticano 00120. Do not give more than one month's notice or less than two days', and indicate the nationality and number of people in your party.

Rome has more than fifty museums, some ranked with the most important in the world. Many of the collections are housed in palaces or Renaissance villas that would be a pleasure to visit even if they were empty. Below is a list of some of the most important. Remember that opening hours often change without notice.

The Vatican Museums, Viale Vaticano. Open October to June, Monday to Saturday, 9:00 A.M.–2:00 P.M.; July to September, Monday to Friday, 9:00 A.M.–5:00 P.M., Saturday, 9:00 A.M.–2:00 P.M. Closed on Sunday except the last Sunday of the month when the hours are from 9:00 A.M.–2:00 P.M. (9:00 A.M.–5 P.M. during the summer). This museum holds one of the most important collections of antiquities and Renaissance art in the world. Your trip to Rome should include at least one visit.

The Capitoline Museums, Piazza del Campidoglio. Closed on Monday; open Tuesday to Sunday, 9:00 A.M.–4:00 P.M., and on Saturday also from 9:00 P.M.–11:30 P.M. These include the Palazzo dei Conservatori, the Museo Nuovo in the Palazzo Caffarelli, and the Capitoline Picture Gallery. This complex of museums has an impressive collection of art, especially an outstanding collection of antique Roman sculpture.

Museo Nazionale Romano, Piazza della Repubblica. November to April, Monday to Saturday, 9:30 A.M.–4 P.M.; May to October, Monday to Saturday, 10:00 A.M.–5:00 P.M.; Sunday and holidays until 1:30 P.M. Here is a fine collection of antiquities, many of them found in Rome.

Galleria Borghese, Via Pinciana. Closed on Monday; open Tuesday to Saturday, 9:00 A.M.–2:00 P.M., Sunday, 9:00 A.M.–1:00 P.M. This is located in the Casino of the Villa Borghese, which was built in the seventeenth century by Cardinal Scipio Borghese who started the collection with some of the best works of his time, including several masterpieces by Bernini.

National Museum of the Villa Giulia, Piazza di Villa

Giulia. Closed on Monday; open Tuesday to Saturday, 9:30 A.M.–4:00 P.M., Sunday, 9:30 A.M.–1:30 P.M. The villa was built by Vignola in 1550 for Pope Julius III. It contains a splendid collection of pre-Roman antiquities found in the necropolis of Veii, Praeneste, Cervetri, and other Etruscan towns.

National Gallery of Ancient Art, Palazzo Barberini, Via delle Quattro Fontane 13. Closed on Monday; open Tuesday to Saturday, 9:00 P.M.–2:00 P.M., Sunday, 9:00 A.M.–1:00 P.M. This collection of Italian and European paintings from the early Renaissance to the seventeenth century is housed in an imposing baroque building begun in 1625 by Carlo Maderno and completed by Bernini.

The Doria Pamphili Gallery, Piazza del Collegio Romano. Open Tuesday, Friday, and Sunday, 9:00 A.M.–1:00 P.M. The Palazzo Doria was begun in 1435 and completed only in 1660, so it spans two centuries of architectural styles. The gallery contains the Doria family collection of paintings and objets d'art, including paintings by Titian, Raphael, Caravaggio, and many others. It is the finest patrician collection in Rome.

The Museum of Rome (Museo di Roma), Palazzo Braschi, Piazza di S. Pantaleo. Closed on Monday; open Tuesday to Sunday, 9:00 A.M.–2:00 P.M. The museum documents the various aspects of Roman life from the Middle Ages onward, including a collection of watercolors by Roesler Franz.

The Galleria Spada, Palazzo Spada, Piazza Capo di Ferro 13. Closed on Monday; open Tuesday to Saturday, 9:00 A.M.–1:30 P.M., Sunday, 10:00 A.M.–1:00 P.M. This is an important museum of baroque paintings shown in four of the sumptuous rooms of this marvelous palazzo (discussed in Walk 3).

National Gallery of Modern Art, Viale delle Belle Arti. Closed on Monday; open Tuesday to Saturday, 9:00 A.M.–2:00 P.M., Sunday, 9:00 A.M.–1:00 P.M. This is a large collection that presents the evolution of nineteenth- and twentieth-century Italian art.

Palazzo Venezia Museum, Via del Plebiscito. Closed on Monday; open Tuesday to Saturday, 9:00 A.M.–2:00 P.M., Sunday, 9:00 A.M.–1:00 P.M. A visit to the museum is the best way to see the interior of Cardinal Barbo's palace, which was begun in 1455. The collection has paintings, bronzes, wood and ivory sculptures, ceramics, and tapestries. The visit includes the Sala del Mappamondo, Mussolini's office.

Accommodations

Rome's long tradition of tourism gives this city an especially wide variety of places to stay. These range from some of the most luxurious hotels in Europe to the simple *pensione*, "boardinghouse." In between are a great number of possibilities based on price, style, amenities, and location. Standards at all hotels are listed in the *Annuario Alberghi d'Italia* published by the Italian State Tourist Organization; this book can be consulted at their offices or through your travel agent. Do make these arrangements as soon as possible, since Rome is always crowded, and the choice hotels are booked well in advance. Also remember that mail to Italy often seems to take the slow boat via China.

Most frequent travelers to Rome have a favorite hotel, which says something about the gracious hospitality this city offers. It also reflects the many distinctive personalities these establishments embody, be they luxurious or not. If you are traveling in the grand style, the Grand Hotel should fit the bill in every way. Located between the Via Veneto and the Piazza Esedra on Via V. E. Orlando 3, its marble columns, frescoed ceilings, voluptuous drapes, and Venetian chandeliers encompass all the details of *fin de siècle* luxury. If you prefer the more intimate and casual elegance of a small establishment there is the Hotel Raphael, nestled in a quiet green corner of Largo Febo, just a block from the Piazza Navona. Or try the Hotel Forum on the Via Tor de' Conti in a sixteenth-century convent that overlooks the Forum of Trajan. The Hotel Inghilterra on Via Bocca di Leone in the middle of Rome's elegant shopping district is where Henry James stayed and, despite the time and renovations, it looks like it could be a setting for one of his novels. If you prefer all the modern conveniences and amenities of a large American chain there is the Cavaliere Hilton on Via Cadlolo in Monte Mario with 400 rooms, a swimming pool, tennis courts, and conference rooms; it is away from the center of the city in a more residential section of town. The Hotel Parco dei Principi has many of the same conveniences but is closer to the center on the north side of Villa Borghese Park—Via Mercadante.

There are also small, moderately priced hotels on quiet streets in the historic center. These include the Hotel Cardinale on Via Giulia and the Hotel Rinascimento on Via del Pellegrino. The Hotel del Sole al Pantheon has made a reputation for itself as a simple, clean establishment, and it overlooks one of Rome's most spectacular sites, the Pantheon.

Across the river, in the vicinity of the Vatican and just a short ride from the center of Rome, you will find the best prices. The Hotel Columbus, on Via della Conciliazione, in a fifteenth-century building with frescoed ceilings, is about as close as you can get to St. Peter's. The Hotel Arcangelo on the Via Boezio and the Hotel Cicerone on the Via Cicerone are both comfortable and quiet.

Pensiones are numerous and are by far the cheapest places to stay. The Isa on Via Cicerone and, in the historic center, the Navona on Via dei Sediari and the Sole on Via del Biscione have all been highly recommended.

Rome also offers apartment-hotel accommodations, called *residenzas*, for visitors planning longer stays (at least two weeks). The Residenza di Ripetta on Via di Ripetta was a comfortable home for me while I was apartment-hunting.

Transportation

There are two airports in Rome. The main international and national airport is Leonardo da Vinci in Fiumicino, twenty-six kilometers southwest of Rome near the sea. A modern *autostrada* connects Fiumicino with Rome, and both taxi and bus transportation are available. As taxis are assigned days when they can work only out of the airport, the fee for going into the city is higher than for going to the airport—the meter is doubled to pay for the taxi's return to the airport. You should count on spending at least thirty dollars to get into town. Bus transportation is, however, very cheap and easy. As you come out of customs you will see a booth with a sign for the bus. Go there and buy a ticket (less than two dollars), and just outside the door is a spot from which a bus leaves every twenty minutes. The bus takes you to the Air Terminal on Via Giolitti, next to the main train station. From there you can easily catch a taxi to your hotel or take a city bus.

The other airport, Ciampino, is thirteen kilometers southeast of the city and is used exclusively by private aircraft and charter flights. This is also the city's military airport. Although there is city bus service (bus number 135) on the Via Salaria outside the airport gates, you need a ticket, which is not always available at the airport's newsstand. The bus also takes you only as far as Piazza Vescovio on the northern end of the city. So, unless you are very familiar with the transportation system, I suggest you take a taxi from Ciampino.

The train station, the Stazione Termini, is a large modern structure built between 1938 and 1950 on the Piazza dei Cinquecento. This is the main train station for all the state railways, including those with international connections. In addition to the services one usually finds in a train station—newsstands for a map of the city, coffee shops, shoeshine boys—this one also has a tourist information center in case you have arrived without a hotel reservation, and an *albergo diurno*, "day hotel," where you can take a shower and even have your hair done. In front of the train station is one of the main stops for the city transportation system (your map of the city should also give the bus routes) as well as a large taxi stand.

This station also serves the Lazio Line for trains to nearby towns in the region such as Palestrina, Frascati, and Fiuggi. You go downstairs for the subway station with services to Ostia and EUR.

Chances are you will not be traveling by bus when you arrive or leave Rome because the train system is so good. Bus service is, however, efficient for some of the small towns near Rome, or you may be interested in the tourist coach services. There is no central bus station in Rome. On the northeast corner of Piazza dei Cinquecento on Via Gaeta are the buses of the Azienda Tramvie Autobus Comunali (A.T.A.C.) to Tivoli. On the southwest side of the Piazza, in front of the train station, are the buses of the S.T.E.F.E.R. company to Colonna, San Cesareo, Palestrina, and Fiuggi, as well as the S.I.T.A. buses to Terracina, Sperlonga, Gaeta, Naples, and beyond. The Piazza della Repubblica is the terminus for the luxury auto-pullmans of the Compagnia Italiana Autoservizi Turistici (C.I.A.T.) with transportation to Naples, Assisi, Perugia, Florence, Pisa, Rapallo, Genoa, and Siena.

Taxis are still a bargain in Rome and cheaper than in other Italian cities. They are clearly identified by a sign and their bright yellow color. Though it is possible to flag one on the street, the usual procedure is to go to a taxi stand, marked by a large blue sign. Because of inflation the meter often does not display the correct price for the ride. The driver should be able to show you an official listing that gives the equivalent for what the meter shows. In the back of the taxi there is a listing of the extra charges in Italian, English, and French. These include night fares, holiday fares, pieces of luggage, and extra people. There are also gypsy cabs with no taxi sign or meter; you should avoid these unless you are desperate—and then bargain before you get in the car.

The entire city is serviced by a very good bus system that, while often crowded and uncomfortable, is still the easiest way to get about town other than walking. You must first buy an A.T.A.C. ticket at a bar or newsstand. Remember that there are four rush hours in Rome—mornings from 8:00 to 9:30, twice during the lunch break from 1:00 to 2:00 and from 4:00 to 5:00, and evenings from 7:00 to 8:00.

Bus stops are marked *"Fermata"* and give the numbers for the buses that use it along with a listing of the main stops made by that line. The final destination point will be listed last. There is a prescribed etiquette for bus riders in Rome: you enter from the rear of the bus, unless you have a monthly pass, and exit from the center of the bus. Stick the ticket into the card punch machine in the direction of the arrow; keep the stub until you have left the bus or you may be charged a fine. Pay attention to your route because you will have to maneuver your way to the exit with a polite *"permesso"* before the bus arrives, otherwise you may miss the stop entirely. Don't be surprised if your return trip is different from the trip going; this is often the case because of all the one-way streets in the city.

With much difficulty, caused by the numerous archeological sites, three subway lines have been built in the past thirty years. The first line of the Metropolitana, completed in 1952, runs from the Stazione Termini to the Via Cavour, the Colosseo, the Circo Massimo, the Piramide, and on out to EUR. The second line starts from the Stazione Termini and runs to Piazza Vittorio Emanuele II, San Giovanni in Laterano, Via Tuscolana, Cinecittà, and Osteria del Curato. The third line, just opened in 1981, starts at Ottaviano, just a few blocks from the Vatican, and runs to Piazzale Flaminio, Piazza di Spagna, the Stazione Termini, and Anagnina.

Another form of transportation popular with tourists is the horse-drawn carriage available at Piazza di Spagna, Piazza S. Pietro, and the Trevi Fountain. They are not cheap, and you should establish the price before you get in for a ride.

Food and Drink

Above all, Romans like to eat, and eating is an all-day ritual. So much respect is given to their produce and cuisine that you will be tempted at every turn: in the shops the windows are filled with decorative displays of hams, salamis, cheeses, breads, and pasta; the restaurants entice you with succulent samples of cold platters and fresh fish; the open markets are a dramatic collage of some of the most beautiful produce you will ever see; the street vendors offer tempting slices of coconut, melon, and, in the winter, roast chestnuts; and even the bars have their counters piled high with an assortment of *tramezzini*, crustless sandwiches. You can snack all day, but dinner is sacred, and you must leave room for at least three courses. At mealtimes you are doing more than just nourishing your body; you are attending one of Rome's best shows. For lunch this begins at 1:00; for dinner not before 9:00. Always, it is a theater of colors, flavors, odors, sounds, and gestures, but from April through October, when the tables move outdoors, the people-watching is at its best. Then, too, you will be amused by countless street musicians and entertainers. There is no need to rush to a movie; the spectacle is right there, coupled with a delicious plate of pasta.

As eating begins in the morning, let's start there. A *cappuccino*, rich Brazilian coffee with steamed milk, and a *cornetto*, a sweet crescent-shaped roll, are the standard Roman breakfast, which is usually taken standing at a counter. First you pay the cashier, then you take your *scontrino*, "receipt," to the bar and give your order (and a 100 lire tip) to the man behind the *espresso* machine. While *cappuccino* is the typical morning coffee, drunk only until noon, you can have your coffee in a variety of other ways. *Espresso* is the highly concentrated black brew that can be made *lungo*, watered down, or *macchiato*, with just a dab of milk. If you don't like steamed milk there is *caffè e latte*, coffee with plain cold milk, or, if the coffee is too strong for you, try a *latte macchiato*, which is a glass of steamed milk with a drop of *espresso*. Those who want a little kick in their coffee can have a *caffè corretto*, with a bit of brandy, and there's always *caffè hag*, decaffeinated coffee, which is available the world over. During the summer you can have iced coffee, black or with milk, *caffè freddo* or *cappuccino freddo*. Coffee is a good way to begin the day, but it is also a good excuse for a break anytime, and, of course, it's the only way to end a meal.

Almost every bar has a plate of *tramezzini* for a quick snack, but larger bars provide additional selections, including pastries and ice cream. The largest have a *tavola calda* and *tavola fredda*, hot and cold prepared dishes usually eaten right at the counter. Though tables and chairs are provided in these establishments be prepared to pay double for the pleasure of sitting. These bars also offer the only possibility of a clean restroom.

Roman ice cream has a justly deserved high reputation, and the *gelaterias*, "ice cream parlors," are another favorite place to grab a snack. This ice cream is made only with eggs, cream, sugar, fresh fruit, and natural flavorings. Try Giolitti's, Rome's most popular parlor, on Via Uffici del Vacario 40. The best ice cream comes from the Bar San Filippo in the northern neighborhood of Parioli, Via di Villa San Filippo 8; another, less fashionable, favorite is Alfredo Pica on the Via della Seggiola. In any case, wherever they make homemade ice cream it is bound to be delicious.

Italy is a country of regional cuisines that vary greatly from north to south. In Rome you eat primarily *cucina romana*, though there are some restaurants that specialize in dishes from other regions. As a rule Roman cuisine is not refined, which is not to say that it isn't tasty, it is just a hardy, peasant form of cooking that uses a variety of pasta. Among the best are: *penne arabiata*, a spicy tomato sauce on macaroni; *spaghetti alle vongole*, sweet small clams cooked in their shells with garlic; and *bucatini alla Matriciana*, large macaroni with a tomato, cheese, and bacon sauce. Standard main courses include tripe, salt cod, sweetbreads, brains, oxtail, and salt pork, but there are also more luxurious foods, such as fish (especially in Trastevere), baby lamb, suckling pig, and veal.

Roman bread is among the best in Italy, but if you want *burro*, "butter," you have to ask for it. Vegetables and salads are served as separate courses. Unless vegetables are fried these are served cold and dressed in lemon juice and oil. Some of the best Roman dishes fall into this category: *carciofi alla giudia*, fried artichokes; *fiore di zucca fritti*, fried zucchini flowers stuffed with mozzarella cheese; and *funghi porcini*, a huge brown-and-white fleshy mushroom that is usually grilled with garlic. Dessert is customarily fresh fruit.

Your meal is not complete without a bottle of wine and *acqua minerale*, "mineral water." Italians seem to have an unquenchable thirst for *acqua minerale*, which has nothing to do with the tap water's being untasty or polluted, because it is neither. It is a habit, but it is also consumed for health reasons. The impressive labels always contain a testimonial by an eminent professor of medicine and a chemical analysis of the bottle's contents. The professor explains in technical terms that the water will relieve digestive miseries, kidney ailments, or whatever. The analysis is as complicated and comprehensive as any blood test. This is all taken very seriously and some waters are better for some things than others: Sangenini for children's digestion, Fiuggi and Uliveto for people with kidney problems, Chianciano for liver problems, and Crodo for dyspepsia and colitis. Neri, Claudia, and San Paolo are alkaline waters and good for hangovers. Both mineral water and wine are quite inexpensive, and most restaurants have a wide selection of wines from all over Italy. The regional wine is not very special, and while house wine is fine and even cheaper, it sometimes has preservatives (especially the white) that can leave you with a throbbing headache.

If you are willing to take the time, one of the nicest lunches is a picnic in Villa Borghese Park. This also gives you an opportunity to shop for bread, wine, cheese, and salami along the Via della Croce. You can buy vegetables and fruit at a small outdoor market on one of the side streets. Remember, when going to the market, that you are not supposed to touch the produce, tempting as it may be. Tell the person behind the stand how much you want; he or she will be very good about picking the best for you. The outdoor markets are open only in the morning, and all food stores are closed on Thursday afternoons, except during the summer when they close with everything else on Saturday afternoons.

Aside from the marvelous experience of eating in Rome, you will appreciate the prices. Dining out is relatively inexpensive, and even the fanciest meal with an aged bottle of wine will not cost what it does in the United States.

The perfect way to end your day is to pass the evening sitting at one of the big piazzas—Piazza Navona, Piazza del Popolo, or Piazza S. Maria in Trastevere—over a glass of *Sambuca*, licorice liqueur; *vin santo*, sweet wine; or brandy. There you can continue people-watching until the wee hours of the morning. But I suggest that you avoid the cafés on the Via Veneto—*la dolce vita* is now but a memory there.

Tipping

A 15 percent service charge is added to hotel and restaurant bills, but you should leave a small tip in addition. At the hotel tip the porters and service personnel as you would anywhere; in the restaurants leave 5–10 percent of your total bill for the waiter. When buying a drink at a bar leave a 100 lire coin on the counter or, if you sit at a table, 5–10 percent of the bill. While cab drivers do not expect a tip it is customary to leave them with small change.

You should be generous to custodians who do special favors for you, such as opening doors to churches, cloisters, and sections of museums not generally open to the public. In such cases it is appropriate to give them the equivalent of a dollar.

Telephone, Telegraph, Post Office

Public telephones are available throughout the city, particularly in bars, but you must use a *gettone*, "token," to operate them. *Gettoni* may be purchased at a bar or newsstand; they are worth 100 lire and can also be used as money. If you are planning to use the phones it is best to carry a few *gettoni* with you. Each token gives you a five-minute conversation; when you begin to hear a clicking sound just add another. In general calls outside Rome but within Italy take six *gettoni*. International calls can be made from your hotel room, but you may be charged as much as twice the normal rate. An easy way to make your calls is at the S.I.P., the main telephone office, located on the Piazza S. Silvestro. It's open twenty-four hours a day, seven days a week. There are also S.I.P. offices at the Stazione Termini and at Leonardo da Vinci airport. Like the American system, long-distance calls are cheaper on Sundays, but overall they are always far more expensive than calls made in the United States. If possible, arrange to have calls made to you at a certain time and place or use that much ignored method, the telegram. Telegrams cost about 500 lire a word and are delivered the next day. It is one of the most efficient and reliable ways to communicate. The main post office at Piazza S. Silvestro also has a telegraph office, open Monday through Friday from 8:00 A.M. to 9:00 P.M., and Saturday from 8:00 A.M. to noon.

You can buy stamps at any tobacconist, usually located in bars and identified by a "T" sign outside. The mailboxes along the street are red, but it is wiser to go directly to the post office to mail your letters. Neighborhood post offices are open from 8:00 A.M. to 2:00 P.M., but the main office, Palazzo delle Poste, also at Piazza S. Silvestro, is open Monday through Friday from 8:00 A.M. to 9:00 P.M. and on Saturday from 8:00 A.M. to noon. The Vatican, as a separate principality, has its own mail system; the post office there is on the piazza in front of St. Peter's. It is open Monday through Saturday from 9:00 A.M. to 5:00 P.M. All mail should be marked "air," and if you are especially concerned about the delivery of a particular letter send it *espresso*, special delivery.

Packages sent out of the country must be tied with a

string, not sealed with tape, for customs purposes. If packages weigh more than 1 kilo (2.2 pounds), the end of the string must be attached to a *piombi*, a small lead clasp that can be purchased at a stationery store or *cartoleria*.

Money and Banking

Banks are open from 8:30 A.M. to 1:20 P.M., Monday through Friday. Most banks cash traveler's checks, but be prepared to stand in several lines and spend more than a few minutes. You must have a passport to make this transaction. The Banco di Santo Spirito, with branches around town, usually has the best exchange rate for the dollar. The American Express Office (Piazza di Spagna 38, tel. 67-64) is open from 9:00 A.M. to 5:00 P.M. You won't have any language problems there, but you will face huge crowds during the summer tourist season. In a pinch you can usually cash a traveler's check at a hotel, but the convenience will cost you.

While credit cards may be used for shopping and in some hotels and restaurants, Italy is still run on cash, so check before counting on using credit.

A Value Added Tax (I.V.A.) is included in the price of all luxury items. In Italy, as opposed to other European countries, you cannot be reimbursed for this tax. The only exception is very large purchases that are shipped out of the country by the dealer.

Shopping

In recent years Italian design has gained a terrific reputation the world over, and it is almost superfluous to say that Rome is a shopper's paradise. Even knowing this, you will be surprised by the opulent window displays along the main shopping streets at the foot of the Spanish Steps. This area centers on the Via Condotti, south along the Via del Corso to Via Frattina and north to Via della Croce. Here you will find all those familiar names: Gianni Versace, Fendi, Missoni, Carlo Palazzi, Valentino, Gucci, Bulgari, Ginori, Mila Schön, Buccellati, Ferragamo, Pratesi, and Roberta di Camerino. Needless to say, this is not a place for bargain hunting, although there are good sales in July and February. This is where you buy quality—the very best money can buy. A word of warning about shopping in these stores: you will be treated as well as you are dressed.

Rome is full of shopping areas. Less expensive ready-to-wear shops are found on the Via del Corso, Via Tritone, and Via Nazionale. The best bargains in nonname leather goods and shoes are found on the Via Cola di Rienzo in a neighborhood near the Vatican. On our walks you will find small neighborhood craft and specialty shops. Although there is a major department store, La Rinascente, this is not the Roman way of shopping.

For the lover of antiques there are many exciting possibilities. Some of the bargains left for the dedicated hunter are in prints, etchings, and music scores. They are sold under the sign *"Libreria-Antiquaria."* The Piazza Borghese is famous for its stands of old books and prints. You get more of a feel for Roman history in an hour of browsing among these prints than in days of reading. Rare, old, first- or second-edition prints command high prices, but there are numerous eighteenth-century prints of piazzas, churches, and monuments that are quite reasonable. The illuminated parchment music sheets, some dating as far back as 1630, are also in abundance. At much higher prices are fine Italian drawings, antiques, and reproductions.

Do remember the shopping hours. They are normally from 9:00 A.M. to 1:00 P.M. and from 3:30 P.M. to 7:30 P.M. In the summer shops reopen at 4:00 P.M. and close at 8:00 P.M. All shops are closed on Sunday; and from September through April shops are closed Monday mornings. From May through September they are closed on Saturday afternoons.

On Sunday mornings you can shop as the Romans do at the Porta Portese flea market. While not the best flea market in the world, it is quite a spectacle. This is the only place in Rome where bargaining is still expected and you can find anything—coffeepots, car parts, cheap clothing, books, ballet shoes and drafting sets sold by the Russian immigrants, antique furniture, and seventeenth-century ceramics. For something very special you will have to look hard and arrive as early as 7:00 A.M.

See the list of selected shops at the end of the book.

Emergencies

The most important number to know in case of an emergency is that of the American Embassy (tel. 46-74), located at Via Vittorio Veneto 119A. They have a list of all American-trained physicians and dentists and can explain the procedure for reporting thefts or accidents. Rome also has an English-speaking hospital and clinic, the Salvator Mundi International Hospital, Viale delle Mura Gianicolense 66–67 (tel. 58-60-41). If you lose your passport you will not be able to go very far—it is needed to cash money and to register at a hotel. The American Consulate at the Embassy can provide you with a new one in a matter of hours. While chances are slim that you will ever recover stolen property, it is worth filing a report with the Italian police for insurance claims and tax deductions.

Pharmacies have late-night and holiday rotations that are posted at the nearest pharmacy. If none are nearby dial 110 for information. If you are taking medication you should bring a supply with you; many American products are not readily available in Italy.

A Word of Warning

You are not likely to be in any physical danger as you walk around the city, but there are some conditions of which you should be aware. Among the many reputations Rome holds is one for its cunning motorcycle thieves who grab for purses, jewelry, and anything else of value. You can also get hurt as they swiftly breeze by you taking their plunder. The best thing, of course, is to not carry a purse or wear jewelry, but this isn't always possible, especially when you are traveling. If you do wear jewelry be discreet; those thin gold chains are a favorite. As for your purse, you will notice that most Roman women wear their shoulder bags across their chest, not just dangling from the shoulder. Follow their example and walk with your bag toward the buildings and not the street. Buses are another danger zone, keep your wallet and purse close to you. One other thing: beware of the gypsy children—they have been skillfully trained to steal from you as you give them money. It is best not to be taken in by their pitiful acts, but to ignore them. They are very persistent, and you may have to be quite stern.

The traffic is as crazy as it seems, so make sure the cars have come to a complete stop before crossing the street; where there are no lights, cross at the white zebra markings, and use underpasses when they are available. As you follow the walks in this book, you will notice that there are usually no sidewalks, and cars and motorscooters will come whizzing by at terrifying speeds. Stay close to the buildings and look around the corner before crossing an intersection.

One thing women may find disarming but needn't worry about is the overtures made by men. These are harmless displays of one of Italian men's favorite pastimes, women-watching. Just remember that any acknowledgment is a form of encouragement. Keep walking. If flirting becomes a major annoyance during your trip it may be because you are calling attention to yourself. It is wise to respect the city's dress code, which is generally elegant and rather conservative.

Glossary of Architectural Terms

architrave: the molded band or group of moldings that rests immediately above the columns.

atrium: originally the principal room in an ancient Roman house; later it became used to define the porch enclosed on three sides and attached to the front of a basilica.

barrel vault: a semicylindrical vault with parallel and evenly spaced support structures.

basilica: an early Christian church with a broad nave ending in a semicircular apse and flanked by colonnaded aisles; the basilica type of chuch in its simplest form has a wooden roof, brick walls, and an interior decorated with mosaics and frescoes.

belvedere: a structure or tower on the top of a building commanding a fine view; from *bel*, "beautiful," and *vedere*, "to see."

campanile: a bell tower next to a church.

capital: the uppermost part of a column or pilaster, crowning the shaft.

cella: the part of an ancient Roman temple within the walls, as distinct from the open porticoes; it contained the image of the deity.

corbel: a projection from the wall or structure to support a weight lying or resting on top of it.

Corinthian: the most elaborate of the three Greek orders of architecture, characterized by its bell-shaped capital enveloped with acanthus leaves.

cornice: the horizontal molded projection that crowns the façade.

cross-mullions: the crossed bars dividing the windows into panes.

Doric: the oldest and simplest of the Greek orders of architecture, distinguished by low proportions and saucer-shaped capitals.

entablature: the wall resting upon the capital of columns and supporting the pediment or roof plate; it is divided into an architrave, the part immediately above the columns; a frieze, the central space; and a cornice, the upper projecting molding.

frieze: that part of an entablature between the architrave and the cornice; usually a sculpted or richly ornamented band.

groined vault: a vault with solid angles formed by the intersection of two arches.

herms: a statue consisting of a head supported on a quadrangular pillar.

Ionic: one of the three Greek orders of architecture, distinguished by the spiral volutes of its capital.

lintel: the horizontal piece spanning an opening or carrying a superstructure.

loggia: a roofed, open gallery that is part of the main structure.

parapet: a low wall or railing.

parastade: a pier produced by thickening the end wall of a porch, usually treated as a pilaster.

pediment: the triangular space forming the gable of a two-pitched roof, used as a decoration over porticoes, doors, and windows.

pergola: a colonnade of beams and poles supporting an open roof, usually treated as an arbor or trellis.

peristyle: the inner court of an ancient Roman dwelling.

pilaster: a rectangular architectural device that is used as a pier but treated as a column with capitals, shaft, and base.

portico: a colonnade or covered walkway.

spandrels: the space between the curved arch and the frame.

stelae: a slab or pillar of stone used as a gravestone.

tondo: circular painting or sculptured medallion.

Tuscan order: a crude version of the Doric order of architecture with unfluted columns and a general lack of ornamentation.

tympanum: the recessed space of a pediment within the frame of the upper and lower cornice.

A Brief History of Rome

The story of Rome's founding is steeped in mythology and goes back to the end of the Trojan War, circa 1200 B.C., when Aeneas, escaping with his father Anchises on his back, landed on the coast of what was called Latium. Three hundred years later, Rea Silvia, a vestal virgin descended from those Trojans, gave birth to twins, Romulus and Remus, whose father was the god Mars. According to the law of the time, Rea Silvia was punished for her infidelity by being buried alive. The twins were left to drift on the Tiber, which carried them to the foot of the Palatine Hill where they were found and kept alive by a she-wolf and raised as shepherds. On this spot they later decided to build a city. On April 21, 753 B.C., Romulus began to build a wall around the Palatine Hill; the city that rose here was called Roma Quadrata because of the hill's square shape. Modern excavations have uncovered portions of this wall and the necropolis that belonged to this earliest settlement.

Favored by its central position on the Italian peninsula, by the proximity of the sea, and by the bold character of its inhabitants, Rome grew rapidly in importance. Under its seven legendary kings—Romulus, Numa Pompilius, Yullius Hostilius, Anicius Marcius, Tarquinius Priscus, Servius Tullius, and Tarquinius Superbus—it successfully waged war against the Latins and the Etruscans. Toward the close of this "period of the kings," a new civic community was organized; its constitution was memorialized by the erection of the Servian Wall. Also built at this time were the Temple of Jupiter Capitolinus, the Circus Maximus, the Carcere Mamertinus, and the Cloaca Maxima, which was intended to drain the swampy site of the Forum. The energetic development of the city under the kings of the Tarquinian family came to an end in 510 B.C. when the city became a republic ruled by two consuls.

Despite a protracted period of internecine struggle between the plebeian and patrician classes, Rome became strong enough finally to conquer the Etruscans of Tarquinii and Veii, who had continued to threaten the city. Shortly after this victory Rome was almost completely destroyed by the Gauls in 390 B.C. But she recovered to conquer the Latins, the Samnites, and the Tarentines, and finally Pyrrhus, at which time, 275 B.C., Rome became mistress of Italy.

Rome flourished. She built fleets, conquered Magna Graecia and Sicily, and challenged the naval prowess of Carthage. Hannibal transferred the Second Punic War to Italy and inflicted severe defeats in the north. But the Romans marched on to conquer Spain and moved the Punic wars back to Africa. In 146 B.C., at the end of the Third Punic War, Carthage was defeated and Rome began a period of aggressive conquest. New countries were disarmed, taxed, and treated as provinces under the control of a Roman magistrate, a proconsul who had wide parameters of power and the opportunity to acquire great fame and wealth. All of Asia Minor, Syria, and Palestine were brought under Roman rule, and Julius Caesar bore the Roman eagles to Gallia Transalpina and Britain. Soon, Rome ruled the Mediterranean. Cato the Censor asked himself, "What will become of Rome when she no longer has any State to fear?" This was the republic's major problem during its last years.

In 49 B.C. Caesar crossed the Rubicon at the head of his troops and marched into Rome; thus began another era in the city's history—the Roman Empire. Caesar became dictator, and his administration included reforms of the calendar, the census, money, and weights and measures. His greatest work, however, was the unification of the Roman world under one leader and under one system of law.

Julius Caesar's murder was a historical blunder; as Cicero said, the tyrant was dead but the tyranny survived. The civil war that followed made it plain to all that good government was no longer possible, except under a beneficent tyrant, and no man was better fitted to play that part than Caesar had been. Though most of Caesar's successors were also murdered, the Roman Empire lasted another five hundred years.

Until the time of Augustus Caesar, Rome was anything but a handsome city. But her steadily increasing power over the then-known world demanded that she display the pride of a capital city, and the funds were available to do so in an impressive manner. Augustus's reign also provided an unusual forty-five years of peace. The result was magnificent; of all the ancient

Roman monuments, those built during the reign of Augustus are among the best. In the Campus Martius rose the original Pantheon, the Portico d'Ottavia, the Mausoleum of Augustus, and the Ara Pacis. Also credited to his reign are the Basilica Julia, the Domus Augustiana on the Palatine, and the Forum of Augustus with the Temple of Mars. No fewer then eighty-two temples were restored by Augustus, and the brick in Roman architecture that we admire today came into use at that time, supplemented by travertine from Tivoli or marble from Carrara, Paros and other Greek islands.

Augustus's successors followed his example in the building of public monuments, each man striving to surpass his predecessors. In this respect Nero (A.D. 54–68) displayed the most unbridled ambitions. In A.D. 64 he reduced the city to ashes in order to rebuild it in a more modern style. Most of Nero's work, however, was destroyed by his successors, including his "Golden House," a palace with gardens that extended from the Palatine Hill across the valley of the Colosseum and up the Esquiline Hill.

The Flavian dynasty continued the tradition, building the Colosseum, to this day considered a symbol of Rome's power, and the Triumphal Arch of Titus, which commemorated the destruction of Jerusalem. Under Trajan, Roman architecture received a new impetus and may have reached its zenith. The Forum of Trajan, with its column named after him and its reliefs now found on Constantine's Arch, are eloquent testimonies to this period's achievements. Under the next emperor, Hadrian, the majestic dome of the Pantheon was raised to dominate the city's skyline, and the Temple of Venus and Roma and his Mausoleum (now Castel S. Angelo) were also added to the city's inventory of great architecture.

Under Marcus Aurelius the Stoic there was a period of such peace and prosperity that to this day the Roman belief exists that "the good old times" will return when the equestrian statue of Aurelius, once gracing the Campidoglio, is again gilded in gold. But this peace was short-lived; during the century following the reign of Marcus Aurelius the empire was beset with civil wars, barbarian invasions, famine, and the plague. The decline of Rome as the capital of the ancient world began under Diocletian in 284. Despite all this adversity, contributions to the city's landscape were made during this epoch: the column of Marcus Aurelius, the Arch of Septimius Severus, the Baths of Caracalla, the huge Thermae of Diocletian, and the Aurelian Walls—all of which stand today much as they did then.

Diocletian divided the empire into east and west, but it wasn't until Constantine moved the seat of government to Byzantium in 330 that this division became a reality. It marked a turning point in the history of the city and the empire. The last important ruins of antiquity, the Basilica Thermae and the Triumphal Arch, bear Constantine's name. Statistics about Rome at this point indicate that the city had 19 aqueducts, 8 bridges, 425 streets, 1,790 palaces, 46,602 homes, 11 thermae, 856 baths, 1,352 street fountains, 36 triumphal arches, and 10 basilicas. After Constantine's reign no new works were begun, and the city fell into a long period of decay.

The Roman religion was based on the belief that the gods intervened in human affairs with rewards and punishments for good and bad actions. Propitiated by sacrifices and offerings, the gods' favor was always sought on any projected enterprise. The chief religious officials were the Pontifex Maximus; the minor pontifice; the flamens; the augurs, who interpreted the mood of the gods; and the vestal virgins, who kept alive the sacred fire of Vesta that had been brought from Alba Longa. It wasn't a sophisticated religion but rather one steeped in tradition, and tradition formed the basis of Roman law and order. Though generally tolerant of various religious beliefs, Christianity contradicted Roman religion and rule at almost every level—the belief in only one divinity, the condemnation of idolatry, the assertion of human equality, and the belief in future punishment for evildoers. Despite three centuries of persecution the Christians gained increasing strength and organized themselves into independent, self-governed republics. By the time Constantine issued his celebrated decree in 313, which granted Christianity equality with other religions, the bishop of Rome was in a position to be recognized as an official of the state. This office, which became known as "pope" after the Romans' Pontifex Maximus, quickly filled the vacuum of power left by the decaying empire. When Alaric the Barbarian appeared before the walls of Rome in 408 it was Pope Innocent I who acted as the city's representative. In 451, Pope Leo I saved Rome from Attila the Hun; and in 455 his intercession softened the blows of Genseric the Vandal. After these events the Romans regarded the Pope as their leader and defender, a position that was further strengthened by the fall of the Western Empire in 476.

The great struggles and victories of Christianity helped preserve Rome from total destruction. The city's transformation from pagan to Christian was accompanied by the gradual development of the papacy as the supreme ecclesiastical power in the West. Pope Leo the Great (440–461) and Pope Gregory the Great (590–604) are credited with this scheme of aggrandizement. Their objective was the independence of Rome from Byzantium, the subjection of the Eastern Church to the Court of Rome, and the conversion of the Germans. In 727 the Longobard king gave the ancient Etruscan town of Sutri to the pope, and this was the first step in the formation of the Papal States. This act was reinforced in 755 when Pepin, at the pope's request, defeated the Lombards and gave a portion of their territory to the papacy. On Christmas Day in 800, Charlemagne, son of Pepin, was crowned augustus and emperor by Pope Leo III in St. Peter's—an act that marked the beginning of Rome's medieval history. This "Holy Roman Empire" endured until the abdication of Francis II of Austria in 1806.

Characteristic of this period are the once-numerous towers of red brick that stand in such strong contrast to the monuments of ancient Rome. This style of architecture was developed during the Carolingian epoch, though most of the towers we now see were not erected before the twelfth century. During this time the great monuments of antiquity were doomed to desecration and destruction. Gregorovius gives us a colorful description of their fate:

> Charlemagne had already set the example of carrying off ancient columns and sculpture to adorn his cathedral at Aix-la-Chapelle; the nobles and even the abbots took possession of magnificent ancient edifices which they disfigured by the addition of modern towers; and the citizens

established their work-shops, rope-walks, and smithies in the towers and circuses of imperial Rome. The fisherman selling his fish near the bridges over the Tiber, the butcher displaying his meat at the theater of Marcellus, and the baker exposing his bread for sale, deposited their wares on the magnificent slabs of marble which had once been used as seats by the senators in the theater or circus and perhaps by Caesar, Mark Antony, Augustus, and other masters of the world. The elaborately sculptured sarcophagi of Roman heroes were scattered in every direction and converted into cisterns, washing-vats, and troughs for swine; and the table of the tailor and the shoemaker was perhaps formed by the cippus of some illustrious Roman matron for the display of her jewellery. For several centuries Rome may be said to have resembled a vast lime-kiln, into which the costliest marbles were recklessly cast for the purpose of burning lime; and thus did the Romans incessantly pillage, burn, dismantle, and utterly destroy their glorious old city.

Upon Charlemagne's death a turbulent period ensued for the papacy. The Crusades against the Turks in Jerusalem began and lasted two hundred years. The city was repeatedly besieged and captured by German armies, and within the city itself various families fought for control. These increasing civic and national crises led Pope Clement V (1305–1316) in 1309 to transfer the papacy to Avignon, where it remained until 1377. During these years Rome was successively governed by Guelphs and Ghibellines, Neapolitans and Germans, Orsinis, Colonnas, and Caetanis; and, for a brief period in 1347, by Cola di Rienzo, who succeeded in restoring the ancient republican form of government. This was an unhappy time in Rome's history. Poverty, war, and disease reduced its population to less than 20,000 inhabitants.

A change was inaugurated with the return of Gregory XI (1370–1378) to Rome in 1377. The schism between the Eastern and Western churches engaged the attention of the popes immediately upon their return, and it was not until 1420 that Pope Martin V began to restore the city, which had deteriorated both physically and socially during the so-called Babylonian Captivity. Under Pope Julius II and Pope Leo X, Rome, aided by vast sums of money that flowed into the papal coffers, attracted the greatest artists of the Italian Renaissance. Slowly the city regained its pride and again transformed itself into a capital, this time of the Christian world.

Yet even at this point in time Rome was not safe from barbarian invasion. In 1527 the city was sacked by German troops of the Imperial General Charles of Bourbon. Restoration after this attack, as well as further embellishments, occupied succeeding popes. The population increased; palaces were built by members of the Papal Court; popes and cardinals restored old churches and vied with each other to build new ones. Their efforts, combined with what has been left of ancient Rome, are what distinguishes Rome from other Italian and European cities.

In the 1700s, Italy was divided into a number of small states. Genoa and Venice were republics; the king of Sardinia held Savoy, Nice, and Piedmont; Lombardy was under the last emperor of the Holy Roman Empire, Francis II; Tuscany, Modena, and Parma were under dukes; the pope ruled the states of the Church; and a Bourbon was king of Naples and Sicily. In 1798 the French, under the leadership of Napoleon, entered Rome and declared a republic. Pope Pius VI was taken prisoner and died in France in 1799. This occupation was but one step in Napoleon's plan to conquer all of Italy and the Holy Roman Empire. In 1810 the French senate proclaimed Rome their second capital, and in 1811 Napoleon conferred the title of king of Rome on his newborn son. In 1815, when Napoleon finally fell, the Congress of Vienna divided Italy among the conquerors: the north (except Genoa, which fell to Victor Emmanuel, king of Sardinia) went to Austrian princes; the Bourbon family obtained Naples and Sicily; and Rome was restored to the pope along with the Papal States.

A general revolutionary movement spread throughout Italy in 1848. It was headed by Mazzini, whose aim was to create a United Italian Republic. Insurrection broke out in Rome; after the pope fled south to Gaeta a triumvirate of Mazzini, Saffi, and Armellini proclaimed Rome a republic and entrusted its defense to Garibaldi. This, however, did not last long because the French came to the defense of the pope and his territory. While Victor Emmanuel was proclaimed king of Italy in 1861, it wasn't until 1870, when the French troops left to fight the Prussian War, that the Italians were finally able to capture Rome and, in 1871, make it their capital. This ended the papacy's temporal power and its rule over Rome.

After World War I a Fascist movement was organized by Benito Mussolini. It grew rapidly. In October 1922 the Fascists marched into Rome; King Vittorio Emanuele III invited Mussolini to form a government, which he did and which prevailed until the middle of World War II, when it was overthrown on July 25, 1943. During the Fascist reign, in 1929, the Lateran Treaty was signed declaring the Vatican an independent sovereign state. From September 1943 until its liberation by Allied troops in 1944, Rome was occupied by Germans.

In 1946, Vittorio Emanuele III abdicated. In December 1947 the Constituent Assembly approved a new republican constitution. Since then there have been numerous governmental crises, but the Italian people have maintained a strongly democratic and united republic.

When Rome resumed her place as capital of Italy much was done to improve the amenities of the city, often at the cost of the picturesque. Old quarters, such as those of the Campitelli and Suburra, were leveled and new quarters were built outside the walls to accommodate a rapidly increasing population. The climax of replanning was reached in the 1930s. Broad thoroughfares were built and many of the historic monuments were isolated from the surroundings. The construction plans facilitated the excavation of important areas, especially around the Forum. The most significant development, however, was the establishment of the Esposizione Universale, EUR, which is now an important business center and suburb on the edge of town—Mussolini's equivalent of the late-nineteenth-century monument to Vittorio Emanuele that dominates the city skyline.

The Artisans
and the
Bourgeoisie:
Around the
Piazza Navona

○

This walk forms a wide semicircle around one of
Rome's most important and beautiful landmarks, the
Piazza Navona, in an area said by many Romans to be
the heart of the city. Rather than visit celebrated
Renaissance and baroque attractions we will meander
down narrow streets crowded with the inhabitants of
this once prosperous bourgeois quarter. It is remarkable how much the neighborhood still reflects its
late-fifteenth-century origins, when it blossomed
as a center for artisans, intellectuals, merchants, and
tourists.

It is also remarkable how much life has been crowded into this small area, embraced by a half-loop of the
Tiber River. The earliest documentation still available
indicates that this was the private reserve of the Tarquins, those Tuscan tyrants who were so hostile to the
Roman population confined on the Palatine Hill.
When they finally drove the Tarquins out, the Romans
consecrated the low-lying plain to their favorite deity,
Mars, the god of war. During the republic the Roman
legions conducted their maneuvers here, on the Campus Martius, and the population on the surrounding
hills used it for sport and recreation. By the time of the
empire this expanse of open field provided the space
for a new monumental quarter. The Pantheon, the
Thermae of Agrippa (the first of those public baths
that were to become such a rage in Rome), the Basilica of Neptune, and other structures were built in a setting of gardens and porticoes.

But fires, war, and time destroyed the grandeur of
the ancient Campus Martius. After the sixth century the
destruction of the aqueducts forced much of the city's
population from the hills onto this plain near the river's edge, providing them with both easy access to water and predictable disaster during winter floods. Only
when the Church reestablished its power and prestige
after the Great Schism did the area regain some of its
grandeur, reinterpreted in the Renaissance mode. Because of its proximity to the Vatican this became an

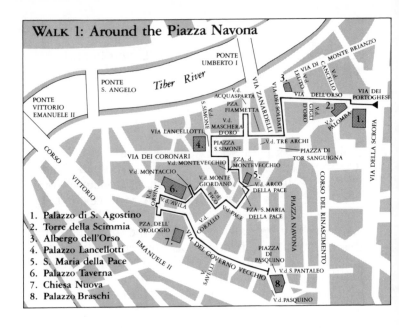

WALK 1: Around the Piazza Navona

1. Palazzo di S. Agostino
2. Torre della Scimmia
3. Albergo dell'Orso
4. Palazzo Lancellotti
5. S. Maria della Pace
6. Palazzo Taverna
7. Chiesa Nuova
8. Palazzo Braschi

ideal residential district for nobility, upper-class merchants, and clergy. It also became a tourist center with many hotels, restaurants, and shops to serve the visitors and pilgrims to the Vatican. The physical renewal initiated in the fifteenth century continued through the end of the eighteenth as the blocks around the medieval street network became dense with new developments, and the remaining medieval structures were replaced with residential and institutional buildings.

Except for the first block of our walk we will be on streets of the Ponte and Parione *riones,* "quarters," of the city. These divisions, originally imposed by Augustus Caesar for the purpose of governing and administrating the city and now used only by the post office, identify sections of town and conjure up tales about the city's history. *Ponte* means "bridge," in this case the quarter's lifeline to the Vatican. *Parione* derives from the Latin for "wall," and probably refers to the barrier around the Roman port that once stood on the river's edge.

Our walk will begin at the corner of Via della Scrofa and Via dei Portoghesi. There, and for a block, we will be standing in the confines of the *rione* of S. Eustachio, a name that dates back to the early days of Christianity in Rome. Legend has it that S. Eustachio was a man named Placidus who played an important part in the Dacian campaign as a general in the army of Trajan. One day, while hunting in the mountains between the Tiber and Praeneste, he saw a stag at bay and clearly defined between the antlers was a grave face "with eyes that penetrated his soul." (This vision of the head of the Savior between the antlers of a stag is now on the coat of arms for that *rione*.) Placidus returned to Rome and was baptized, along with all the members of his family, under the name of Eustachius. This act had immediate and disastrous consequences: he lost all his property and was forced to migrate to Egypt, where his wife was kidnapped by pirates and his children reportedly were taken away by wild beasts. Eustachius's leadership and valor were not forgotten in Rome, however, and when Trajan faced another war, this time against the Persians, he commanded that his best general be found. Eustachius was discovered working as a hired laborer in Egypt and was brought back to Rome, where a more tolerant emperor, Hadrian, had recently taken the helm. For a short time Eustachius's life reverted to its former dignity; his campaign against the Persians was a success, his wife and children were found, and he was honored in Rome with a great triumphal procession. But when he refused to perform the traditional sacrifice of the victor to Jupiter, a ceremony held here on the Campus Martius, he was condemned to death along with all the members of his family. This is not an unusual story of martyrdom during the early days of Christianity, but the courage and faith of this Roman general made a very deep impression in this fledgling community: it is one of only two of the city's twenty-two *riones* that bears the name of a Christian saint.

If you would like to fortify yourself with a quick bite before you begin your walk, or just feast your eyes on sumptuous displays in an Italian delicatessen, step into Volpetti's, just behind you at Via della Scrofa 32. You should at least take a peek; many Romans drive across town just to shop here—one of the two or three best *rosticcerie* in town. The shelves have wine from all over Italy and the counters are piled high with gourmet delights. And you don't have to wait to sample; there is a counter where you can order a sandwich or a plate of any of the prepared items on the shelf.

This done, return to the Via dei Portoghesi. Only the

optical shop to the right, on the corner, is a reminder of modern exigencies. The bar, the pharmacy, the wine shop, the tobacconist, and the barbershop all look as if they have been here for the last hundred years, and they probably have. A few yards to your left, at no. 12, is the entrance to the Palazzo di S. Agostino. This palazzo was originally built to house the Augustine Order, whose main church is a block away (it is one of the earliest Renaissance churches and is important for its artistic treasures). The building, now occupied by the city's Ministry of Justice, presents us with a courtyard that is rather bland considering the artistic heritage associated with this religious order. When occupied by the monks, followers of St. Augustine, it was a fifteenth-century-style cloister. Only the tombstones in the portico remain to give a hint of this courtyard's more gracious past. These tombstones, including that of Cardinal Piccolomini, nephew of Pope Pius II and a fellow humanist and patron of the arts, are typical of the workshop of Andrea Bregno. The reliefs are in the manner of Nino da Fiesole. Both Bregno and da Fiesole were important stonecutters and sculptors during the Renaissance.

This palazzo also houses the Angelica Library, one of the best research libraries in Rome. Its location here reminds us of one of this neighborhood's characteristics: until recent times this was considered the center of Rome's intellectual life and, therefore, a favorite location for printers, publishers, and booksellers. A 1526 census shows that twenty-four publishers and booksellers were located in the immediate vicinity, along with numerous writers. The publishing trade began in Rome at the end of the fifteenth century and blossomed during the seventeenth and eighteenth in conjunction with the art of engraving, which was to become one of Rome's most flourishing trades. In this neighborhood Lafrery printed his *Speculum Romanae Magnificentiae*, an important documentation of Roman archeological sites; de Pérac printed his famous plates; and the offices of di Rossi provided the Vatican with the basis for its collection "Calcographia Camerale" that includes, among other important engravings, the plate for the great map of Rome by Nolli published in 1748 by Giangiacomo di Rossi. Today the publishing trade is not nearly as active here, but the tradition is carried on by the many antiquarian book and print shops concentrated in this section of town.

To your right, behind an iron gate, is the national church of Portugal, S. Antonio dei Portoghesi, crowned by heraldic angels blowing trumpets. Founded as a pilgrim hospice in 1417 the present church was begun by Martino Longhi in the mid-seventeenth century and continued by Carlo Rainaldi and Cristoforo Schor until 1695. The two virile figures holding up the side vaults, along with the magnificent angels that seem capable of flying across the tile roof of the Palazzo di S. Agostino, achieve the delightful, theatrical effect that is so central to baroque architecture. If the church is open, it's worth a visit for its collage of rich marbles. Missing since the eighteenth century, when Rome was occupied by the French and a number of Rome's treasures were shipped to various points in Europe, is the chapel of the baptistry decorated by Luigi Vanvitelli and Nicola Salvi. It was dismantled stone by stone and taken, along with the paintings and silver candelabras, to Lisbon, where it now stands in the Church of S. Rocco.

Directly in front of us, above the *barbiere* sign, is the tower of an old Frangipane fortress that was incorporated into a sixteenth-century residence. This is known to all Romans as the Torre della Scimmia, Tower of the Monkey. Readers of Hawthorne will recognize it as Hilda's tower in *The Marble Faun*. He describes the view from where we stand:

> . . . indeed what might be called either a widening of the street, or a small piazza. The neighborhood comprises a baker's oven, emitting the usual fragrance of sour bread; a shoeshop; a linen-draper's shop; a pipe and cigar shop; a lottery office; a station for French soldiers, with a sentinel pacing in front, and a fruit stand, at which a Roman matron was selling the dried kernels of chestnuts, wretched little figs, and some bouquets of yesterday. A church, of course, was near at hand, the façade of which ascended into lofty pinnacles, whereon were perched two or three winged figures of stone, either angelic or allegorical, blowing stone trumpets in close vicinity to the upper windows of an old shabby palace. This palace was distinguished by a feature not very common in the architecture of Roman edifices; that is to say, a medieval tower, square, massive, lofty and battlemented and machiolated at the summit.

At one of the angles of the battlements stood a shrine of the Virgin, such as we see everywhere at the street corners of Rome, but seldom or never, except in this solitary instance, at a height above the ordinary level of men's views and aspirations. Connected with this old tower and its lofty shrine there is a legend which we cannot here pause to tell; but for centuries a lamp has been burning before the Virgin's image, at noon, midnight, and at all hours of the twenty-four, and must be kept burning forever, as long as the tower shall stand; or else the tower itself, the palace, and whatever estate belongs to it, shall pass from its hereditary possessor, in accordance with an ancient vow, and become property of the Church.

I will pause to recount the legend to which Hawthorne refers because it gives the tower its Italian name. The event took place in the seventeenth century when the house was inhabited by the Scapucci family. One day a young married couple's pet monkey carried their small child to the top of the battlements. The infant's cries attracted attention, and the father was summoned to the scene. Standing in the center of the street he invoked the aid of the Madonna and whistled to the ape who then obediently climbed down the tower along a waterpipe, clutching the child in its arms. As an offering of thanks for this miracle the father erected the shrine to the Madonna, which we see at the summit of the tower. The lamp is still kept burning, as Hawthorne describes, and though the palace is not in the hands of the Church, it is owned by a quasi-religious group. I imagine the wind must have blown out the candle for a few minutes!

There is also a legend dating back to the Middle Ages having to do with the origin of the name Frangipane, the family that built this tower. In 725, during an especially vicious flood of the Tiber, Flavio Anicia rowed around town in a boat dispensing bread to stranded people. When they saw him coming they cried out, *"Frange nobis panem,"* Latin for "divide some bread with us." He and his descendants became known as Frangipane, a name they later adopted; they also added to their family crest a large loaf of bread between the feet of lions. The Frangipanes were one of the most powerful families in eleventh-century Rome.

In medieval times these towers played decisive roles in the clan fights betwen papal and antipapal factions.

Their purpose is sometimes vividly described by chroniclers who make them sound like part of a Hollywood stage set with siege towers, fortified walls, and moats. In actuality only a few of these towers were so heavily fortified. Many were built as status symbols; the higher the tower, the more prestige. The Torre della Scimmia was built late in the thirteenth century, and this late date, along with the remaining travertine ornamentation, indicates that it was probably constructed with status rather than warfare in mind.

From Hilda's tower we take the street to the right, Via dell'Orso, past the Albergo Portoghesi with its Parisian-style streetlamps. But that's the only thing about this street that is not Roman. Named for a famous hotel located at the far end, this street has undergone several transformations since the fifteenth century. In 1480, Pope Sixtus IV paved this road for the first time and it became known as the Via Sistina. In 1488, when another Via Sistina was built, this became the Via Pontificium, after the papal processions here. In 1516 it became a section of the Via Recta Papalis, again after the papal parades; and when this route was changed, it assumed the name Via dell'Orso, Street of the Bear. The name isn't the only thing about this street that's changed over time. Originally known for its livery stables and hotels, in the 1800s it became known as a street of antique dealers. In fact, Cardinal Fesch, uncle of Napoleon I and Napoleon's ambassador to the Vatican, is said to have found the first piece of Leonardo da Vinci's painting of S. Jerome in a shop on this street. Thanks to Cardinal Fesch's passion for collecting, we can now see the entire panel at the Vatican Museum. In this century the antique shops have moved to Via dei Coronari, Via Giulia, Via Babuino, and Via dei Cappellari. Today, in their place, the ground-floor shops belong to artisans—carpenters, jewelers, gilders, lampshade makers, furniture restorers, brass workers, and upholsterers. All these crafts can be seen as you walk down the street. If you find yourself here in June you may also see the annual outdoor handicrafts show.

As the street became less fashionable so did its façades, but it is being improved now that high rents can be had any place in the center-city. No. 64–67, with the jewelry shop on the ground floor, is still part

Restorer's shop on Via dell'Orso

of the large palazzo that was attached to Hilda's tower in the late 1500s. To your right you will pass two streets reminiscent of the Middle Ages: the Vicolo dell'Orso, which ends suddenly after a few steps because a building has obstructed its passage, and the Via del Cancello, named after a gate that once protected pedestrians from the river's edge.

To your left, on the corner of Via dell'Orso and Via della Palomba, is no. 74, an eighteenth-century building of particular interest at the time of this writing because it is all closed up and covered with signs announcing that it has been illegally restored. This is an increasingly familiar example of some of the current urban renewal and legal battles taking place in the historic center of Rome. Restoration is welcome and helpful, but the city is trying hard to protect the rights of long-term tenants and the integrity of the original architectural plans. It is not an easy project to undertake, and, as we see here, violations can lead to bureaucratic battles (in this case, more than six years long). In the meantime this building stands empty in a city where the need for housing is critical. I am told that in the courtyard behind the locked gates is a beautiful three-tiered antique fountain.

On the right, at no. 28, is another recently restored building, the Palazzo Antonio Massimo. As it was important enough in the topology of this neighborhood to appear on Bufalini's map of sixteenth-century Rome, this is an especially welcome sign of the general face-lift given this section of town. It is also good to see that the courtyard has not been sanitized and still houses the print and graphic art shop that is so in keeping with the neighborhood's character.

A few yards from here, to your left, is the beginning of Via dei Gigli d'Oro (Street of the Golden Lilies). The name comes from the lilies painted on a sign that indicated a hotel or restaurant, but the street's landmark was the women's public baths located somewhere along its way. These baths were installed at the end of the fifteenth century to accommodate the female pilgrims and populace of the area, but it also brought courtesans, for whom this amenity made the neighborhood an attractive place to live.

Past the Vicolo del Leuto and a dozen yards to your left, near no. 87, is a small corner created by a building that juts a couple of feet out onto the street. Here rests a fragment from a Roman sarcophagus on which there is an image of a lion attacking an antelope. Equally picturesque is the house itself with its portal dating from the 1500s and the wild bushes clinging to the waterpipe up the front of the building.

At the end of the street to your right is the former hotel, the Albergo dell'Orso, that gave this street its name. Legend has it that Dante stayed here when he made his famous pilgrimage to Rome for the Holy Year of 1300. As most experts agree that the building dates from the mid-fifteenth century and was not open as a hotel until the Jubilee Year of 1475, this legend must be apocryphal. However, the rooms have seen numerous other dignitaries: Rabelais stayed here at the beginning of the sixteenth century; and when Montaigne arrived in 1581 to be made an honorary burgess of the city, this was considered the best hotel in town. (He writes of his stay at the Albergo dell'Orso in his essay on vanity.) Goethe also is said to have found temporary lodging here when he came to Rome in 1786. These illustrious figures, along with numerous foreign cardinals, nobles, ambassadors, ministers, priests, artists, scientists, and poets, all associated this charming building with Rome. And, as was customary during the Renaissance, many of them commemorated their stay by having their coats of arms painted on the wall in the room they used.

By the end of the nineteenth century this building was still open as a hotel, but the dignitaries had moved to more fashionable lodgings in the area around the Spanish Steps, and their cooks, maids, and coachmen found quarters here. In the 1930s the city chose to save the building from complete ruin and restored it to its sixteenth-century splendor. In 1937, on the anniversary of Rome's birthday, April 21, it was opened as an elegant restaurant/nightclub. Well into the 1960s this was one of the finest and most glamorous evening spots in town, but these days I recommend only a drink to see the lovely interior.

During the restoration a medieval projection, probably an outhouse that had been walled in for centuries, was opened up. To the shock of the workers and the delight of storytellers the skeleton of a man was found intact. There were no traces of this man's identity or history, but rumors of a sinister murder made such an impression on the neighbors that they still talk about it as if the discovery had just been made. (In fact, until I researched the event I assumed that this proof of the "atrocities of the medieval world" was found during my stay in Rome and not, as it had been, well before I was born.) Even without the gruesome discovery, the restoration of this ancient hotel seems to have fascinated local residents. The hotel is a symbol of a more glamorous past and a source of great pride among the older generation whose families have, as they say, always been here. This is not true of many of the younger people I talked to, on account of the huge post–World War II immigration to Rome.

Walk to the front of the hotel; it faces a wall and steps that lead up to the street which runs along the river. Until the 1800s the hotel stood at the crossroads of Via dell'Orso and Via di Monte Brianzo, one of the main arteries of the medieval and Renaissance city because it connected the northern section of the city to the Ponte S. Angelo and the Vatican. Some historians say that Rome's hotel industry began in this area, the Albergo dell'Orso being just one of many dating from the fifteenth through seventeenth centuries. In the sixteenth century the area around the Campo dei Fiori also picked up the flourishing business of housing and nourishing pilgrims; and by the seventeenth the Piazza di Spagna was included. Today there is hardly a section of Rome that doesn't cater to this trade, yet this neighborhood now does so less than most.

On the front of this charming building is an arched loggia supported by ancient marble columns. The loggia had been decorated with fragments of marble frescoes, traces of which are still visible. A story is told that when the hotel opened, back in 1475, the owner asked a painter to decorate the façade of the building with two bears. The painter wanted six scudi to paint the bears with a chain that tied them to the portal, or four scudi to paint them without the chain. Taking the cheapest offer the owner had a bitter surprise when after a period of rain the fresco almost disappeared. In response to the owner's complaint the painter said, "You didn't want them chained to the wall, so they ran away." I can only say that I am glad the building hasn't disappeared entirely as so many of these early Renaissance houses have.

There is little left in this area to remind us of the days of the Roman Empire except for a few hints in the names of streets and some marble fragments. For example, there was once a port at this point of the Tiber that was used for the delivery of marble, so important to architectural design during and after the time of Augustus. The port is gone, but a reminder of that heritage is embedded in the wall on the corner of Via dell'Orso and Via dei Soldati: a beautiful sculptured animal, which many say gave the hotel and street its name. (I, however, would call the animal a lion, not a bear.) Unfortunately, what we see now is an imitation; on the night of March 8–9, 1976, the original, dating back to the Roman Empire, was stolen. In an example of community spirit the artisans on Via dell'Orso commissioned Vincenzo Piovano, who has a shop here, to carve a new one. The Via dei Soldati, which we will take, is itself a reminder of the ancient Campus Martius: it is named for the soldiers' barracks that once stood here.

Via dei Soldati was a commercial center for wine and woodwork during the Renaissance. Today its narrow dark length is of little interest; even the shops have small entrances that lead into dungeonlike spaces. Except for the building at no. 29, a charming

Renaissance palazzo with a devilish face carved over the portal, what we are looking at are the imposing and faceless backs of grand baroque palazzi. To your left, beyond the Vicolo dei Soldati, is the back of the Palazzo Altemps, a Spanish seminary. This building is an example of a number of sites so irritating to serious students of Rome: it is almost impossible to visit its works of art or examine its architectural points of interest, yet it contains an important collection of antique marble, an important library, and a chapel that has the distinction of housing the only papal tomb located in a private residence, that of S. Aniceto, the eleventh pope, who reigned from 155 to 166. At one time the chapel was open to the public one day a year, on the feast day of St. Aniceto, and one could at least catch a glimpse of the impressive courtyard with loggia and elaborate stucco work and the frescoes of Romanelli, but no longer.

The end of the street opens onto the Piazza di Tor Sanguigna, named after the medieval tower at no. 8 on the far left-hand corner. The tower was built by the Sanguigni family, who controlled the immediate area until the fifteenth century. The restaurant Passetto, before the tower, is also of some importance to visitors, as many consider it to be one of the finest restaurants in Rome.

Don't walk the length of the piazza—we will cross the street at the newsstand—but for information's sake note the modern building at the far end that borders the Piazza Navona. In this building, at street level, is an excavated site that allows you to see some of the stones and columns remaining from the substructure of the Stadium of Domitian (A.D. 81–96), which gave the Piazza Navona its present shape. These remains were exposed in 1938, when the avenue to your right (Via Zanardelli) was built with the intention of opening this end of the piazza to view from the Palace of Justice across the river. The plan so outraged the Romans' sensibility that the modern building was erected to replace those that had already been demolished.

Go past the newsstand and across Via Zanardelli toward the gas station and bar on the other side of the street. Walk along the street, which for no obvious reason is called a piazza (Piazza Fiammetta), to its end and turn right onto another street, also with a slightly inappropriate name, Via degli Acquasparta (this one I would call a piazza because of the island of trees in the middle of a rectangular square). Here stands another delightful fifteenth-century house known as the Casa di Fiammetta. In the sixteenth century this house, still a private residence, belonged to the celebrated courtesan Fiammetta Michaelis, the mistress of Caesare Borgia (people often mistake this Fiammetta for her namesake, Boccaccio's lover). Fiammetta was part of that charmed circle to which Castiglione, Sadoleto, Bembo, and Raphael belonged. On warm summer nights this privileged group enjoyed dining out, perhaps occasionally under the trees in front of Fiammetta's house but most often in the garden of their friend John Garitz. They entertained themselves by reading verses that were, in the spirit of the Renaissance, an extraordinary mixture of paganism and Christianity—the Virgin and the saints glorified as classical goddesses. This was a time when the classical ideal of beauty was being rediscovered, and, like the humanists, Fiammetta and her colleagues imagined that they were modeling themselves after their classical predecessors, the famous *hetaerae* of Greece and Rome. Fiammetta composed verses, studied the classical authors, cultivated the art of conversation, and surrounded herself with illustrious men. She was a very active and prominent figure in Rome, and even built herself a chapel in the exclusive church of S. Agostino. This chapel, along with the tombs of other courtesans, was removed from the church during a surge of prudishness. The courtesans' contribution to the social fabric of Rome during the Renaissance cannot, however, be so quickly dismissed.

Courtesans were unusually plentiful in Rome, where a large clerical population and the guarantee of tourism provided a clientele. Those of the highest strata were educated women, esteemed as much for their company and conversation as for their physical attractions. The greatest of them was Imperia, who lived during the reign of Pope Julius II (1503–1513). Her beauty and charm were famous throughout Europe, and among her many admirers was Agostino Chigi, the most powerful Roman banker of his day. She lived in such magnificence that the Spanish ambassador, on a visit to her residence, is reported to have had to spit into the face of his servant because it was the only nonprecious object in the room.

Pietro Aretino, who lived in Rome during the 1520s and 1530s, delighted in depicting the lowlife of the courtesans. In his risqué *Ragionamenti*, a wise and witty older courtesan named Nanna gives advice to a pretty young apprentice about how one rises to the top of their profession. She talks a great deal about manners, but also tells the girl to keep some fashionable pieces of literature, such as Aristo's *Orlando Furioso* and Petrarch's poems, on her table so that her suitors will think she is well-read.

Alvigia, in Aretino's *Cortegiana*, delighted in the appearance of wealth and showing off in public. One can imagine her strolling through the streets in her best finery, accompanied by numerous servants, and looking down at everyone along the way—an image not unlike the spectacle of a cardinal walking down the street, as described by other writers of the time. Added to this picture of luxury were her choice of pets —parrots and monkeys, animals that were both exotic and costly.

Fiammetta shared her high position in Roman society with other great courtesans who may also have lived in this neighborhood: Tulia d'Aragona, a poet prominent in the 1520s and 1530s; Camilla of Pisa, who published elegant letters to well-known literary figures; Marema-non-vuole, known for her recitation of Latin and Italian poetry; and Pantha, a favorite of cardinals and one of the best-known courtesans of the time.

Back to Fiammetta's house, which couldn't be more charming. Although it does have all the elements of a house from the 1400s with its arched windows and portico, there is hardly a brick left from the original structure. Despite criticism made about its overrestoration, my excitement when I first "discovered" it, on my initial wanderings through Rome, was tremendous. This excitement is generated as much by the house as by the setting—it stands alone with some trees on a piazza with other buildings of interest from the 1500s, nos. 11 and 16.

Retracing our steps to the Piazza Fiammetta and the back of the house (don't miss any of the details, such as windows, gates, and chimneys), we find ourselves at the beginning of Via della Maschera d'Oro. This is the street we will take, but before we go on, let me point out something interesting off the main route. To your left, go down the Vicolo S. Trifone, which forms an angle with the beginning of Via della Maschera d'Oro; after a few steps you'll find yourself in the narrowest street in the city, Via dei Tre Archi, named for the three arches that surmount it. Despite the trash, which may also qualify this as the dirtiest street in Rome, it exudes the romance of centuries past. Here one's imagination is never jolted to reality by the appearance of a car. The romance, however, ends as soon as the sun sets, when walking its short course becomes a dark and frightening experience.

Return to Via della Maschera d'Oro, named for the paintings on the façades of all the buildings that may have made them seem at one time like golden masks (or it may just refer to the mask hanging on one of the façades). In any case this street must once have been spectacular. As with all of these painted façades, few traces are left—just enough to excite the imagination. Immediately to your right note the miniature arch that connects the Casa di Fiammetta to the huge Palazzo Gadi, which runs the full length of the Via della Maschera d'Oro. The entrance to this palazzo is at no. 21. Now a military court, it was built in the beginning of the sixteenth century and painted between 1524 and 1527 by the most famous duo of the chiaroscuro and graffito art, Polidoro da Caravaggio and Maturino da Firenze.

According to art historians this was the best and most complete example of their work. As fate would have it, today there is not a trace of the painting, and only during this century was a print found at the Albertina Museum in Vienna that verified the documentation. (The best extant example of Polidoro and Maturino's work is seen on the Palazzo Ricci, Walk 3.) The print shows us a truly extraordinary work of art: on the ground floor, between the windows, *trompe l'oeil* niches were drawn with figures of famous men of antiquity; along the second story a long depiction of people boarding a boat in the Orient or Egypt and landing in Lazio; next were scenes from Roman history; above that, allegorical figures depicting the gods. Unfortunately, all we see today is a rather dark and plain façade without even the architectural details of most buildings (the painting was meant to provide all the adornment). We can, however, see faint examples of this style on two houses across the street.

The first, at no. 7, is also by Polidoro da Caravaggio and Maturino da Firenze. It was painted at the request of Antonio Milesi, a literary figure of Rome just before the sack of 1527. Milesi belonged to the same group as Bembo and Castiglione, and may even have included Fiammetta among his friends. The design on this house was so popular in late-sixteenth-century Rome that many engravings were made of it, and it was often used as a background in drawings. As Vasari and other artists agree that the design on the Palazzo Gadi across the street was by far superior, the attraction here may have had something to do with the literary reputation of its owner or, more probably, its scale, which is certainly smaller and easier to capture. In 1576, Cherubino Alberti carved the mask suspended in the hands of a cherub hanging in the center of the façade. Until the twentieth century the painting was still clearly visible, but today all that can be seen are the shadows of the story of Niobe: daughter of Tantalus and wife of the king of Thebes who was punished for her motherly pride and turned into a stone that continued to weep for her children. On this house even the courtyard was painted, which, while not unusual, was rare.

The house at no. 9 was restored in 1943 and preserves better examples of graffito than the rest. These, however, are not by Polidoro and Maturino but by an artist named Jacopo Ripando. It is ironic that the work of the greater artists has disappeared while that of a lesser artist remains. We get an excellent representation of the style but without that touch of inspiration of which only great artists are capable. The decoration is divided thematically by floor, as usual: on the first are images of *putti* and animals; on the second, women holding vases full of fruit, cornucopias, and musical instruments; on the third, tritons, sirens, and cupids; and above the series of arched windows that once probably formed a loggia are images of dragons. Between the windows were scenes from the history of Rome.

These monochrome paintings imparted dignity and antiquarian flavor. They were decorative and cheaper than travertine or colored marble, and allowed the modest builder to participate in the classical revival. This style, which became extremely popular during the first three decades of the sixteenth century, always included scenes from mythology or Roman history.

Across from the house at no. 9 and the Vicolo di S. Simone is a plaque in the wall of the Palazzo Gadi. It says, "The Prince Frederigo Cesi, a Roman, who in spite of persecution and maligning statements maintained his ardor for the scientific method. A brilliant investigator of nature and the illustrious founder of the Accademia dei Lincei, gathered here in his family home the learned men of the area and his friend Galileo." The Accademia dei Lincei (Academy of the Lynx-Eye), founded in 1603, is Italy's equivalent of France's Académie Française. We must remember that this plaque describes a courageous act, as Galileo was far from popular in Rome at the time. In fact, from 1630 to 1633 he was imprisoned in the Villa de' Medici by order of the Inquisition Tribunal.

I have often enjoyed a rest on the stone base built into the corner of Via della Maschera d'Oro and Vicolo di S. Simone. From here you can admire the angel "flying" from the corner of the Palazzo Lancellotti at the end of Via della Maschera d'Oro. It is also a good spot for observing Roman life as the street is not busy with traffic and there are few tourists. The sight from this corner is characteristic of the harmony and tranquility of eighteenth-century Rome. Just beyond the palace with the angel is a large area now undergoing restoration and rehabilitation. In the late 1930s those blocks were expropriated by the city government for demolition and reconstruction. The war's arrival prevented completion and the area lay in abandon until the 1970s. Today these houses are now slowly being made habitable and are scheduled for use as public housing.

Included in that area, before the construction of the river embankment, was Rome's most glamorous theater during the eighteenth and nineteenth centuries, the Teatro Apollo, more commonly known as the Teatro di Tor di Nona. Its walls were painted by Podesti, Coghetti, Capalti, and Fioroni, and it was here that Verdi's *Il Trovatore* and *Un Ballo in Maschera* had their premieres.

Walk a few more yards down Via della Maschera

d'Oro and turn left onto Via Lancellotti, which is dominated by the palazzo for which the street is named.
Built by Cardinal Scipione Lancellotti at the end of the
sixteenth century, the palazzo was constructed from a
design by Francesco da Volterra and finished under
the direction of Carlo Maderno. Domenichino, in the
only architectural work he is known to have executed,
designed the huge portal (no. 18) with columns supporting a balcony. This was one of the many portals
that were kept closed in Rome from 1870 until the
signing of the Lateran Treaty in 1929, a gesture of the
"black nobility," thus called because they were aligned
with the pope against the republic and the nobility
that supported its formation. You may still see a form
of protest against this antirepublican gesture on the entrance column, the bright-red letters V.V.E. for "Viva
Vittorio Emanuele II."

This building, with its long line of architraved windows crowned on high by a beautiful cornice, is a typical example of the elegance of baroque palazzo
architecture. The courtyard, though not open to the
public, is one of the most interesting aspects of its design: it includes a portico, a loggia, and on one side a
wall decorated with antique marble and stucco. The
formal reception rooms are painted with frescoes by
Agostino Tassi and del Guernico. I have been able to
see small sections of this impressive work during
strolls after dinner when the shutters were not closed
and the lights were still on. (This is something I suggest you do during your stay in Rome. Walk through
any part of old Rome and keep your eyes open for the
few unshuttered windows; it is the only way to see the
many beautiful interiors of this city.)

Across from the entrance to the Palazzo Lancellotti
is the Piazza S. Simone, adorned by a fountain that presents yet another example of community spirit. This
piazza was created in 1939 as part of the plan I described to eliminate the shabbier buildings in the area
and replace them with new ones. One of the only con-
solations of World War II is that it prevented Mussolini
from changing the whole texture of Rome. For a long
time this space lay vacant, a very noticeable disconti-
nuity in this neighborhood of densely packed streets.
When the city government decided, in the 1960s, to
remedy the dilapidated blocks near the Lungotevere

The fountain at the Piazza S. Simone

the antique dealers of Via dei Coronari organized themselves to preserve the heritage and beauty of their street. They lobbied for a fountain and got this one designed by Giacomo della Porta. Built initially for the Piazza Montanara, it stood there until that area was cleared away by Mussolini's urban plans (see Walk 2). For a while it was placed in the orange garden on the Aventine Hill, but it has now found an appropriate place here, where the destruction in the thirties did not lead to the construction of an avenue. To the nearby residents and shopkeepers the fountain is more than just a decoration, it is an important source of the refreshing waters of the Acqua Paola aqueduct.

The simple house now occupied by the Hosteria dell'Antiquario was probably built in the seventeenth century. While this building does not have any distinguishing architectural elements, the restaurant has distinguished itself as the inventor of *spaghetti alla checca* (spaghetti with a cold, raw tomato sauce), now a standard item on Roman menus. The restaurant has gone through several owners since that moment of delectable creativity, but it remains a delightful summer dining spot.

Via dei Coronari runs along the southern side of the piazza, and while we will only walk across it, its history is very important in the development of this neighborhood. In ancient times this was a section of the Roman Via Recta, which began in the area of the Piazza Colonna and connected the Via Flaminia, leading north out of town, to the bridge over the Tiber. The Via Recta traversed the entire Campo Marzio and comprised what is now Via del Collegio Capranica, Via delle Coppele, Via S. Agostino, Via del Curato, and Via dei Coronari. The half-kilometer stretch now known as Via dei Coronari was the first straight street opened by the Renaissance papacy in its effort to impose an urban plan on the medieval city. Under the direction of Pope Sixtus IV (1471–1484) the street was literally cut out of the medieval clutter that overran the original Roman street and paved. It became the most important access to St. Peter's Basilica, and from the 1400s through the 1500s the most trafficked street in Rome.

The name of Via dei Coronari (Street of the Rosary Makers) comes from the numerous shops that sold devotional objects and trinkets to the stream of pilgrims on their way to the Vatican during the Renaissance. As more streets were built to connect the city to the other side of the river, commerce was dispersed and the Via dei Coronari lost its status as the most important pilgrim route. Nevertheless, it has remained a significant residential and commercial street since the Renaissance.

Today its commerce is almost exclusively that of the antique dealers who have filled all the ground-floor shops and given the street a worldwide reputation as the center of the antique trade in Rome. The Antique Dealers League, formed to maintain Via dei Coronari's *cinquecento* charm, has had notably successful results. I've already commented on the fountain in the Piazza S. Simone. They have also installed copies of the original Renaissance lanterns along the Via dei Coronari, and though these are lighted only for special occasions and fairs, they do add a touch of authenticity. Despite such incongruous notes as the skyline dotted with TV antennae, the toy store just waiting for the arrival of Pac-Man, and the number of shops selling eighteenth- and nineteenth-century English furniture,

Via dei Coronari still has the aura of old Rome. The committee has brought new life to the street, which has always been picturesque but at the beginning of this century was a bit dilapidated. For two weeks every year they hold an important antique fair, which brings flames to the torches and crowds to the street. It is a fun diversion if you are here in mid-May.

Across from the fountain, at Via dei Coronari 30–32, is a small eighteenth-century palazzo with two plaques on its façade. These are to remind us that on this site in 1585, Pope Sixtus V built a permanent home for the Monte di Pietà, now known as the municipal pawn-shop. In 1752 the pawnshop was transferred to a new building located on the Piazza Monte di Pietà, just a block away from the Piazza Trinità dei Pellegrini (Walk 3). The origins of this institution date back to 1439 when a cardinal and a Franciscan friar founded it, not for profit, but to protect the Roman population from the evils of usurers. Today it is often referred to as the Mount of Impiety for its high interest rates that, never-theless, in this time of high inflation are competitive with the banks'. Despite such sentiments it is a very es-tablished institution in this city. When I first moved to Rome, one of the tips I received was that I should send my fur coat to this pawnshop for storage rather than a furrier. Whether or not this is the best storage vault in town is beside the point; pawning and borrowing is a custom in which all of Roman society indulges to pay for the house or the airplane tickets for the summer holiday. And, sure enough, you should see the traffic jam of fur coats (many carried by chauffeurs) in front of the Monte di Pietà the week after Easter!

Next to it, on the left, is the Vicolo di Montevecchio, which leads us into a part of this neighborhood that is captivating precisely for its shabby elegance. But this residential quarter spotted with artisan shops is chang-ing, as is most of the center-city, in the new spirit of renovation. The first sign is at the juncture of the street with the Piazza di Montevecchio, where an elegant aw-ning announces Pino and Dino's restaurant. These two brothers run an expensive place whose cuisine verges on chic nouvelle Italian. During the summer months you can savor a plate of pasta under the shadow of the Palazzo Chiovenda at no. 5–7; now sadly fallen from its old estate, its arched courtyard has been walled in and converted into workshops. The palazzo is said to be by Baldassare Peruzzi, but it is probably just a good imitation. Housed in the ground floor of this palazzo is one of my favorite night spots, L'Arciutto, where after 10:00 P.M. you can listen to Italian ballads. The owner/singer, Enzo Samaritani, likes to say that the space he occupies was Raphael's studio. Why not? Many people make such claims in this city.

Wind your way through this piazza to your left as you face the restaurant. After passing several simple houses of seventeenth-century construction you will see a narrow passage at the far left-hand corner of the piazza. This leads us to Via dell'Arco della Pace and puts us directly in front of the entrance to Bramante's cloister for the Church of S. Maria della Pace—a spot easier to know about than to find!

Before we go into the courtyard look to your left at the recently restored medieval house, no. 10. Once this house had a double-arched ground-floor portico, which was probably closed in 1475 when a law was passed that outlawed them in Rome. Today we still see the columns and the iron rings that were once used, in conjunction with a stick of wood, to make a clothesline. In the area immediately adjacent to S. Maria della Pace are several fifteenth-century houses distinguished by their small round-topped windows. These houses are as rare today as they were abundant in Rome before 1870.

The entrance to the cloister is at no. 5; if it is closed when you get there, you really must come back. In 1855, Burckhardt called this spot "small and neglected" but added that it represented "an architectural revolution." No longer in a state of neglect, the cloister's calm and dignified atmosphere can now be appreciated without distraction. Built between 1500 and 1504 under the patronage of Cardinal Carafa, whose family emblem is above the entrance door, the cloister is considered one of Bramante's masterpieces in Rome. The design illustrates a favorite theme of his early work: the simple arrangement of two spaces over one with the central pillar of the upper tier resting on the crown of the arch below. Standing in the middle of the court you can also appreciate the dome of the church to which this cloister is attached. As part of the summer festival in Rome, concerts of Renaissance music are held here in June and July.

Leave the cloister, turn left, and walk under the arch, Arco della Pace, the source of this street's name. We now enter the Piazza S. Maria della Pace, undoubtedly one of Rome's most picturesque. The plaque on the wall immediately to your left says: "It is forbidden for anyone to build buildings, add stories, make any changes to the exterior or any renovations in this piazza of S. Maria della Pace, or its environs, or on the adjacent streets. If anyone dares to disobey this pronouncement they will be penalized . . . June 27, 1659." This emphasizes the degree to which the construction of this church's façade was tied to the development of the area around it.

Walk to the middle of the piazza to a point from which you can study the entire effect of the church and the piazza. The portico accenting the front of the church is reminiscent of the antique porticoes built throughout the city by the ancient Romans. Its curved lines, both concave and convex, blend with the other façades to make this one of the most typical and harmonious examples of baroque architecture in Rome.

Since the Middle Ages there has been a church on this site. It is said to have been the church of the *acquarellari*, "water salesmen," who delivered water from the Tiber in wooden casks to sections of town cut off from a supply of water. In this church was an image of the Virgin Mary, which, legend tells us, started to bleed after it was hit by a stone. In 1482, Pope Sixtus IV came to the church to venerate this celebrated Virgin and to give thanks for the peace he had just established on the peninsula following the assassination of Giuliano de' Medici in the Pazzi conspiracy. The pope chose to change the church's name to S. Maria della Pace and ordered a more elegant church to be built on the site. Work on it was continued by his successors. Under the reign of Julius II in the sixteenth century Agostino Chigi, the great banker, poured part of his family's wealth into the construction of a private chapel and the completion of the church. The façade was constructed by Pietro da Cortona in 1656–1661 under the reign of Pope Alexander VII.

As a result of Alexander VII's interest the church became one of the most fashionable in town. It was also
the only place where one could attend mass in the afternoon. Getting to the church, however, was not an
easy task. The street leading to its main entrance was
narrow, and those on either side were even worse. The
passage next to the apse of the neighboring church on
the right was not even wide enough for a carriage, the
means of transportation that by the mid-seventeenth
century was *de rigueur* among Roman nobility. The
access on the left allowed for only one carriage, which
led to many petty quarrels over procedure. This transportation problem, along with the façade, was the issue Cortona dealt with in his design for this piazza.
By destroying a row of houses he created an impressive approach to the church, enough room for the carriages to turn around, and a symmetrical piazza of
unusual shape. In the design for the façade he joined
the church to the adjacent buildings and streets to create a single architectural unit.

"This masterly entrance," as John Gibbs called Cortona's design in the early eighteenth century, deserves
a careful look. The upper part of the façade is articulat-
ed by a curved order of Corinthian columns and pilasters. Below that is the bold half-oval porch with
unevenly spaced Tuscan columns. The line of the façade is extended by a wall that has outlets to the adjacent streets and two quarter-oval bays that mask the
surrounding buildings.

The interior of the church is also very special. Since
it is closed, except for one hour during mass at 10:00
A.M. on Sundays, I will describe some of its highlights.
The body of the church consists of a rectangular space
lined with chapels that ends in an arch leading to an
octagonal, domed apse. The figures of Strength and
Prudence over the arch and Peace and Justice on the
entrance wall are by C. Foncelli. The Chigi chapel was
decorated for Agostino by Raphael with a fresco of the
four Sibyls: Luma, Persia, Phrygia, and Tibur. They are
depicted as each receiving a revelation from an angel.
This chapel was finished after Raphael's death by Sebastiano del Piombo. Another chapel, the Cappella
Cesi, is a superb example of high Renaissance sculpture decoration. Built by Antonio da Sangallo the

Entering the Piazza S. Maria della Pace

Younger in 1525, the vault was later decorated with stucco and fresco designs by Sicciolante da Sermoneta. During the time of Cortona's work on the piazza the size of this chapel was slightly reduced to widen the Vicolo della Pace. Other important works are by Peruzzi, whose paintings made Arthur Symon never tire of this church for "their strength, their gracious severity, and profound purity." There are also works by Raphael Vanni, Orazio Gentileschi, and Stefano Maderno.

Certainly, this is not just another Roman church, and it is a shame that it has been almost abandoned by the Church. Today, rather than a parade of elegant nobility, it attracts only the few cognoscenti who know when the door will be open, the devout locals, and a crowd of hippies who find refuge under the portico. As always it's a favorite of artists, for whom the façade's dramatic display of light and curves creates an ideal scene. Most recently Bertolucci made the most of its shadowed curves in his movie *La Luna*.

To the right of the church you can see the late Gothic campanile, or bell tower, of the adjacent church, S. Maria dell'Anima. This is the German national church; though its façade is on Via dell'Anima, its entrance is on this piazza at no. 20. Take a quick look in the door—the high polish and cleanliness bespeak a northern temperament, an atmosphere that can hardly be more different from that of S. Maria della Pace or other Roman churches. Nevertheless, this church is important for its frescoes and seventeenth-century tombs, including that of Pope Hadrian VI (until the current one, the last non-Italian pope). The son of a ship's carpenter in Utrecht and the tutor of Emperor Charles V, Hadrian VI is best remembered for his efforts to reform the extravagances of the Papal Court. To the relief of everyone in Rome, and art historians since, his reign lasted but a year, from 1522 to 1523.

Leave the piazza on the street that faces the Church of S. Maria della Pace, the Via della Pace, and turn right with the street, which keeps the same name. This brings us into a truly popular section of the neighborhood. On the corner is a delightful old-fashioned *birreria*, "beer hall," in the ground floor of the Palazzo Gambirasi, a huge building extending from Via della Pace to Vicolo degli Osti and over to Via dell'Arco della Pace. This building, designed by G. A. di Rossi, was altered by Cortona in 1656–1657 when he created the piazza of S. Maria della Pace; at the end of the seventeenth century it became the home of a priest named Donato Gambirasi who adorned one of the façades with heraldic crayfish (the Italian word for crayfish is *gambero*). Gambirasi also built a belvedere that bears his name. These seventeenth-century structures are interesting derivatives of the medieval towers in that they served the same purpose, symbolizing the family's eminence and wealth. They became popular not necessarily as a means of spying on the life of the neighborhood, or for outdoor dining and sunbathing (which is the case today), but rather as perches from which a nobleman could survey his dominion.

At this point we enter a several-block section of the neighborhood that is not identified with any great masterpieces of architecture or any particularly captivating tales. During the day this section of Via della Pace is filled with fruit and vegetable stands. It is a typical neighborhood market, unlike the large one at Campo dei Fiori, which services all of the center-city. At the end of the street, where the wall of a house cuts the width of the passage, is an interesting *edicola* to the Virgin: it is the only one I have noticed in Rome made of wood and its charm is accented by the wall colored with graffiti and the local water tap below. This *edicola* commemorates the Church of S. Bagio della Fossa, once the home of the confraternity of olive vendors, ringmakers, and combmakers. The church was destroyed in 1812 by the Commission of Improvements when they widened Via della Pace.

The Via della Pace ends at the Piazza del Fico; there turn left. The inscription on the house to your left tells us that Marcantonio and Giambattista Fappa created this piazza at their own expense in 1634. This same Marcantonio designated a trust in his will of 1673 for the education of poor children in this neighborhood, with preference given to those who live on the piazza.

Make a right-hand turn onto Vicolo del Fico. It is one block long and lined with lower-middle-class residences and ground-floor shops specializing in the making of chairs. At the end of the block we make another left onto Via di Monte Giordano.

This area gives us an opportunity to reflect on the history of these kinds of dwellings. Early in the Renaissance the typical workman's or artisan's home was a small detached unit with two floors. The ground floor held the workshop or storeroom, and the living quarters were above. During the late Renaissance two things occurred to change this design. First, the urban scheme introduced and enforced by the papacy required orderly and aligned streets. Second, Rome's population grew so quickly that speculators were determined to get maximum use of the land, especially land so near the city's business center and the Vatican. These requirements led to the standardization of building components and the appearance of a block of three-storied attached houses on a single street with a series of workshops on the ground floor. Behind the façade there was usually a small courtyard and outbuildings. On this street we see examples of small dwellings looking much as they did in the seventeenth century.

Immediately to your left, at Via di Monte Giordano 4–6, is a typical example of a house of the 1500s. Next to it, at no. 7–9, is the house known as that of Teodoro Ameyden, a famous Flemish scholar who settled in Rome at the end of the sixteenth century. The house, built in the beginning of the sixteenth century, is three stories high with arched windows encased in carved travertine. Over the main door is a fading inscription: UNDE EO OMNIA CIOE ("Where things come from, where they all go"). This house is now in rather sad shape, but it retains the elegant charm of its age, highlighted by the flowerpots in the windows.

Across from this house is a dead-end street worth investigating. Called the Vicolo del Montaccio, this street takes its name from the steep hill you are climbing. Numerous legends explain the origin of this hill, including one that has it as the pile of earth left after digging the foundations for Hadrian's tomb across the river. A more likely explanation is that it was created by both the accumulation of silt from the ancient port at this point in the Tiber and from the remains of archeological ruins. For a long time the hill was known as the *Mons Ursinorum* for the Orsini family who, beginning in 1296, controlled the area. Giordano Orsini, who gave it the name it has now (Monte Giordano), was a civic leader during the time the papacy abandoned Rome for Avignon. More specifically he is re-

Laundry decorating a late-Renaissance building

membered for his help in coalescing support for Cola di Rienzo's brief republic and also as the senator who received Petrarch at the Campidoglio in 1341. If the door at no. 9 is open you can see the apse of the ancient church of SS. Simone e Guida.

Return to Via di Monte Giordano and follow its curved path. The buildings on your right, which all back onto Monte Giordano, recall a passage from Benvenuto Cellini's autobiography that, despite its bombast and narcissism, does give an interesting documentation of life in sixteenth-century Rome. Cellini tells us that he once lived in one of the houses resting on the slope of Monte Giordano. This position proved advantageous to him during the heavy floods of 1530 when he was unable to open the front door; instead he climbed out a second-floor window in the back of the house with all his jewels and found safety on the top of the hill.

For centuries this hill has been an important landmark in this area, which is one of the lowest and flattest points in the city's terrain. The Orsinis seemed to have a predilection for establishing their fortresses on mounts created by the rubble of ancient Roman ruins, and this location served them as a bridgehead from which to control the only means of access to the Borgo. From the top of their fortress they also had an expansive view of Monte Mario, Trastevere, and the Tiber. The fortress they built was immense, covering the entire hill and extending to the river. All around it was land controlled by them and occupied by their vassals. When Dante came to Rome in 1300 it must have made an impression on him, as it is one of the few nonreligious sites he mentions in his *Divine Comedy*:

> Just so the Romans, because of the great throng
> in the year of the Jubilee, divide the bridge
> in order that the crowds may pass along,
> so that all face the Castle as they go
> on one side towards St. Peter's, while on the other
> all move along facing towards Monte Giordano.

This site was the Orsinis' first base in Rome. From here, branches of the family moved to the Campo dei Fiori and the Teatro di Marcello, establishing themselves as one of the most powerful families in the city. Their ranks included two popes, forty cardinals, and an equal number of senators and leaders in the government of Rome and the kingdom of Naples. References to internecine warfare among nobles in Rome during the Middle Ages and later almost always mention the Orsini family and their great rivals, the Colonnas. In order to ensure the Pax Romana of 1511, the pope made a member of each family a papal prince.

For five centuries the Orsinis controlled and ruled from this hill. The huge fortress was slowly divided among different branches of the family, the dukes of Bracciano, the counts of Pitigliano, and the signori of Marino. To the right, on Via di Monte Giordano, we see the sixteenth-century façade of the building constructed by the dukes of Bracciano.

After one block, we reach the imposing entrance to the Orsini fortress. Now gentrified as a palazzo and known as the Palazzo Taverna, it is hard to find a more impressive entrance. The sight of it on a steep incline drooping with ivy, covered by a huge iron gate through which you can see a vaulted entrance with a fountain and more green in the background, can't help but provoke curiosity, at least to inspect the garden. The gate, said to be created by Baldassare Peruzzi, has the family crests of both the Orsinis and the Pamphilis woven into its lace design. The palazzo's ponderous structure is softened both by the elegant fountain for the Acqua Paola designed in 1618 by Felice Antonio Casoni and by the monumental entrance vault built in the nineteenth century. Although this palazzo is not architecturally important, one can get an idea of its size and many components from the central courtyard. It is also a pleasant reprieve from the noisy streets.

There are five principal and distinctive structures inside this gate. The oldest is to the left, where we see the remains of a medieval structure. There we enter a fifteenth-century courtyard with an outside staircase and a marble portal bearing the inscription *"Ex Olympo."* This marble may have come from an ancient tower on the site known in medieval times as the Major Tower. The building over the grand entrance facing the central court is the Palazzo dei Duchi di Bracciano. It contains a beautiful fifteenth-century portal with the Orsini emblem and shows traces of a loggia, as dictated by the style at the time of its construction. Across from it, on the same side of the yard as the fountain, is the Palazzo of the Conti di Pitigliano with an entrance leading into its own court. Between these two buildings, on either side of the main courtyard and opposite the oldest section of this compound, is the newest wing, constructed in 1807 to connect the two palazzi. Through the arches of this new wing is the courtyard of the Palazzo degli Signori di Marino. In it is a tower, known as the tower of Augusta, built in 1880, and a third-century Roman sarcophagus now used as the bowl of a fountain. The fifth distinct structure is the ex–Church of SS. Simone e Guida, now engulfed by the various constructions and used as a residential space. Other structures are attached to this complex but, as they do not share the same main entrance, they are not defined as part of the Palazzo Taverna.

Despite their warlike tendencies the Orsinis did make this an elegant home; in the fifteenth century it was considered one of the finest in Rome. Brutally sacked in 1527, it was well enough restored within twenty years to become the home of Cardinal Ippolito d'Este, who was known for his magnificent displays of wealth and culture and who created the Villa d'Este in Tivoli. During Cardinal d'Este's stay the poet Torquato Tasso was a frequent guest. The Orsinis stayed here until 1688, when they began to have financial problems. From 1688 to 1888 the Gabrielli family occupied the compound. They restored, modernized, and tried to unify the property, constructing the new wing with the tower of Augusta, named after Placido Gabrielli's wife. Napoleon's family was linked through marriage to Gabrielli's and to this residence. Cardinal Luciano Bonaparte, Napoleon's great-nephew, lived here and entertained the Empress Eugènie during her stay in Rome. In 1888 the Gabrielli family became extinct, and the compound was purchased by a Milanese family, the Counts of Taverna, whose name the palace still bears. As with all these huge palazzi, this one is today divided into numerous private apartments and offices.

In an article about her life in Rome for *The New York Times*, Muriel Spark had this to say about her apartment in this palazzo:

The main room was enormous, a Renaissance Cardinal Orsini's library and the upper walls and ceilings were painted with classical scenes and Orsini emblems. I did not try to furnish it, but made a sitting room in a remote corner while the rest of the room, with its polished Roman tiles, was for walks. (It would have made a good skating rink.) In one of the corridors a Roman pillar had been let into the wall. . . . The Palazzo Taverna, with its fountain in the great courtyard, its arches and small courtyards, was fun to live in and my echoing cardinal's room was to many of my friends one of the wonders of the world. . . . After dinner everyone in the palazzo would go down to the courtyard to take the air with the neighbors.

She goes on to comment about something that distinguishes Rome from other European cities: in its historic center there are no exclusive neighborhoods, and the rich and poor seem to live proudly next to, above, and below one another. This palazzo still has a medieval flavor about it, surrounded as it is by a poorer section of central Rome. (I will never forget an overly protective Roman gentleman warning me about walking through this area. He described the inhabitants as descendants of the Orsini soldiers, "a bunch of ruffians and hoods." Never mind that the Orsinis left more than three hundred years ago and that he himself lived in a similar neighborhood, occupied by both the rich and the poor. His concern only became clear to me when I discovered that he was a member of the Colonna family, who since the thirteenth century has pitted itself against the Orsinis. It wasn't the socioeconomic factors or any realistic possibility of danger that bothered this man, but the Via di Monte Giordano's association with the Orsinis and their henchmen.)

Leaving the Palazzo Taverna through the main gate we walk straight onto the Via degli Orsini. Here to our right, at no. 34, is an entrance with a fountain at the end. This looks better from the street; it is meant to be seen framed by the long entry hall. On March 11, 1876, the man who was to become Pope Pius XII was born in a room of this palazzo.

To your left on the corner, with its entrance on the Via del Governo Vecchio, is the Palazzo Boncompagni. This was built in the sixteenth century by a member of an important Jewish family, Salomon Corcos, who, after converting to Catholicism, adopted the name and emblem of Pope Gregory XIII, a Boncompagni. The dragon associated with that name appears on the capitals of the columns that flank the main entrance.

Straight ahead, on the other side of the intersection, is the Piazza dell'Orologio and the Palazzo dello S. Spirito. This palazzo was originally begun by Borromini in 1661 at the request of Virgilio Spada, but was left unfinished at the time of Borromini's death in 1663. Pope Alexander VII later ordered his nephew to buy it and complete it at his own expense, so now, except for an engraving by Falda, few traces remain of the great architect's design. The vestibule and court-yard probably retain more of Borromini's plan than the rest, in particular the arrangement of the court with superimposed arcaded loggias, now blocked up.

The clock tower, to your left as you face the pa-lazzo, gives this piazza its name. Built in 1640, this work of Borromini turns its concave face toward the traffic moving up Via dei Banchi Nuovi and Via del Governo Vecchio from the Ponte S. Angelo for the benefit of the papal processions that made these two streets so important during the high Renaissance. To finish the effect Borromini embellished the intersec-tion of Piazza dell'Orologio and Via del Governo Vec-chio with a beveled corner and a scuptured tabernacle.

The building that makes this corner and on which sits Borromini's tower is called the Oratorio. It was built in 1572 for S. Filippo Neri by Pope Gregory XIII and Cardinal Cesi from a design of Martino Longhi the Elder. (The entrance façade is on the Corso Vittorio Emanuele II.) The Oratorio institutionalized some-thing new in the religious life of Rome; it was built as a monastery for an order of religious men, the Oratori-ans, who continued their careers in the secular world. Pier Luigi da Palestrina was a member of this order, which attached a great deal of importance to religious music, often in semidramatic form. It is through this association that we acquired the musical term *ora-torio*.

In his *Italian Notebooks*, Goethe refers to S. Filippo Neri as the "humorist saint." Neri captured the hearts of the Romans (who made him their patron saint) with his charm, kindness, and sense of humor, which was sometimes masked by eccentricity. "The church," Goethe says, "cleverly brought into its circle a man who of independent mind took his point of departure from where the holy could unite with the worldly, the virtuous with the things of everyday, and each harmonize with the other." It was this man that the Oratorians try to emulate and to his memory that this building with its elegant bell tower was erected. Today it houses the Vallicelliana Library, the first ever open to the public in Rome; the Institute of Roman Studies, which includes the Capitoline archives; and the monastery of the Oratorian Brothers.

Return to the Via del Governo Vecchio, which is to the right as you face the entrance to the Palazzo Taverna. This street was an important part of the route used to link the two major basilicas, St. John the Lateran and St. Peter's. Especially after the coronation of a new pope, a spendid procession marched along its path as the new pope went to the Lateran to take possession of his title as bishop of Rome. These parades were very elaborate and colorful; they were celebrations meant to establish the pope as the temporal ruler of Rome. Triumphal arches were constructed and decorated with hangings and figures symbolic of the cultural and political policies expected of the new pope. For Pope Leo X's procession, one of the most extravagant ever, scores of arches were erected along the Via del Governo Vecchio to symbolize Leo's role as peacemaker, as a force behind the Lateran Council, and as a patron of the arts. In the style of the time, pagan symbolism was mixed heavily with Christian. Agostino Chigi's arch included the figures of Apollo, Mercury, and Pallas to show the power, splendor, and politics Chigi expected of the new pope. Pope Paul III was depicted, during his procession, as Androcles with the lion from which he extracted the thorn of heresy representing his tasks during the Counter-Reformation. These processions included elaborate festivities such as masked dances, bullfights, showers of perfumed oranges, and floats.

In 1623, when the governor of Rome moved into a palazzo here, the street was given the name Via del Governo; before that it was called Via di Parione. The descriptive *vecchio,* "old," came after the governor moved to the Palazzo Madama in 1741. Though it is no longer used for processions it still maintains an air of pageantry; Borromini's clock tower and the decorative corner are but two examples of the many architectural details suggestive of this tradition of pageantry. Via del Governo Vecchio is a good example of the typical Renaissance residential quarter. Both sides of the street are lined with elegant houses whose styles, dating from the fifteenth century to the seventeenth, are vivid illustrations of the social prosperity of that time and the tastes of the clerical, aristocratic, and merchant circles that dominated Rome. Here merchant/artisan houses stand next to the palazzi of members of the Papal Court. While the styles may be the same, the merchant/artisan houses always had workrooms and shops on the ground floor and the nobility and clergy had elegant courtyards. These buildings, with their infinite number of architectural and decorative details, define the character of the street, which winds its way crookedly along what was once a medieval path. Aside from the architecture you can also enjoy some window-shopping; the street is filled with antique shops, boutiques, and examples of a new fad in Rome—boutiques, coffee shops, and wine bars. Along the side streets are numerous artisan shops specializing in the making and restoring of antique furniture.

Via del Governo Vecchio 3, the entrance to the Palazzo Boncompagni Corcos, is decorated with a huge shell and two columns ending in the head of a dragon. The house at no. 12–13 was built in the 1400s and has the arched windows and doors typical of that period. Each floor is defined by a travertine molding; on the fourth floor is a loggia that still has iron hooks for stringing the laundry. To your right continues the high spare wall of the Oratory, while at no. 14–17, to your left, is a house built in the sixteenth century. In contrast to the earlier house this one has a base of rough-hewn stone, a fashion made popular in Florence at the beginning of the fifteenth century. On the ground floor is an arched portal and three shops. The fourth level is a kind of loggia with arches divided by Doric pilasters that hold an architrave of the same style, and above that is a variation on this theme that has rectangular spaces, elaborate capitals, and a much richer architrave. In the 1600s this building was attached to others along the Vicolo dell'Avila and the Via di Monte Giordano, forming a large unified block. At that time a belvedere was built near the corner of Via del Governo Vecchio and Via dell'Avila; it is richly decorated with stucco and has since been enclosed. A tablet attached to this house in 1882 says that Pietro Cossa was born

Local knife sharpener

here on January 25, 1830. He was a playwright who used stories from Roman history in his dramas.

The section of Via del Governo Vecchio that is part of the *rione* Ponte ends at the intersection with Via del Corallo, two short blocks away on your left. On that corner is the seventeenth-century sign put up by Pope Benedict XIV that marks the confines of this region. We now enter the *rione* of Parione. On the other side of the street by the corner of Via della Chiesa Nuova is another elaborate corner design with a painting of the Virgin, Child, and saints framed in stucco. Above that an inscription records the opening of this street in 1675. Just beyond Via del Corallo, on your left, is the governor's palace that gave this street its name. The Palazzo Nardini (no. 39) is now in a terrible state of disrepair and has been taken over by a radical feminist group. The occupation of this building is a sensitive issue in the neighborhood; they are squatting in this building, which was abandoned for restoration. As they are not a very tame group of women I suggest you stay on the street and catch a glimpse of the courtyard through the open gate. (My camera was snatched away from me and my film taken out when I tried to photograph the exterior of this building.)

The Palazzo Nardini was constructed between 1473 and 1478 by Cardinal Stefano Nardini when Pope Paul IV called him to govern Rome. The building has the characteristics both of a fortress, with its diamond-shaped hewn-stone façade and towers from an earlier medieval construction, and of an elegant Renaissance palazzo, with its finely carved portal and the large, square windows. The courtyard is probably the most interesting part of the palazzo, decorated as it is with distinctive fifteenth-century octagonal columns and graceful porticoes. This style of inner-courtyard articulation became popular in Rome, but it was still new at the time of this construction. What we see through the main entrance is only one of three courtyards encircled by this large palace, so large it covers a full block. The plaque to the left of the entrance tells us that after Cardinal Nardini's death in 1475 the building became the property of the Salvatore al Laterano hospital and the Academy of Humanistic Art. In 1624 it was deeded to Pope Urban VIII, who chose to make this palazzo again the seat of the governor of Rome. After the governor moved to Palazzo Madama, Palazzo Nardini became a court of law until 1964.

Across from the entrance to the Palazzo Nardini is another special sight, the small sixteenth-century Palazzo Turci (no. 123). Its façade of Doric pilasters alternating with round-topped windows is an excellent example of the application of Bramante's architectonic principles to a small residence. In fact, such a good job was done that for a long time the design was attributed to Bramante himself. Across the façade is an inscription telling us that Pietro Turci, a writer for the Papal Court, had the building constructed in 1500 for the comfort of himself and his descendants.

This palazzo, in conjunction with the next two on the same side of the street, nos. 121 and 118, gives us an easy and delightful study of the changes that took place in the design of small dwellings from the fifteenth through the seventeenth centuries. The house at no. 118, with its flat façade and pointed windows, was built in the 1400s; the Palazzo Turci at the turn of the century in 1500; and the house at no. 121, with square windows framed in travertine and topped with pediments, in the 1600s. The texture of the façades changes along with the shapes and ornamentation around the windows and doors. All of these houses have ground-floor workspaces that are used as shops.

On your left, no. 48 is the Palazzetto Sassi, once famous for its great collection of art and sculpture. Martin van Heemskerck (1498–1574) has left us a sketch of the courtyard when it was cluttered with important Roman and Greek marble sculpture; among them were the *Venus Genitrice*, *Apollo*, and *Hermes*, all of which later became apart of the Farnese family collection. An inscription on the wall of the house informs us that Fornarina, the baker's daughter who captured Raphael's heart, lived in the house. Indeed, a 1518 census tells us that a Sienese baker occupied a house belonging to the Sassi family.

Another inscription on the Palazzetto Sassi tells us that it was restored in 1867, a time when the Via del Governo Vecchio was going through a renaissance of its own. This started in 1855 when the first gaslights in Rome were hung on this street. (To commemorate this event the city government in 1966 installed copies of the original gaslights.) Later, many of the houses were restored in response to the construction of the Corso Vittorio Emanuele II, which led the residents of the Via del Governo Vecchio to believe that their property might be devalued. Both of these events helped maintain the prestige this street deserves and today Via del Governo Vecchio is one of the best preserved examples of a Renaissance street in Rome.

Across the street is the Pizzeria Baffetto, an eatery that I'm sure has brought more people to this street than its rich history and architecture. A favorite on the list of students coming to Rome for its cheap meals, it is also known among the residents of the city as one of the best pizza restaurants. It is so crowded at dinner that the line interferes with traffic on the street. While pizza is a national dish, it has become even more popular these days as it combines the necessity of a cheap meal with the Romans' fancy for eating out.

A block away, on the corner of Vicolo Savelli, is another 1400s house. At one time it was covered with the monochrome frescoes we saw samples of on Via della Maschera d'Oro. Now the only trace of decoration is on the corner—a beveled pilaster with a carved lion's head above which is a marble bracket with carved ribbons that probably once held a sizable family emblem. The cornice is decorated with the figure of a dragon, telling us that this building once belonged to the Boncompagni family.

Next door, at no. 104, is a sixteenth-century house decorated with a series of medallions in stucco representing celebrated personages. On the top floor is an amusing *trompe l'oeil* painted in the recess of a blocked-in window that shows the then owner of the house dictating to his secretary. The stucco decorations around the windows and the door (including the medallions) were added in the 1700s when this house was almost completely remodeled. Don't overlook the cornice, richly decorated with rosettes, women's heads, and shells.

Across the street, at no. 62, is the Palazzo Fonseca, one of the few buildings not to have been renovated in the last hundred years. It is a beautifully proportioned building with an ancient well still in its courtyard. Next to it, no. 66, is said to be the smallest house in Rome; it is now engulfed by the adjacent structure.

On the right-hand side of the street are a few more interesting details. On the façade of no. 96 is an *edicola* of the Virgin surrounded by stars and an oval stucco frame. A few yards further, at no. 91, is a seventeenth-century house with delightful decorations: an exotic face over the door, shells on the window frames of the second floor, and leaves on the cornice. Walk another block and the street ends at the triangular Piazza di Pasquino.

Before we reach the statue for which this piazza is named, we pass a church on the left, the Church of the Agonizzanti. Its name hints at its mission, which from the seventeenth to the nineteenth century was to pray for those souls condemned to death. On their way from prison to the scaffold, prisoners were brought here for their final religious rites. A placard outside the door identified the day's victim and promised plenary indulgence to all the faithful who after confession and communion assisted at the services in behalf of the "sufferer."

Before this piazza became known as di Pasquino it belonged to the bookmakers; President de Brosses writes of the statue of Pasquino in the *places des librairies* in his *Lettres d'Italie*. The shops on the square were full of bookstalls, printing presses, and editors' workshops. In fact, the first guidebook to Rome in a foreign language (German) was printed here by Mauricio Bona.

We will end our walk with a story about Pasquino, a folk hero in Rome and one of that famous group of "talking statues" that have contributed so much to Rome's popular culture. I am referring to the mutilated, third-century sculpture of Menelaus supporting the body of Patroclus, to your right on the corner formed by the intersection of two streets. The statue was discovered during the repaving of the nearby Via dei Leutari and positioned here by Cardinal Oliviero Carafa in 1501.

This statue, which Bernini considered the finest piece of ancient sculpture in Rome, owes its name and fame to its reputation as a critic and censor of Roman affairs. The name it bears comes from that of a tailor who at the turn of the fifteenth century had a shop across the way. He wove garments for the Papal Court and entertained his customers with gossip and cynical comments about the pope, cardinals, courtiers, and events of the day. After the tailor's death the statue, which had been used as a steppingstone for crossing a muddy street, was dug out and set up just outside the shop once belonging to Pasquino. Immediately it became known by the Roman people as Pasquino, as if it were a reincarnation of the well-known tailor to whom all salacious criticism of the government had been attributed.

Every year on the feast of St. Mark a procession passed this way, and Cardinal Carafa had Pasquino temporarily remodeled in plaster and draped with cloth for the event. Each year the statue assumed the character and attributions of a different deity: Jupiter, Mars, Apollo, Minerva, and others. The university lecturer charged with the statue's transformations initiated among his pupils a competition of Latin epigrams for the occasion. These were posted on the pedestal of the statue. The competition came to an end in 1517, and though these epigrams were more pedantic than witty, they set a precedent for the expression of anonymous political opposition and satire. By 1520, Pasquino became the established mouthpiece in Rome for all popular criticism.

Once Pasquino became a popular oracle it was only natural that he should have a dialogue. It didn't take long for the people to find an appropriate partner in another statue, that of Marforio, the river god. Questions were affixed to his body to which Pasquino responded. Marforio, however, was removed from the edge of the Forum near the Mamertine prison and locked away in the Capitoline Museum. This action did not end the notorious dialogue with a number of other statues; Abate Luigi (Piazza Vidoni), Madame Lucrizia (Piazza San Marco), Babuino (Via Babuino), and Facchino (Via Lata) joined the ranks of "talking statues." Pasquino is even said to have enticed the statue of Gobbo on the Rialto in Venice to participate in his discourse. These statues kept up a lively fire of wit and repartee that caused enough of a panic in the Vatican that Pope Hadrian proposed to have the offensive statue thrown into the Tiber. He was dissuaded by Tasso who said that "like frogs, Pasquino would even croak louder in the water." Later Pope Benedict XIII imposed a "penalty of death, confiscation of property and disgrace to the family name of whomever, whatever their position, including priests, writes, prints, or disperses libels which have the character of a pasquinade." During the conclave for the election of Pope Pius VIII the environment became so tense that the statue was guarded by sentinels.

Before 1870, Pasquino acted as a substitute for a free press and scarcely an event took place in Rome about which he did not pronounce judgment. Many of these are untranslatable as they are puns on words such as the comment on Napoleon's occupation of Rome: *"I Francesi son tutti ladri"* ("the French are all thieves") to which Marforio responded, *"Non tutti— Ma Bona Parte"* ("not all, but a good many"—Bonaparte). Others have become common pasquinades (the English word comes from this statue's reputation) such as "What the barbarians didn't take the Barberini did," in reference to the stripping of bronze from the

Pantheon for making the Baldacchino at St. Peter's.

I still see an occasional sheet of paper posted on the base, which reads "I owe my existence to Cardinal Carafa 1501," but they lack the bite of some of the best of the original. Upon the death of Pope Paul III, Pasquino claimed that the pope (at the age of eighty-one) had died in childbirth having aborted two still-born cardinals. His epitaph for Queen Christina of Sweden was "Queen without a realm, Christian without faith, and a woman without shame." When Napoleon's government instituted the Legion of Honor, Pasquino had this to say: "In fierce old times they balanced loss, by hanging thieves upon a cross, but our humaner age believes, in hanging crosses on the thieves." Many people think that Pasquino's swan song was his interpretation of S.P.Q.R. after the events of 1870: *"Sanctus Pater Quondam Rex"* ("The Holy Father Once a King").

With the establishment of the republic and a free press, anonymity was no longer necessary and Pasquino's tongue quieted, but that audacious, satirical wit is native to Romans and jokes are still told that might well be attributed to this statue's spirit. When Mussolini built the avenue from the Vittorio Emanuele monument to the Colosseum and called it the Via dell' Impero, Romans joked, *"Che cosa è la Via dell'Impero? È la Via che conduce alla più grande rovina d'Italia"* ("What is this street of the empire? It is the street that leads to the greatest ruin of Italy").

Our walk ends here at the Piazza di Pasquino, just behind the entrance to the Museum of Rome in the Palazzo Braschi, which towers over the statue of Pasquino. If you have the stamina and time I suggest a visit. The museum contains paintings, drawings, and photographs that illustrate the life of the city from medieval times to the last century. Included in the collection are depictions of the papal processions down the Via del Governo Vecchio and the festivities held during the sixteenth and seventeenth centuries in the Piazza Navona, just a block away on Via di Pasquino. The entrance to the Museum of Rome is off the Via di S. Pantaleo.

2

The Empire, the Church, and the Jews: The Jewish Ghetto

○

Starting Point: Corner of Via del Teatro di Marcello and Via del Foro Olitorio (next to the church)

This walk leads us through an area of Rome between Michelangelo's beautiful square, the Campidoglio, on the Capitoline Hill, and the Tiber. It is one of the most evocative neighborhoods in the city, with remnants of twenty-six centuries of the city's history, much of it closely allied to the history of the Jewish people in Rome. In ancient days this area was filled with markets; later, with temples; and during the time of Augustus it became the site of some of the city's greatest splendors. For many centuries Rome received its diplomatic, political, and commercial visitors here. Great triumphal receptions were celebrated in the Portico d'Ottavia, the Teatro di Marcello, and the Circus of Flaminius. The Foro Olitorio, the oil and vegetable market, and the nearby Foro Boario, the meat market, established a center of commercial activity between the city and its outlying regions that lasted until the eighteenth century. It was in this zone that the local Romans had their initial contact with foreign traders, first the Greeks and later the Etruscans. Even during Rome's demise (in what was referred to as the dark ages, when many sections of the city had been abandoned and the population fell to 17,000), this quarter maintained its position of power and commerce. The Counter-Reformation forced the Jewish population into a small, walled ghetto near the Tiber and surrounded these walls with the splendid baroque architecture that came to symbolize the papacy's wealth and power.

Today this quarter has lost its political importance and is isolated from the most trafficked areas of modern Rome. Nevertheless, it maintains a strong emotional connection with the past. Here the grandeur of the Roman Empire, the simplicity of the Middle Ages, the elegance of the late Renaissance, and the functionalism of the twentieth century blend dramatically but unpretentiously with an equally dramatic history of the Jews in Rome. Though now well assimilated, Jews still predominate in this area, making it a distinct neighbor-

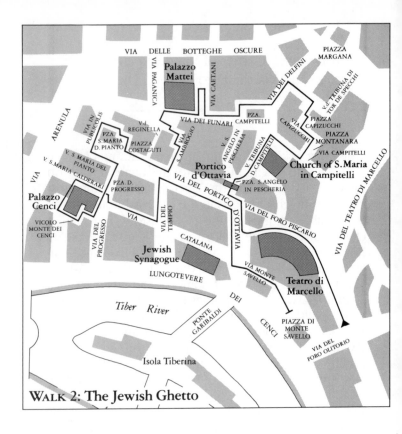

WALK 2: The Jewish Ghetto

hood with a sense of community that is atypical of modern urban life.

We will begin our walk on the corner of Via del Teatro di Marcello and Via del Foro Olitorio. These streets and the modern buildings on your right as you face the Via del Teatro di Marcello are the product of Mussolini's passionate drive to revitalize Rome. He isolated the splendors of Rome's imperial past and in doing so destroyed much of the city's medieval fabric. Whole quarters were replaced with wide streets and new buildings, such as this example of modern architecture, which now serves as the city's registry. Across the street to the left are two structures that survived his razing; while not part of the neighborhood they do relate to the history of this area before it was so clearly detached by this major thoroughfare. On the corner is a Roman ruin referred to as the Portichetto de Via della Consolazione; it's a fragment from the last decades of the first century B.C. when the Foro Olitorio was occupied by a series of porticoes. Seen from this corner, what remains are two arches supported by semicolumns of the Tuscan order. Opposite that are three arches with parastades that anchor a corniced architrave. This remnant was once incorporated into the structure of a medieval house, and a few walls and columns still remain from that phase of history, but its days of greatest splendor can now only be imagined. During those days privileged citizens walked sheltered from the rain and the heat beneath the arches. Needless to say, this became an architectural phenomenon only at the time of the empire, when a taste for luxury and comfort superseded the previous austerity of Roman life. In speaking of the porticoes the poets—Martial, in particular—alluded to the delight of their warmth and sunshine while outsiders shivered in the chilly winter wind.

The columns of such porticoes were often made of the rarest kinds of marble and had gilded Corinthian capitals and floors laid with jasper and porphyry. Each portico contained a museum of sculpture, pictures, and enclosed gardens with thickets of landscaped boxwood, trees, lakes, fountains, and waterfalls. Even more incredible than their design is the fact that by the end of the fifth century these porticoes extended from the Forum to the area of St. Peter's Basilica, an expanse of almost two miles. It is interesting to note that this architectural device has not been used in Rome since then but is still popular in northern Italian cities.

To the left of the portichetto, on Via del Teatro di Marcello, is a medieval house that dates from the twelfth century. It has undergone a great deal of restoration, but its tower and its arched bifurcated and trifurcated windows still convey the charms of another era. This is an especially imposing view at night when the lights from the Campidoglio outline it against the wooded hillside.

Next to us on the northeast corner of Via del Teatro di Marcello is the Church of S. Nicola in Carcere. Although this church is of little artistic importance it is unique in that it stands within all or part of three temples that are among the few remains of the republican era. This is a spot of great archeological and historical importance. Explanations of the church's name, "St. Nicolas in Prison," carry us back through some of that history. One explanation has it that during the early

Middle Ages the immediate area was a stronghold for Greek immigrants who introduced the cult of St. Nicolas to Rome. This saint spent much of his life in prisons so the ascription could just be a natural association with his name. Another, more romantic, explanation is that the church was built on the foundations of an ancient prison that was remembered in Pliny's history of Rome by the Emperor Appius Claudius's contemptuous statement that it was the *"domicilium plebis Romanae."* Legend has it that in this prison a young woman kept her dying father alive by feeding him with the milk from her breast. This act of charity so impressed the Roman senate that they decreed the man's life spared and commemorated the occasion by erecting a temple to Piety. This legend was revived in Lord Byron's poem, "Childe Harold's Pilgrimage":

> There is a dungeon in whose drear light
> What do I gaze on?—Nothing—Look again!
> Two forms are slowly shadowed on my sight—
> Two insulated phantoms of the brain:
> It is not so / I see them full and plain,
> An old man and a female young and fair,
> Fresh as a nursing mother—but what doth she
> there,
> With her unmantled neck and bosom white and
> bare?
> But here youth offers to old age the food,
> The milk of its own gift: it is her sire
> To whom she renders back the debt of blood
> Born with her birth—No he shall not expire
> While in those warm and lovely veins the fire
> Of health and holy feeling can provide
> Great Nature's Nile, whose deep stream rises
> higher
> Than Egypt's river; from the gentle side
> Drink, drink, and live, old man! Heaven's realm
> has no such.

Discrepancies also exist about the age of the church. First written mention of it seems to refer to Pope Urban II (1088–1099), and a plaque at the entrance bears the date 1128. Oral tradition, however, has it much older, and a plaque can be found inside the church bearing the date 369. But since most scholars have not found examples of churches that date earlier than the seventh century built in the ruins of pagan temples, this plaque was probably brought from another site. Inside there is also a column, to the right of the entrance, with votive inscriptions from the seventh or eighth century.

Numerous restorations have completely altered the original plan typical of early Christian churches in Rome—a basilica with three naves divided by antique columns. Now it is dressed in eighteenth-century garb but with a sixteenth-century façade by Giacomo della Porta (the coat of arms of Cardinal Pietro Aldobrandini, who commissioned the façade, looms over the entrance). In the fifteenth century the church was decorated with frescoes, a mosaic floor, a choir, and a marble bishop's chair. Even the frescoes by Orazio Gentileschi are now gone. Instead, our attention is drawn to the very antique origins, a remnant of which is the extremely rare urn of green prophyry under the main altar.

In 1932 the church was freed from the many dwellings that surrounded it and obscured the façade and the three temples (believed to have been dedicated to Janus, Juno Sospita, and Hope) that are part of the church's structure. These temples date from the second century B.C., the time of the Punic wars. The temples were very near one another, so that when the church was built on the cella of the middle temple its side walls enclosed the remaining columns of the other two. On the Via del Foro Olitorio side of the church six lateral columns of the original Doric temple remain. On the other side seven columns are embedded in the wall; these are from an Ionic temple. The middle temple was the largest and richest of the three, and the façade of the church includes three columns from the front of this temple. Most of the middle temple is in the basement of the church and can be visited Thursday mornings at 10:00 A.M.

Since the eleventh century, when S. Nicola in Carcere was known as the "church of Petrus Leonis," it has been under the protection of the lords occupying the Teatro di Marcello, which is to your right as you face the church. In 1286, Pandolfo Savelli donated to the church a bell made by Guidotto Pisano, and that bell still rings in the campanile, the base of an old me-

Fragments of marble columns around the Teatro di Marcello

dieval tower. Today, the ancient theater is a palazzo divided into apartments and one of its occupants continues to see to the general upkeep of the church, including a weekly delivery of flowers.

Walk twenty yards to your right as you face the church. You will see the Teatro di Marcello and the archeological park around it. Note also the two columns from one of the republican temples standing beyond the side of the church. Walk down the steps into this area strewn with the ancient fragments.

In his *French and Italian Notebook* Charles Dickens says, "I soon struck upon the remains of the Theater of Marcellus which are very picturesque and the more so from being closely linked in, indeed identified with the shops, habitations and swarming life of modern Rome." The approach to the theater has changed since the days Dickens walked here. The theater remains an imposing sight with its curving arched wall open to the city; but since the 1930s it stands like a monument, isolated from the commerce of the city.

The small open area here, near S. Nicola in Carcere,

the Teatro di Marcello, and the adjacent avenues, was once a maze of buildings and narrow streets. In the heart of the densely populated area was a piazza bound on one side by the theater, whose arcades were used as shops by blacksmiths and scrap-iron dealers. This piazza served as Rome's central meat market and was a gathering place for day laborers in search of work.

Piazza Montanara, named for the mountain people who converged here to sell their goods or seek employment, was a center of Roman street life from the Middle Ages. It is still described with much nostalgia by older Romans who keep alive, in a way etchings and photographs never can, its former color and vitality. Peasants, many in costume, always filled the piazza; they enjoyed a famous puppet theater there, and they used the services of the town scribe who read and wrote their personal communications for them. As a visitor to Rome in 1786–1788, Goethe was captivated by this scene. He met the Roman people here, a place far removed from the Rome of the Catholic Church and the palaces of the gentry. Here also he met the famous Faustina of his *Roman Elegies*; she was the daughter of the owner of the local restaurant-bar.

The Teatro di Marcello may be one of the oldest inhabited buildings in the Western world. First a Roman theater it was afterward, by turns, a fortress, an elegant Renaissance palace, and, today, a complex of apartments and offices. Built by Augustus and dedicated to his nephew and intended successor, Marcellus, son of Ottavia, it was inaugurated in A.D. 11 with great pomp, ceremony, and not without incident. During the festivities the ivory stand from which Augustus was viewing the spectacle broke and sent him tumbling into the crowd of senators and dignitaries. Accounts of this event claim Augustus rose with great dignity and commanded that the spectacle resume.

Augustus, referring to himself as "an adventurous man of the world" on the dedication plaque, offered this theater to the Roman people for assemblies and grand spectacles. Not until the reign of Domitian (A.D. 181–196), however, was this function realized with the greatest flair. Then theater and poetry were introduced as part of the celebrations that were held in March in honor of Minerva, the goddess of wisdom.

This feast was called the *quinquatrie* because it lasted five days; *quinquatrie* is a name still used for the carnival festivities before Lent.

This theater has always been considered an exceptional piece of architecture. Vitruvius writes of it as the finest building of its kind, providing a model for the (now much more famous) Colosseum. It was so well conceived that the senators and the people each had their own entrances, exits, and halls. Massive enough to hold ten to fourteen thousand spectators, the structure was built of travertine and had three tiers of arches—Ionic, Doric, and Corinthian—with fifty-two columns in each. Only twelve arches from the first two tiers survive; the third tier disappeared in the course of various alterations and spoilage that is so much a part of Rome's architectural history. By the first century the theater must already have been in a state of ruin since it helped provide the building material for the construction of the Ponte Cestio, the bridge between the small island in the Tiber and Trastevere on the other side. The accumulated debris of centuries created the hill now called Monte Savello, and completely covered the first tier of arcades until the theater was restored in the 1930s. The shops, therefore, that Dickens and Goethe wrote about were in fact in the second tier of arcades.

In 1086 the ruin of the theater became the fortress of the Pierleoni, a Jewish family turned Catholic in the eleventh century who built their base of power as bankers and businessmen in the Jewish neighborhood of Trastevere. The Pierleoni are sometimes spoken of in contemporary Italian history books as the "Rothschilds of the Middle Ages." Their conversion brought them a strong political alliance with the papacy and their greatest moment was the election of a member of the family as pope. Although this occurred during a schism, and Pope Anacleto II is now considered an antipope, this event signaled the acme of power for this Jewish family and also a period of great hope for the Roman Jewish population in general. The Pierleoni's move to the Teatro di Marcello is also significant because from here they were able to control the island, the main bridges to the left bank of the river, and the entire periphery of the Capitoline Hill, which at the time was the city's commercial center and one of its most populated areas. The fortification they built within the theater's ruins consisted of numerous towers, one of which can still be distinguished in a square terrace that rises high above the building.

In the thirteenth century the Pierleoni's power was assumed by the Savelli family, which took over the fortress and established a very active fiefdom for themselves. It was under their patronage in the sixteenth century that Baldassare Peruzzi built a patrician home on the remains of this Roman theater. In doing so he enclosed what remained of the third tier of arches and constructed a huge palazzo that covered the full semicircle of the theater and contained several courtyards with gardens.

Evidence of the size of the palazzo and the complex network of spaces it created within the original Roman design can be attested to by the story of a Jewish countess who hid in its secret chambers throughout the Nazi occupation of Rome. In 1712 the Orsini family became lords of the palazzo, which is known to this day as the Palazzo Orsini. This family first appears in Roman history in the early half of the twelfth century; their claim to fame, besides producing forty cardinals and two popes, is as the greatest enemy of the Colonna family, considered Rome's oldest family. Their battles were such that Pope Julius II, in his effort to bring peace to Rome, was forced to give one of his nieces in marriage to Virginio Orsini and the other to Marcantonio Colonna. At the same time he made the two heads of the families barons and prince associates to the papal throne. Today the gatekeeper at the Palazzo Orsini, now one of Rome's most elegant apartment buildings, will point to the bears standing on the gatepost as the only remains of the Orsini family. On the other hand the Colonnas, who also had their palazzo (on the Corso Vittorio Emanuele II) designed by Peruzzi, have managed to keep their residence, one of the few palazzi in Rome that has not become a public building or been divided into apartments.

As you walk around the ancient theater you can't help but be amazed by its height and volume. The arcades are now occupied by the famous cats of Rome, who are fed their daily meal of spaghetti by one of the more eccentric neighborhood women. The shadows of these arcades also provide a haven for drug users.

Recently the city erected a fence with gates, open only during the day, that completely surrounds the theater and its piazza in an effort to discourage these people, who sometimes set up temporary housekeeping here. Because of the fence you may have to walk back up the stairs to the walkway along Via del Teatro di Marcello and reenter the archeological grounds of the theater by the main gate, about thirty yards to your left.

Immediately north of the theater and to your right from the main entrance are three marble columns with a richly carved entablature. These are the remains of the southeast corner of the first temple dedicated (in 431 B.C.) to Apollo, the Greek god of light and the protector of letters and art. Apollo was also thought to have healing powers and as the city was being devastated by plagues the temple was dedicated to him for this attribute. Today the threat of plague is gone, and these glistening white marble columns, surrounded in late spring by red poppies, appear instead to pay homage to Apollo the sun god.

The temple's remains are part of a restoration done in 33 B.C.; they were resurrected in 1940 from fragments found in the course of excavations. This is one of the best examples of Augustan period architectural decoration, which was strongly influenced by the Greeks. Look carefully at the corniced capitals, the cordoned base, and the frieze adorned with intricate patterns of leaves, oxen horns, and branched candlesticks. Pliny described this temple's lavish interior as being richly decorated with colored marble from Africa and an entablature depicting scenes of war and a triumphal procession. Fragments of this entablature can now be seen in the Capitoline Museum.

To the right of the Temple of Apollo, surrounded by a fence, are the foundations of another temple, the Temple of Janus, the porter of heaven. Janus opens the year (January) and is the guardian of gates. The ancient Romans ritualized his persona by opening the gates to this temple during times of peace and closing them during times of war. Since it was built to celebrate the Roman victory over the Carthaginians in 260 B.C., the gates of the Temple of Janus were rarely open for the next two hundred years.

On the hill overlooking these two temples is an in-

teresting thirteenth-century house surrounded by ole-
ander trees and seasonal flowers. Recently restored as
office space for the city's Administrator of Fine Arts
and Culture, the structure is known as the *Albergo della Catena,* "Hotel of the Chains." The name describes
the medieval street that led to it, which must have
been blocked by a rope of chains.

Walk up the first set of stairs that extend to the left
of the ruins to an elevated passageway called the Via
Tribuna di Campitelli. From here you have a great
view of the residential spaces within and above the
Teatro di Marcello. You can also see an open arcade-
turned-terrace that is covered with cultivated and wild
greenery bursting from every available crevice. To the
right is the palazzo's former chapel, a hexagonal space
now perhaps used as a dining room. At the farthest visible point stands an iron pergola wrapped in ivy that
must be the best place in town to enjoy one's morning
coffee. Also admire the elegant fourteenth-century
house that completes the triangular space. We will take
a closer look at this near the end of our walk.

Walk down the stairs and take whichever open gate
(of the two, one is usually locked) leads to the Via del
Portico d'Ottavia. A few steps around to your right
stands yet another monument from Augustus's reign,
the Portico d'Ottavia. In no other part of town can one
so clearly see the meaning of his famous words, "I
found a city of wood and bricks and have left a city of
marble." This portico was first built in 149 B.C. by
Quintus Metellus and then completely reconstructed
by Augustus with richly decorated marble when he
dedicated it to his sister, Ottavia. In Augustus's time it
housed Greek and Latin libraries, as well as the most
celebrated pieces of Greek art to be found in Rome.
These included a group of thirty-four bronze equestrian statues; a cupid by Praxiteles, which was later destroyed by fire; and the famous Medici Venus, found
during a seventeenth-century excavation and now at
the Uffizi Museum in Florence. The original structure
was in the form of a parallelogram 118 meters by 135
meters surrounded by a double arcade of 270 columns
that enclosed the Temples of Juno Regina and Jupiter
Stator. This complex had two entrances, each with a
double atrium and monolithic columns of white marble between two Corinthian pilasters supporting the

A view from under the arch of the Portico d'Ottavia

tympanum. Before us is the principal entrance, which was reconstructed by Septimius Severus following a fire in A.D. 203, as documented on the pediment. Since then the portico has been further altered. Half of it is now blocked off by a church entrance, and the second pediment looks like a collage of fragments (including bits of fluted columns) that were found on the site.

According to Pliny the architects employed by Augustus were two Greeks named Batrachos and Sauros. Because they were not allowed to sign their work they carved lizards and frogs on the fluting of all their columns, thus leaving us the personal touch of the artisan in this age of emperors. One such column, with a lizard and a frog clearly visible on the capital, was used to decorate the Church of S. Lorenzo Fuori le Mura, "Church of St. Lawrence Outside the Walls," and many of the other two hundred-odd columns are also probably preserved in the monuments of Christian Rome.

The Church of S. Angelo in Pescheria, whose entrance is behind the gate blocking off the right-hand side of the portico, is an example of the manner in which the city has constantly adopted its edifices to the cultural mores and taste of the times. Literally inserted into the ruins of the portico in 770, the propylaeum, or vestibule, of the ancient structure forms the porch of the church. In the fifteenth century it was rebuilt in conjunction with restoration done on the ruin, and then in the seventeenth century it was decorated in the style of that time. The entrance arch, which substitutes for two of the original columns, still bears faint traces of thirteenth-century frescoes of the Archangel Michael (for whom the church is named) and of the Virgin Mary and St. Paul. In the twelfth century the church added *in pescheria* to its name when the portico became the site of the central fish market. Later, in the sixteenth century, the appellation was reinforced when the Confraternity of Fishmongers adopted this church as their place of worship.

Old engravings depict the portico and church surrounded by large marble slabs on which the fish were cut and cleaned. These slabs, owned by the local nobles, were rented to the fishmongers at a handsome profit. Until 1880, when the fish market was dismantled, this site was one of Rome's more picturesque attractions, frequently depicted by its community of foreign artists and often described by visitors in their journals.

The plaque in the brickwork by the entrance to the church is a Latin ordinance proscribing that the head and the body up to the first fin of any fish larger than the plaque were to be delivered to the city magistrates. These fish were supposedly used in the soup kitchens for the poor. It was a form of tax, which, the population complained, took the best part of the fish, and was repealed only after the French Revolution in 1798. Note also the oratory to the right, at Via del Foro Pescario 33; built in 1689 it is an image of St. Andrew with an inscription that describes this as "the place of worship for the fishmongers."

One of the most dramatic moments for the Church of S. Angelo in Pescheria was in 1347 when Cola di Rienzo gathered his forces to conquer the city. Born in 1313 just a few blocks from here, Cola di Rienzo grew up the son of a poor family during a time when Rome had been abandoned by the pope and had become a private battleground for the nobility. In keeping with the spirit of the times Cola studied the classics and history and took great pride in his heritage. He yearned for the lost glory of Rome and after his brother was killed in a faction fight Cola di Rienzo decided to conquer Rome. With the help of Pope Clement VI he impressed people with his charisma and his grandiose schemes for the reestablishment of a Rome free from the destruction of the barons. He insisted that the pope return to St. Peter's, that the Eternal City be once again the world's metropolis, and, above all, that the people be sovereign subjects only to God. What is so remarkable about Cola di Rienzo is that he not only dreamed of a revolution, but he achieved it—if only for a short time, from May to December of 1347, and without much success. He is recognized today as the first of the Italian liberators.

The portico and the church stood just outside the walls of the old Jewish Ghetto. Toward the end of the sixteenth century, at the instigation of a converted Jew, Pope Gregory XIII forced the Jews into S. Angelo in Pescheria to listen to thunderous denunciations against them. This practice lasted for more than two centuries and included other churches in the area. Today a very different kind of thunderous roar fills the space of the church: every Saturday evening the charismatic Catholics of Rome come here for their services. With eyes closed and ears open to their soulful music you can almost imagine being in some revival town in the American South.

Go around the left side of the portico through a narrow alley and you will find yourself in the Piazza S. Angelo in Pescheria. This is one of those special nooks of old Rome that becomes a piazza just because it is a dead end. Much of its visual charm comes from the sudden change of scale—a small area closely bound by modest houses and narrow streets. Immediately to the left as you enter the piazza is the vestige of an outside staircase, an unusual sight in Rome, despite the fact that it is a typical architectural device in the nearby countryside of Lazio and Abruzzo.

Behind you as you face the outside staircase, at no. 14 on the corner, is a house characteristic of the eighteenth century with its smooth corners and its cornice decorated with the motifs of animals' heads and shafts of wheat. The ground floor of this building is the dish-washing and storage area for the restaurant Da Gigge-to's on Via del Portico d'Ottavia that backs onto this piazza. Just a few steps up the street to the left, on the Via S. Angelo in Pescheria, look to see if the doors at nos. 9 or 10 are open. If so, you'll see inside, on the staircase, an upright column that was once part of the Temple of Juno Regina. All these houses immediately around the portico are built over and hide a complicat-ed network of excavation paths with numerous col-umns buried in their foundations.

Return to the piazza and walk halfway around the apse of the church to the Via Tribuna di Campitelli. At the intersection you will find two typical Roman sights: the first is the ever-flowing, cast-iron water tap. Each section of Rome is served by a different aqueduct and water source the virtues of which source are con-stantly being debated among Romans, though all the water is fresh and clean. At this tap you can help your-self to some Acqua Felice, named after Pope Sixtus V, who completed the aqueduct in the late sixteenth cen-tury. Here the source is a group of springs about fif-teen miles east of Rome; these springs are fed by water from the Alban Hills that has been filtered through vol-canic tufa. The second typical sight is a marble plaque indicating that this is the *rione* Campitelli, one of twenty-two civic districts. The concept of the *rione*, or quarter of the city, stems from the days of the empire and was reinforced by the fiefdoms of the early Middle Ages. In 1143, with the establishment of the "Com-mune," or city government, these districts legally be-came the basis of the political and civic organization of Rome. At that time there were fourteen *rioni*, twelve on the east bank of the Tiber, and then Trastevere and the island. These have since been reorganized and ex-panded through the centuries, and although they no longer represent distinct political entities they contin-ue to function in other ways as districts.

To the right, at the beginning of Via Tribuna di Cam-pitelli, is a clear view of the Augustan treasure chest that is so much a part of this neighborhood. These Ionic columns were probably used in the Middle Ages to make a portico attached to the house. They were lat-er either engulfed by the structure of a larger building or closed off by order of Pope Sixtus IV, who in 1475 decided that the dark open spaces should no longer provide refuge to criminals. Today, as once-modest houses in Rome's historic center are renovated to make luxury apartments, the columns have been completely exposed and have become decorative details on the façade of an otherwise plain brick house.

The last house, no. 16, to the left at the end of the street, is the Palazzo Lovatelli, the first in a series of palazzi that circumscribe the Piazza Campitelli with the grand architecture of the 1600s. Tucked between two piazzas, this palazzo opens its gate to both, giving the impression, from this entrance, of a courtyard with shops or an elegant covered arcade. Designed by Giacomo della Porta, it was completed in 1620 on the site of the original Church of S. Maria in Campitelli. Here, in the late nineteenth century, Ersilia Lovatelli Caetani held a salon that was famous throughout Europe. Gregorovius, Carducci, D'Annunzio, Liszt, Zola, and Anatole France were among the many whose intellectual energies enhanced this salon's reputation.

The Piazza Campitelli, one of the prettiest and perhaps the most harmonious in the city, is an example of the Catholic Church's plan during the Counter-Reformation to make Rome the most beautiful city of the Christian world "for the greater glory of God and the Church." This movement, a period of self-renewal during the seventeenth century, presented a newly fortified faith with the papacy strongly established in Rome and supported by the city's nobility. It was a time of great wealth and vigor; buildings were designed on the grand scale of the baroque. Here, at the foot of the Campidoglio, the symbol of secular power in Rome, the spirit of that time may be clearly seen. The piazza is a statement of nobility and grandeur with the palazzi of some of the greatest patrician families of the time facing the Church of S. Maria in Campitelli. To create this space the church was moved and rebuilt, and the façade of one of the palazzi was changed to open onto the church. Today the spirit that created this piazza has vanished; it is occupied primarily by city government offices and various cultural organizations. The church is the parish seat for a predominantly Jewish population, and the focal point of the piazza is the restaurant on the corner, Vecchia Roma, known throughout the city for its cuisine and atmosphere.

At no. 1 Piazza Campitelli is the Palazzo Cavalletti, a building of the late 1500s where Rome's last senator, Francesco Cavalletti Rondinini, died in 1870. The windows on the *piano nobile*, thus called because the reception rooms are on the second floor, are adorned in a mannered style with elegant festoons. In recent times an extra floor has been added above the cornice. This sad corruption of the original design, called the attic space, has become a necessity in modern Rome, where housing is scarce. But it was also popularized during the postwar period by members of the large foreign community whose desire for fresh air, sun, and greenery was not satisfied by the local custom of merely walking in the piazza.

The palazzo that houses the restaurant Vecchia Roma is the newest face on the square. Its late, almost rococo architecture is a playful contrast to the strictly classical lines of the Palazzo Cavalletti, built more than a hundred years earlier.

Since the 1600s the Palazzo Albertoni Spinola, at no. 2, has been home for an illustrious Roman family that still occupies a section of it. The building was designed by Giacomo della Porta and completed by Girolamo Rainaldi with a façade that connected it to the palaces on either side. Note the lions' heads (from the Albertoni family crest) on the cornice and moldings. Note, too, above the first window on the left, the round tabernacle to S. Maria in Porticu, which can be seen on several buildings in this district. The tabernacle is a reference to the image of the Madonna on the high altar of the church across the way. According to legend the portrait of the Madonna was brought to Pope John I in 523 by two angels and at the moment of this offering all the bells in Rome miraculously started ringing. This image was carried through the city in great penitential processions during the pestilence of 590 and again in 1656, during the plague. In both cases, wherever the Madonna passed the epidemic ended. She is therefore worshiped as the protectress of Rome against contagious diseases, a powerful symbol to Romans who for centuries were afflicted by such disasters.

The Church of S. Maria in Campitelli, which was built in her honor between 1662 and 1667, is considered to be Carlo Rainaldi's best work. Its façade is made entirely of travertine with a *leitmotif* of strong vertical lines effected by placing huge columns against but not attached to the façade. These columns overpower other elements of the design and seem to reach for the sky with their double pediment. The result is similar to another of Rainaldi's churches, S. Andrea della Valle, in which the first act of *Tosca* takes place. Inside the church the same kind of trick is played: the space is given a sense of amplification, depth, and size that it in fact doesn't have. Baroque design aspires to startle and to create an emotional response; the architect here manages to focus attention on the high altar, which appears large and overpowering. For the price of a few coins you can listen to a tape recording in English near the entrance of the church that will give you a detailed account of the church's artistic contents.

It is heartwarming to know that, in this city of churches, prayers are said for all of us at one time or another. Here we are always remembered in prayers against contagious diseases, which after all includes even the common cold. If you are English and Protestant, you will be happy to know that every Sunday the 11:00 A.M. mass includes a "perpetual intercession for the conversion of England." This was established in 1766 by the Older Pretender, known to his adherents as James III of England.

Back across the piazza at no. 3 is the Palazzo Capizucchi, also designed by Giacomo della Porta. Within this palace is a famous music hall, which serves as a reminder of the explosion in musical interest that took place in Rome during the sixteenth and seventeenth centuries. It is this palazzo's façade that had to be redesigned to face the church and the piazza. Go in the gate, which, because of the remodeling, is off-center; it opens onto a lovely ivy-covered courtyard with a view from the vestibule of the stone steps leading into the living quarters. Today the building is used by the French Cultural Center, and it is purely by coincidence that the *fleur-de-lis* decorating the portal is part of the Capizucchi family crest.

The fountain, purposely placed to the side of the piazza to keep the church as the center of attention, is also by Giacomo della Porta. It is decorated with the coats of arms of all the families whose palazzi we have just admired.

No. 9 is the house of a religious order connected to the church. This palazzo and the one on the other side were originally designed to match, and do, in seventeenth-century engravings. The building at no. 6–7, now a city government office for the Cultural Minister, is known as the Palazzo Flaminio Panzio, Pope Paul V's architect at the turn of the seventeenth century. The palace was given this name because the inlaid marble pieces are from Panzio's house, which was demolished during the clearing of the Forum in 1933. If the gate at no. 7 is open go through the vestibule to the back. There you will see fragments from the Temples of Apollo and Janus, walls of ancient Roman houses, the three columns from the Temple of Apollo, and a wonderful view of the Teatro di Marcello. You can also see the front of the medieval Albergo della Catena.

Turn on Via Capizucchi, to the left directly across from the Palazzo Flaminio Panzio. Immediately on the right is the bleak wall of the Convent of the Tor de' Specchi, owned by the order of Oblates that was founded by Francesca Romana in 1425 for daughters of the aristocracy. The convent is named after a tower that was a city landmark until it was torn down in 1750. The Tor de' Specchi, "tower of mirrors," is associated with medieval legends about the Capitoline Hill and its surrounding buildings. According to one legend this tower was covered with magic mirrors through which the ancient Romans could see and control their entire empire as well as protect themselves from the plots of the outside world.

In the Piazza Capizucchi, at the end of the short street and to your left, you can see what was originally intended as the front of the Palazzo Capizucchi, and also, on the far end, behind the iron gate, an arch built to connect the Palazzo Albertoni Spinola with another family house. The attraction in this piazza, however, is the ivy-covered fifteenth-century house on the right. Though much restored, it maintains the grace of its period architecture in the low-arched doorways and the molding of the windows. Walk around the house and look at the main entrance on Via della Tribuna di Tor de' Specchi 5. Above the door is a crest of a harpy, the symbol of the *rione* (Campitelli), and above that is an intricately carved stone molding. To the left, below the

ivy, is an even older section of the house, with symbols of the Guelph cross on the window representing
the medieval faction that opposed the authority of the
German emperors (the Ghibellines) in Italy.

Return to the street that leads out of Piazza Capizucchi, also called Via della Tribuna di Tor de' Specchi,
past nos. 28 to 30. In a few feet it opens onto the Piazza Margana, named for the Margani family who from
their tower controlled this area in the fourteenth century. It is a quiet spot, isolated from the more active
heart of the neighborhood and apparently lost in
time—though this may be changing with the advent of
a fancy gift and jewelry shop. The less conspicuous
shops at the other end of the piazza are old family
businesses. These artisans, such as the glass restorer,
the ironsmith, and the pharmacist, have been here for
several generations.

I am always attracted to the terrace straight ahead
with its many cacti, succulents, and blossoms; it's a
wild and rather haphazard jungle that overlooks the
cobblestones and concrete of the piazza. Immediately
to the right as you enter the piazza is the Palazzo Velli,
no. 24, built at the end of the seventeenth century. The
building has a large, arched portal of hewn stones, and
over a window on the second floor is an inscription,
worn with age, that reads "Andreas Villus," probably
in reference to the magistrate of Rome from 1592 until
1603. Walk through the portal; at the end of the vestibule, in the small enclosed courtyard, is a fountain
made from a lovely sarcophagus that portrays Apollo
and the Muses.

The Palazzo Maccarani, at no. 19, also has a courtyard that is worth visiting. This one is cluttered, in the
style of the sixteenth century, with antique fragments
of sculpture, inscriptions, and columns. The fountain
in the corner looks as if it were made of volcanic lava
but, in fact, years of accumulated calcium from the
hard Roman water have created this effect. You will
recognize the small tabernacle to S. Maria in Porticu
outside, on the wall of the palazzo, protecting the
house and the piazza from contagious diseases.

Across from the Palazzo Maccarani and to your right
are the remains of the Margani's tower. In 1305, Giovanni Margani bought a house with three columns, a

A street sign on Piazza Margana

gate, and a side courtyard surrounded by a portico of ancient columns. He then broke with the norm by building a tower with an open loggia, one of the first examples of a less defense-oriented style of tower architecture. (Some successive owner closed in the loggia but probably for reasons of space.) Embedded in the wall beneath the street sign we can see one of the three Ionic columns, above it, a carved eagle from the family crest and, to the right, a gateway to the ancient courtyard decorated with fragments of antique cornices.

This piazza also has a restaurant on the corner that is easily confused with Vecchia Roma on Piazza Campitelli (this one isn't as good). The building housing the restaurant embodies the architecture of two different centuries, primarily distinguished by the doors and the angle of its façade. At no. 34 is the seventeenth-century section and at no. 35 is a small entrance with molding typical of the sixteenth century. Above it is the coat of arms of the Albertoni family.

We leave the piazza on the street bordering the restaurant, Via dei Delfini. The street gives us our first glimpse of the commercial life of this neighborhood. Here we have the paint store, a meat store, a shop for household goods, the only local store that sells milk, and the wine bar. Until recently the wine bar was outfitted in the old-fashioned Roman tradition with a marble countertop and barrels of wine behind it. Workmen came here to quench their thirst with the white wine of the Alban Hills, and local housewives brought their empty bottles to be refilled for dinner. But, along with the new shops we saw around the corner, the wine bar has dressed itself up for a more sophisticated, nonlocal crowd. Its lost charm is regrettable, nevertheless this is not a bad place for a light lunch or a drink.

St. Ignatius lived in a small house on the site of the elegantly conceived, late-sixteenth-century Palazzo Delfini at the bend in the street to your right. It was here in September 1540 that he received permission to start the Society of Jesus, or the Jesuit Order. The main entrance, no. 16, leads into a garden that at one time was filled with one of the world's most famous collections of antique sculpture. Today the sculptures are gone and a large part of this garden has been closed by the state to make room for the excavations of the crypt of the ancient Theater of Balbus, built in 19 B.C. by Cornilius Balbus to celebrate his triumph over the Germantes.

Turn right where Via dei Delfini becomes a narrow alley. Here you will encounter a great change of environment, with abandoned buildings standing in an incredible state of disrepair. When I first asked about this condition I was told that it was the result of terrorist bombings, a theory not entirely without credit since the neighborhood, near the headquarters of both the Italian Communist party and the Christian Democratic party, has had more than its share of terrorist-related activity. The truth, however, is a more familiar one. The block was bought up by the Bank of Rome and sits empty. It is interesting that this situation, in a city with a serious housing shortage, doesn't raise protests from the neighborhood. Instead, denizens would rather believe the terrorist story, perhaps in part because their efforts are already concentrated on keeping landlords and speculators from displacing people for renovations. As you walk around the old city you will see a number of buildings with banners hanging from windows espousing this antidisplacement cause. It is one of the most emotional issues in Rome.

The narrow end of Via dei Delfini leads right into Via dei Funari. This street is named for the ropemakers who plied their trade here. Immediately to your right is the recently cleaned façade of the Church of S. Caterina dei Funari. This, one of the few examples of late-Renaissance architecture in Rome and built on the site of a monastery founded in 1000, was designed by Guido Guidetti, an apprentice of Michelangelo's during the construction of the Piazza del Campidoglio. The church has a lovely chapel designed by Vignola that can be seen on Sundays at 10:30 A.M. In marked contrast to the chapel and the façade is the bizarre and unattractive bell tower that houses bells brought from Germany by St. Ignatius. Step back into the Piazza Lovatelli so that you can see it. The bell tower was added to one of those simple but elegant medieval towers that were such a dominant characteristic of this neighborhood in the fourteenth century. To make matters worse, recent restoration has made the top look like a decoration for a wedding cake. This restoration is referred to coldly as the sacrilege of S. Caterina.

As part of the church St. Ignatius founded here an institution for poor and homeless girls that became a sort of finishing school providing wives for the local artisans. On the day of her marriage each girl was given an attractive dowry of fifty scudi from an endowment supported by the rich courtesans of Rome. Isabella de Luna, a famous sixteenth-century courtesan whom Bandello writes of in his novels about Rome, was one of this institution's most generous patronesses.

The first intersection to your right is the Via Caetani. Here you can see the spot, marked by a plaque, where Aldo Moro's dead body was found in March 1978. Italy was almost immobilized when the Red Brigade kidnapped the then-favorite candidate for election as Italy's head of state. After he was held for three months his body was dropped here. The event marked a turning point in the course of modern Italian politics and was a startling finale to any remnants of the famous *la dolce vita* in Rome during the 1950s and 1960s.

On the corner of Via Caetani and Via dei Funari stands the Palazzo Mattei Giove, the grandest of several built by the Mattei family, whose complex of palazzi cover an entire city block from Via Caetani to Via Paganica and from Via dei Funari to Via delle Botteghe Oscure. This family was run out of Trastevere in the 1400s after their violence became unbearable to the local population. They settled in this part of Rome and built their stronghold on the remains of the ancient Theater of Balbus. By the 1500s the Mattei family was again firmly established, with members holding such titles as Duchi di Giove, Marchesi di Rocca Sinibalds, Duchi di Paganica, and Principi Romani. Among their sources of wealth were the tithes they collected as the custodians of the bridges over the Tiber, and later of the gates to the Ghetto.

In the 1400s they began a massive building project including five palazzi whose construction continued until the end of the 1600s. As a consequence of a decree by Pope Gregory XII in 1574—that all new construction in the city could not be free-standing and had either to be directly attached to the adjacent buildings or connected by a wall—the Mattei palaces were separated only by interior courtyards and different styles of architecture. Since the seventeenth century this block has been called the island of the Mattei. We will look at two of the palazzi during our walk, both the first one and the last one to be built.

The Palazzo Mattei Giove at Via Caetani 32, designed by Carlo Maderno between 1598 and 1618, was the last. It is a severe building except for its rich, heavy cornice decorated with the emblems of the family crest. Stand up against the building for the best view, since it is one of the most impressive cornices in town. The façade is the same on both the Via Funari and the Via Caetani sides, with a large entrance leading from an atrium into a vestibule. The entrance off Via Caetani faces the grand staircase while the other has a view of a classical courtyard that looks like an outdoor museum, and beyond that, a garden courtyard. Walk into the palazzo. The entire public space is richly decorated with stucco and ancient reliefs of marble encased in the walls. In the vestibule is a precious group of marble figures, "The Sacrifice of Mitra" (the Persian god in whose name fire was adored), "Apollo and the Muses," and a Bacchanalian shrine. The first courtyard is decorated with statues and more antique reliefs, including one on the left entitled "The Hunt in the Great City of Calydrone," which was sculpted by Meleagro. There is also a beautiful "Rape of Persepine." If you go up the grand staircase you will pass more sculpture, vases, and a beautifully stuccoed vault. This leads to a loggia lined with imperial busts from the sixteenth century.

A plaque from 1616, in the first courtyard, states that Astrubale Mattei was a fastidious collector who documented all of his purchases, restorations, and commissions for seventeenth-century reproductions. This is one of the earliest examples of collector responsibility in the history of art collecting.

Leave the building through the gate facing the Via dei Funari and turn right. You will come upon the most beautiful fountain in Rome; its sensual charm soothes nerves frayed by the traffic and noise of the city. Known as the Turtle Fountain, it was designed by Giacomo della Porta to display the Acqua Felice, and it was sculpted by the Florentine artist Taddeo Landini.

Four young, beautiful boys with the limber arches of dancers stand on dolphins, and each lifts a turtle into the vase of the fountain. Ideally the fountain should be viewed in a carefully landscaped garden where one can listen in silence to the flow of water and see the fountain's beauty in harmony with nature. D'Annunzio, one of Italy's greatest poets, wrote: *"La Fontana di Giacomo—a la fresca—serenità con voce roca e pianamettea parole come una fontana-magica dell'età cavalleresca."* ("The fountain of Giacomo— in the open—serenity with a voice of rock and words of quietness like a magic fountain of the days of chivalry.")

Neighborhood folklore has it that the fountain was designed by Raphael or Bernini—who but the greatest could conceive such beauty! In fact, Bernini may have added the turtles when he restored the fountain in 1658; the original design called for dolphins to match the base. Another legend has it that the fountain was built overnight. Across the piazza, at Via dei Funari 19, you will see a blocked-in window. According to this legend one of the dukes of Mattei in the 1600s gambled away his entire fortune in a night. When his prospective father-in-law heard of this he told the duke to find himself another wife. The duke, enraged by this insult, decided to prove that even without money he remained a great and powerful man, so he had this fountain built overnight in front of his house. The next day he invited his future father-in-law to the house. He opened the window exclaiming, "See what I can do in such a short time, a wretch like me." He won the hand of the girl and she, in return, blocked the window so that standing inside her home she would never see the fountain that resulted in her marrying such an irresponsible man.

No. 19 is the oldest Mattei palace. Built in the first half of the sixteenth century by Nanni Baccio Bigio, it incorporated a fifteenth-century house that was on the property. Entering through the Renaissance doorway we come upon a courtyard and what is probably the oldest wing of the palazzo with an outside staircase and open loggia sustained by an elegant portico. This courtyard demonstrates the picturesque variety a fifteenth-century Roman courtyard can have when it unifies rustic and irregular elements with the more

The Turtle Fountain

sophisticated, elegant sixteenth-century lines, such as the capitals and the details of the arcades. Certainly movie scouts have thought so. In the 1950s this court-yard was a favorite setting for cloak-and-dagger and spaghetti-Western movies in which the hero jumped from the staircase onto his horse.

Before leaving the piazza note the palazzo at no. 12, tucked in the far-right corner near the barbershop. The Palazzo Costaguti, with its lovely baroque entrance, was built at the end of the sixteenth century. The building itself spreads without any precise plan, but in-side is an extraordinary collection of baroque art: fur-niture, fabrics, art objects, and frescoes by Guercino, Domenichino, d'Arpino, Lanfranco, Albani, and Ro-manelli. It contains one of the few throne rooms found in a private house. It was customary, until 1870, for the pope to make occasional visits to the houses of Roman princes, dukes, and four privileged marche-se—the Marchese Costaguti, Patrizi, Teodoli, and Sac-cheti. To receive the pontiffs and to underline their privileged status, these nobles always had a throne complete with a *baldacchino*, "canopy." The palaces of these noble families still possess throne rooms and the four marchesi are still known as the *marchesi del baldacchino*. The palazzo, however, is closed to all vis-itors, even distinguished scholars, and may never be appreciated, as it is said to be in terrible disrepair.

Take a short detour down the Via della Reginella, which is straight ahead as you face the fountain. With-in fifteen steps you can see the former entrance of the Palazzo Costaguti, used before the Jewish Ghetto en-croached upon it, and, next to it, fragments in the wall that mark an entrance to the ancient Ghetto. This gate was put up when Pope Leo XII effected the final exten-sion of the Ghetto to include the Via Reginella. The act, which was made in conjunction with Pope Leo's abolition of liquor in bars and restaurants, inspired a wonderful *pasquinade*, "popular saying":

> *Fior de mu ghetto*
> *Papa Leone e diventato matto*
> *Ha chiuso le osterie e allargato il ghetto.*

> Lilies of the valley
> Pope Leo has gone mad
> He has closed the bars and enlarged the ghetto.

This street is still filled with the commercial activities that precipitated Pope Leo's 1825 decision to make it part of the Ghetto. Although it leads to our next destination, the Via del Portico d'Ottavia, I prefer taking Via S. Ambrogio, to your right as you return to the Piazza Mattei from Via Reginella. It is a narrow street that zigzags around buildings and includes a miniature piazza in front of a school. Its surrounding terraces, tile roofs, courtyards, gates, cats, and the obligatory church evoke what must surely have been the atmosphere of this neighborhood two hundred years ago. After you have followed its course, first turning left and then right, you will exit on Via del Portico d'Ottavia. Turn right. This is the center of the neighborhood still known today as the Jewish Ghetto. On the right-hand side of the street and on the Via della Reginella, mentioned above, stand the only Ghetto buildings that were not demolished at the turn of the century when the embankments of the Tiber were built and the streets were widened. The old Via del Portico d'Ottavia was a mere lane; an entire block of houses and another street stood between the medieval and Renaissance houses on the right and the turn-of-the-century buildings on the left. Thus the story of the Jewish Ghetto must now be told as history.

Like many ethnic groups in an alien city the Roman Jews tended to congregate in certain districts. Initially they lived on the left bank of the river in Trastevere. After the pillage of Rome in 1084 they migrated first to the island and then to this area next to the Portico d'Ottavia, where Vespasian and Titus had met with the Roman senate on the day of Rome's triumph over Jerusalem.

The first diplomatic encounter of the Jews with the Roman senate was in 160 B.C., when a mission was sent by Judas Maccabeus to seek the friendship of this great nation. In 139 B.C. a treaty of commerce was signed and by 50 B.C. the Jewish community in Rome seems to have been flourishing. At that time Cicero wrote of the Jewish influence on the city, and Caesar proclaimed an edict that granted them religious freedom. Only after the conquest of Jerusalem in A.D. 70, when Jews were brought back as slaves, were there any real conflicts for Jews living in Rome. For centuries no pious Jew would walk under the arch of Titus in the Forum as it was built to celebrate the conquest of Jerusalem and depicts the plunder of the Temple.

The position of Jews became intolerable in the late Middle Ages when their fate depended less on established dogma than on the whim of various pontiffs. In the thirteenth century, sumptuary laws were imposed on all Jews and heretics, forcing them to wear a mark of distinction. This was at various times a large circle of yellow cloth, a scarlet mantle, and an orange cap. Only licensed physicians, considered public benefactors, were exempt. Other humiliations included carnival races from the Piazza Navona to the Corso in which Jews were pursued by the jeering and laughing lower classes, who in many cases were their worst enemies and oppressors. This practice began in 1468 and got progressively worse until it finally stopped in 1668 when Pope Clement IX accepted instead a tax of thirteen hundred scudi. The true date of infamy for the papacy was 1555. In this year the fanatical Pope Paul IV rescinded all of the privileges the Jews had enjoyed and established the Ghetto, which was based on ghettos in Prague and Venice. The word *ghetto* in fact comes from the Venetian word for "foundries," which occupied the quarter assigned to the Jews in Venice. The decision to segregate the Jews was in large part the product of the Counter-Reformation movement, which feared that any friendship between Jews and Christians would cause a serious danger to the purity of the Christian faith. A hint of Jewish sentiment toward this segregation is the event that took place in 1559, when Pope Paul IV died. At the announcement of his death a mob of Jews broke through the gates of the Ghetto and stormed into the Conservatory Palace on the Capitoline Hill. They overturned the statue of the pope and dragged its head through the streets back into the Ghetto, crowning the pontifical tiara with the hateful orange cap they were forced to wear.

The Ghetto wall was built by Galvestro Peruzzi, son of the famous architect Baldassare Peruzzi, and paid for by the Jewish community. It extended from the Ponte Fabricius to the Portico d'Ottavia, across the Piazza Giudea and back down the river along the Vicolo dei Cenci; the fish market and the Teatro di Marcello were excluded. In 1555 it was 270 meters long and 150 meters wide—less than three hectares—and it housed 3,500 Jews. The main entrance on Piazza Giudea had a large ornamental gate and a fountain by Giacomo della Porta, which Pope Paul commissioned "to relieve the misery of the Jews." The other gate was across from the Church of S. Giorgio della Divina Pietà. In 1577 a third gate was added at S. Angelo in Pescheria. The boundaries of the wall were enlarged from time to time and the number of gates eventually increased to eight. These gates were closed at seven o'clock in the evening in the winter and at eight in the summer. The Mattei family was responsible for guarding the gates in return for a yearly remuneration of 163 scudi and 20 Vatican copper coins.

In some respects the Ghetto provided the Jews with safety from the malice of the Roman populace. Late in the eighteenth century Moses Mendelssohn, grandfather of the composer, wrote to a friend in Berlin and complained bitterly that his movements were circumscribed in this city of self-styled toleration by the cry of "Jew" raised against him and his children when they walked through the streets. He also described boys throwing stones at them as they passed.

In 1853, Gregorovius visited the Ghetto and wrote an enchanting description of the rag shops, the trade practiced by many Jews who were allowed few choices of profession or trade. Before the shop doors lay "scraps of golden fringe; pieces of silk brocade; rags of velvet; patches of red; scraps of blue, orange, yellow, black, and white. I have never seen the like. The Jews might patch all creation with it and make the whole world as varicolored as a harlequin." He goes on to describe the astrologers, diviners, magicians, witches, and crystal gazers who were frequented by the grand ladies of Rome. The Ghetto was undoubtedly full of color and fascination in the eyes of an outsider, but, in fact, it was a miserable place to live. Most of the houses were in a very bad state of disrepair, either half-fallen or leaning from the weight of stories added to accommodate a population of more than 4,000 where only half that many should have been living. The Ghetto was also exposed to the constant inundation of the Tiber and the lower section near the river was a perilous web of narrow muddy streets. The upper part of the Ghetto, traces of which remain on Via del Portico d'Ottavia, was inhabited by Jews of better means who were in the business of lending money or trading silk.

Under Napoleon and again under Mazzini and the Roman republic, Roman Jews enjoyed—in theory—full professional and religious liberty, but the actual end of the Ghetto came only in 1870 when the papacy fell as a temporal power. Soon after the creation of the kingdom of Italy a huge modern synagogue was built on the banks of the Tiber and the king made a point of being present at the opening ceremonies. There was, however, still another persecution to be endured. The position of the Italian Jews before and during World War II has been relatively forgotten in the face of the Nazi murders in Germany and Poland, yet it is estimated that between 1938 and 1944 a quarter of the Jewish population in Rome was murdered.

After the Ghetto walls were destroyed Jews either stayed put or moved into areas immediately adjacent to the former Ghetto. When the area was being completely rebuilt, at the turn of the century, an effort to relocate the Jews in the peripheries of the city and to integrate them with the rest of the population resulted in dramatic failure. For the most part the Jews were unwilling to leave their neighborhood, which to them represented centuries of struggle, fortitude, and pride.

Now back to Via del Portico d'Ottavia. All the shops you are walking past are owned by Jews. In fact, there are only three non-Jewish stores: the wine shop, the chicken store, and the bread store. The Bar Toto, on the right, where you may want to freshen up with a *cappuccino* or an *acqua minerale*, is a meeting place all day long, but in the evening it *really* livens up. Nowhere else in Rome is the *passeggiata*, the traditional evening's walk, taken so seriously as on this street. The people of the neighborhood, along with the Jews who have moved to other sections of town, get dressed in their weekday finest to stroll up and down the street and stop in at Toto's for a quick coffee or aperitif or to exchange the news of the day. The scene is so boisterous that, if unfamiliar with the neighborhood, you might imagine that the *passeggiata* is a political demonstration. In a way it is a demonstration, but of what Gregorovius described as "the solidarity of the family, which is Israel's enduring heritage." He noted that this

Fragments of antique sculpture on Via del Portico d'Ottavia

solidarity kept the crime rate down in the nineteenth century, and the same can be said today of this neighborhood, which is relatively free of the thievery known everywhere in Rome.

Continue down Via del Portico d'Ottavia to the corner of Piazza Costaguti. On your right is a wonderful house called the Casa di Lorenzo Manili that dates back to 1497. The house consists of three sections, one with windows from the 1600s, another with arched windows, and a third with the remains of a crossed window. Lorenzo Manili covered the façade with antique fragments that he took from the Appia Antica. The lion attacking a doe (one of the finest sculptures of a lion in Rome), the relief of a dog and a rabbit (to the right and further down), and the fragments of funerary stelae with four busts are particularly vivid. This work, by a man of modest fortune, is one of the few remaining expressions of the humanistic and archeological passion that seized Rome at the end of the fifteenth century. After three centuries, during which Rome had been reduced to a battlefield, Romans finally sought in the fifteenth century to emphasize their direct connections with the classical past and to revive patriotic feelings for their city. Lorenzo Manili seems to have taken great personal pride in his house. Not satisfied with an inscription bearing his name five times in Latin, he had it repeated as many times in Greek. The inscription also bears the date of the founding of Rome and also the year of the building's inauguration, 2221 according to the Roman calendar. Around the corner, on the frieze of the window that overlooks Piazza Costaguti, a good Roman descendant of Lorenzo Manili carved the words HAVE ROMA to salute the reascendence of his city to its former splendor. *"Urbe Roma in Pristinium formam rinascente . . .* HAVE ROMA."

The store on the corner of Lorenzo Manili's house is famous throughout Rome for its pastries. The secret seems to be recipes of ancient Jewish origin, and while heavy, their ricotta pies and turnovers are delicious.

Turn right from Via del Portico d'Ottavia onto Piazza Costaguti. You will come across a small round iron construction known as the Tempietto del Carmello, which was built in 1759. During the period when the Ghetto boundaries were enforced this was the only church within its confines. The Jews were required to come here four or five times a year to listen to Christian sermons. One can imagine the natural feelings of indignation assuaged when the Tempietto was taken over, thirty-five years ago, by the local shoe repairman. He uses all the available space and loves having his shop right in the middle of the piazza where he can chat with everyone going to the bread store across the way.

The Piazza Costaguti demonstrates the variety in form and function of spaces described as "piazzas." They can be a dead end, as we saw in the Piazza S. Angelo in Pescheria; a juncture of many streets, as at the Piazza Venezia; a mere widening of the street, as at the Piazza Campitelli; or the odd space that just isn't big enough for yet another building, as it is here. This piazza is a vestige of Rome before city planning. Today the piazza is the local soccer field, as it is closed to traffic, but doubles—like so many modest spaces in Rome—as a parking lot.

Cross the L-shaped piazza, turn left onto Via in Publicolis, and walk down to the corner. On the left is a building of unusual architecture for Rome, one that also illustrates the impact of early city planning. It is the Palazzo Santacroce, named for a family that has lived in Rome since 1299. In the late 1400s its members were so wild that Pope Sixtus IV had their house razed to the ground. According to the epigram inscribed over the main door of this palazzo, Antonio Santacroce rebuilt the family home in 1501. In doing so he was instructed by the pope to respect the paths of the existing streets and thus help preserve linear order and not disrupt habitual lines of travel and communication. The palazzo, small in dimension but nevertheless elegant, stands perpendicular to both streets and has a tower at the corner. The structure is a mixture of various architectural elements—a tower, two wings, a courtyard, different kinds of windows and ground-floor shops—that are brought together with the decorative motif of diamond-shaped hewn stone covering the base of the building. This type of decoration is Catalan in origin and is rarely seen in Rome, except for the portal of the Palazzo Nardini (Walk 1). The area above the diamond points was once covered with a decorative band of travertine slabs that created a wonderful light and shadow effect. The diamond-point decoration was originally a symbol of the warrior class, but by the sixteenth century it represented luxury and wealth. Turn left onto Via S. Maria del Pianto; nos. 60, 61, and 62 are all the original shop spaces that were designed for this building. These demonstrate that the noble class at that time was mercantile as well as bellicose.

Following Via S. Maria del Pianto we come back to the beginning of Via del Portico d'Ottavia. This space is called the Piazza S. Maria del Pianto but is still popularly called Piazza Giudea because it is part of the once larger piazza that was divided by the main entrance to the Ghetto. On the right-hand corner there is a church by the name of S. Maria del Pianto, this side is blocked from view by apartments and shops. If you step back and look up you can see the octagonal-shaped dome. This church holds a number of legends. One is that at the sight of a frightful murder, committed in broad daylight, an image of the Virgin that then overlooked the piazza started to cry, thus giving the church its name, "St. Mary in Tears." Another story explains the lack of façade to the despair and tears of the Virgin over the stubbornness of the Jews. Gregorovius also tells an interesting story about the church. During the height of the Counter-Reformation contests of catechism knowledge were conducted here. Boys from all over Rome participated, and the winner was taken triumphantly to the Vatican where he could ask one favor of the pope. The boys invariably asked for bread and wine for the rest of their lives, which gives us some idea of the economic state of Rome during the seventeenth century.

Turn right onto Via del Progresso and enter the large Piazza del Progresso, which at one time formed part of the Piazza Giudea. The "Piazza of Progress" was created at the turn of the century when the old Ghetto was demolished and more modern buildings were erected. The space has now become a large parking lot for the patrons of the wholesale shops nearby. On hot summer days, however, the residents get their chance to enjoy it; families sit outdoors on folding chairs at wooden tables and have their supper. Next to the entrance to the church is a small *vino e cucina*, "wine and kitchen" shop, which fascinates me. Even in the early morning it is filled with older men drinking wine, giving the impression that it is the community center for the retired. Only once have I seen a woman inside, and she was rolling out the pasta. I'm told they serve a very good and cheap meal, but it would seem insensitive to barge in on one of the few strongholds of intimate neighborhood life. The fountain, designed by Giacomo della Porta, once stood inside the Jewish Ghetto across from Manili's house. It is all marble with four masks that spill water into two graduated basins.

Directly across from the *vino e cucina* is the impressive former entrance to the Palazzo Cenci, a huge, many-sectioned structure that covers most of the block.

Proceed straight to the far corner of the piazza and we'll come upon a small ascending street called the Vicolo Monte dei Cenci, which takes us to the current entrance of the palazzo. This incline was created by ancient ruins, probably those of the Circus of Flaminius, which was constructed by C. Flaminius in 221 B.C. and was still standing in the fourth century. For centuries there were arguments about the precise location of the Circus. During the Middle Ages it was thought to have been under the site of the Mattei family houses. However, the discovery of the Severan Marbles, an architectural design of Rome during that emperor's reign, led to the conclusion that the Circus probably extended from the Piazza S. Carlo Cairoli to the Teatro di Marcello and from the Portico d'Ottavia to the river.

Before proceeding up the hill, let me recount the sixteenth-century tragedy of Francesco Cenci and his family so that you will understand the significance of the small church to your left. The Cenci family had held a high position in Rome as early as 914, when a Cenci reached the papal throne under the name of John X. Later four cardinals came from this house. Francesco Cenci was a man with a serious record of evil deeds. The pope effectively banished him from Rome by constraining him to live on a small allowance. Cenci retreated to a castle in Petrella (rented from the Colonna family) where he vented his brutality on his wife and sons, Giacomo and Bernardo, and even tried to violate his daughter, Beatrice. Exhausted and demoralized by his treatment, the family decided to murder Francesco. With the help of a servant, Giacomo killed his father with a hammer on September 9, 1598. They threw his body over the wall and tried to pretend that he had fallen.

Unfortunately, the investigators did not believe the story and arrested the whole family. During the trial only Beatrice would respond to questions; and Giacomo accused the others of the murder. It is said that Pope Clement VIII would have pardoned the Cencis, considering Francesco's turpitude, except for his discovery, at the very same time, of a similar crime committed in the Santacroce family. At their country house in Subiaco, Paolo Santacroce killed his mother with a sword because she threatened to disinherit him. The pope was so angered and shocked by this crime that he decided to condemn all family crimes. In the end the entire Cenci family was decapitated except for Bernardo who, because of his young age, was spared; instead, he was forced to witness the deaths of the members of his family and then sentenced to life imprisonment. The executions took place at the piazza next to Ponte S. Angelo on September 11, 1599.

The Church of S. Tommaso is the family church of the Cenci. It was built in the twelfth century by a Cenci and restored in 1575 by Francesco Cenci. In the Mid-

"Get out of our quarter Fascists and Bourgeoisie"

dle Ages it was known as the millers' church because of the number of wheat mills that worked along this point of the Tiber. Every year, on the anniversary of the Cenci executions, the Confraternity dei Vetturini (the Confraternity of Coachmen) has a mass said at S. Tommaso, and it is only on this day that the church is open.

Beatrice's tragedy especially captured the people's imagination. Her remains are buried under the high altar at S. Pietro in Montorio. A portrait of her by Guido Reni can be seen in the Corsini Picture Gallery, and Shelley based a play on her story. The scandal caused the confiscation of the Cenci property, which included a good part of what soon became the Borghese family estate, now Villa Borghese Park.

As we walk up the hill the street curves into a small piazza that contains the most elegant of the Jewish restaurants, Piperno's. Especially during the summer this is a delightful spot for outdoor eating, protected as it is from the traffic. The frequent presence here of long Mercedeses with watchful bodyguards suggests that the clientele includes many Italians concerned about security. Straight ahead the marble fragments decorating the wall of the Cenci palace are remnants of the spirit of Roman revitalization that Lorenzo Manili's house so enthusiastically exhibits.

Turn to the right at the end of the Vicolo Monte dei Cenci and you will see what is now the front of the Cenci palace, a jumble of structures from various periods. A medieval arch connects the main palazzo with a curious Spanish baroque-style frame to a smaller one on the side. The palazzo, now a condominium, houses the Italian headquarters of the Rhode Island School of Design—an institution less susceptible to the gloomy legend than sentimental Italians.

Walk through the piazza and under the Cenci arch. This spot more than others in Rome suggests to me what the visual and sensual experiences of the Middle Ages, pleasurable and otherwise, may actually have been like. We emerge on Via S. Maria Calderari. Here to your left, at no. 23, is an arch of brickwork flanked by two travertine columns that for many years were thought to have been part of the Theater of Balbus. Architectural drawings dating from the sixteenth century show the ground floor and the elevation of the building and indicate that the brick arch belonged to a double portico with an upper story of arcades. The recent arrangement of the fragments of the Severan Marbles locates the Theater of Balbus at the Palazzi Mattei and suggests that this portico is probably related to the Circus of Flaminius. It is now the site of the local firefighting force, which lounges in the relative security of a Rome constructed largely of brick and concrete.

Turn right as you face the firehouse and the Via S. Maria Calderari will lead you back to the Piazza del Progresso. Once there, take the street that enters the piazza on its south side, straight ahead and a bit to the right. This is the Via Catalana, named for the large population of Spanish Jews that settled in Rome at the time of the Inquisition. While still part of the old Ghetto, this section was destroyed and completely rebuilt at the turn of the century. At the end of the block is the new synagogue.

During the many centuries the Ghetto was enforced there were a number of synagogues representing different cultures. In the late 1400s and early 1500s these different backgrounds caused great internal friction within the Jewish community. In this century five schools have been united in a single building, three of Italian origin (Scuola del Tempio, Scuola Nuova, Scuola Siciliana) and two of the Spanish rite (Scuola Catalana and Scuola Castigliana). The great temple that now rises on the banks of the Tiber is a symbol of the regained splendors and solidarity of the Jewish community.

The synagogue, designed by Costa and Armanni, was consecrated in 1904. The plan and structure of the temple echo the East, in particular Assyrian-Babylonian motifs, and avoids any possible resemblance to Christian churches. It is a solid complex of centralized symmetry with a heavy squared base projecting from the side of a central quadrangled body. The upper part of the building is crowned by a large metal dome. The synagogue is a prominent feature of the Roman skyline; visitors in the early 1900s wrote that the dome was almost blinding when it reflected the sunlight.

The synagogue houses the Permanent Exhibition of the Jewish Community of Rome, open every weekday morning from 9:00 A.M. to 1:00 P.M. Among its manuscripts and religious objects are prints that display a clear plan of the old Ghetto, including at least eight streets and five piazzas.

Turn left onto the Via del Tempio and continue one block to the Via del Portico d'Ottavia. From this intersection you can see the entire length of the old side of this street. In the area between Via della Reginella and Via di S. Ambrogio once stood the Portico di Filippo (parallel to the line of houses) built by Filippo, the brother-in-law of Augustus. This, like the Portico d'Ottavia, was richly decorated with marble, filled with works of art, and it contained a temple.

Especially on this street you have a sense of the grandeur of ancient Rome buried and incorporated in the later structures. First, there is the Portico d'Ottavia, with its wings of granite columns jutting from the sidewalk, and in the background the pockmarked travertine arcades of the Teatro di Marcello. When, in 1982, the city dug up the Via del Portico d'Ottavia to put in new pipes for the methane gas used in most homes, numerous fragments of marble were uncovered, including a marble slab from the old fish market and a capital from the Portico di Filippo.

The two houses at nos. 8–11 and 12–15 are especially interesting. The first, a solid but graceful structure of the fifteenth century, ends on the top floor with a loggia whose arches are now closed. At the next house, no. 13, walk into the courtyard; it is dark and dreary but nevertheless provocative. This house was built by the Fabi family, who lived briefly in the ruins of the Teatro di Marcello and whose family tomb is in the Church of S. Nicola in Carcere. At no. 25 is an authentic medieval house, perhaps the only one in the old Ghetto that has not been radically changed by restoration; it is undoubtedly the base of a thirteenth-century tower. Its magnificent portal, now the entrance to a butcher shop, is composed of fragments from a beautiful, ornate molding of imperial times. Surely it is a collector's item in this interminable museum that is the old city of Rome.

The long window above and to the left of the portal is usually occupied by flowerpots and a housebound elderly woman who gazes all day long at the activities on the street. During the hot summer she pulls down the venetian blinds, but her shadow is still visible. Although I've never photographed her myself, I've seen enough cameras angled in her direction to think she must be an important international memory of Rome.

Two of the neighborhood's landmarks are just in front of you. Da Giggeto's, the restaurant next to the tower, is famous for its Roman Jewish cuisine, especially its fried artichokes and fried mozzarella. In the summer you can sit at outdoor tables next to the columns that stretch from the portico. The other is Limentani's, a discount porcelain, crystal, and kitchenware store that extends, endlessly it seems, in the basement of the building across the street from the restaurant. The entrance is on the corner where Via del Portico d'Ottavia curves. This is where every self-respecting Roman buys housewares. If you have time it's quite an experience to walk through room after room piled high with Ginori, Limoges, and other china, and see Christofle silver just lying around in huge open boxes.

To your left past the portico at no. 28–29 is the Casa dei Vallati. The marble plaque is in memory of the approximately two thousand Jews who were rounded up here and exterminated by the Nazis in 1943. Every year, on the anniversary of this event, the street is cleared for a memorial service at sundown.

The house itself is one of the few free-standing medieval houses left in Rome. We saw the back of it at the beginning of our walk. It was originally built in the thirteenth century and is a good example of the architecture of that period when most buildings were irregular, taking up and then expanding into the spaces defined by the narrow, irregular streets. On the ground floor of the house is a small portico covered by what used to be an outside staircase leading to a loggia. In the interior is an open courtyard with a tower in the middle; this courtyard was a means of getting light and air into the house. The tower was needed for protection from belligerent rivals, and the portico on the ground floor, with its iron gate, was probably used for mercantile purposes.

Across the street from this house is a small view that captures so much of the essence of Rome. Look back toward the Portico d'Ottavia. The constant irregularity in space, height, and style in almost every street and piazza in the old city tempts one to believe that the diversity was intentional. In fact the irregularity is the haphazard result of thousands upon thousands of buildings being constructed at different stages in the city's long history. The view from here contains a tremendous variety of heights and forms—terraces, balconies, a Roman monument still covered with marble, tile roofs, and the cupola of a church.

We walk past the synagogue with a view of the palm trees growing in its small but verdant side garden. On the other side of the street is another view of the immense palazzo built into the ruins of the Teatro di Marcello.

At the end of the Via del Portico d'Ottavia stood one of the gates of the old Ghetto. The church, which has become an island between the busy Lungotevere and the Via Monte Savello, stood just outside the gate. S. Giorgio della Divina Pietà was built in the seventeenth century and has a painting on its façade of the crucifixion with an inscription in bold Hebrew and Latin letters clearly addressing its audience, the Ghetto Jews. The inscription is from Isaiah: "All day long I have stretched out my hands to a disobedient and gainsaying people." In 1727, Pope Benedict XIII, an Orsini pope, made this the seat of the Congregation of Workers of Divine Pity whose function it was to help those who had fallen on hard times. On the Via Monte Savello side of the church you can see a marble box in the wall for "offerings to poor honorable families."

If you continue walking up the Via Monte Savello you will come to the Piazza di Monte Savello. From there you can look down on the ruins of the temples we saw at the beginning of our walk; tucked in the left-hand corner of the piazza is a large gate with two bears on the post for the Orsini family. This is the entrance to the palazzo built on the ruins of the ancient theater. Our walk ends here, full circle through a very small section of Rome that took us from the Republican era to the twentieth century—Rome, the eternal city!

Streets of the Papacy: The Neighborhood of the Campo dei Fiori

○

In the middle of the eighth century, Pepin, king of the
Franks, granted Rome to the Papal Court. This act
saved the city from extinction and also marked a turning point in its social history. Rome, built on the ruins
of a pagan city and nurtured by the heritage of a pagan
empire, became the center of a world religion.

Surrounded by malarial swamps and sparsely inhabited plains, and with no productive life of its own, the
city needed the sponsorship of the Papal Court. During the great papal schism the population of Rome
dropped from 35,000 in 1200 to 17,000 in 1400, because the city failed to develop the flourishing civic
and economic life of other central and northern Italian
cities. Petrarch, one of the pilgrims of 1350, says that
Rome gave the impression of having just been
stormed and pillaged by barbaric hosts. Things remained as such until 1417, when Martin V reestablished the papal seat in Rome. Platina, Martin V's
biographer, says that when the pope returned to Rome
he found the city "in such a state of devastation that it
could hardly be considered a city fit for human habita-
tion: whole rows of houses abandoned by their tenants; many churches fallen to the ground; streets
deserted and buried under heaps of refuse; traces of
plague and famine everywhere." Rome's improvement
was neither sudden nor immediately noticeable, but
simply the fact that the head of the Church returned to
Rome gave the city a new lease on life. The Papal
Court brought wealth and distinction to this struggling
community, and a new tradition of grandeur rose
amidst the ancient ruins. Hundreds of thousands of
pilgrims from all parts of the world brought not only
money, but also the vitality of a cosmopolitan life.

Rome began to flourish again between 1450 and
1650 as each pope proposed a building program and
hired architects and builders to carry it out. Grandiose
plans were drawn up by Renaissance artists who were
anxious to apply their aesthetic theories about geome-
try, divine proportion, and perspective in order to

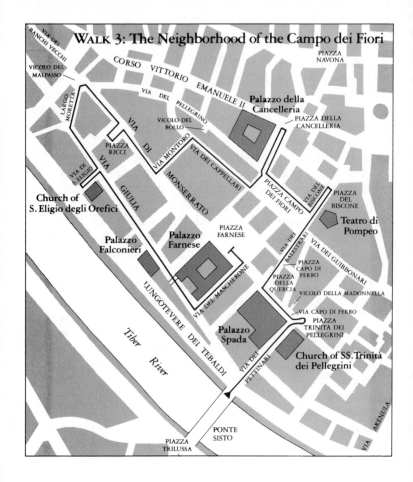

WALK 3: The Neighborhood of the Campo dei Fiori

combine the great Roman and Christian traditions into a single, magnificent vision of a capital. Most of these plans were never carried out; instead, the new Renaissance and baroque city evolved slowly based on incremental plans seldom committed to paper. Yet, despite the lack of a master plan, the twenty popes and the hundreds of architects, craftsmen, and administrators who rebuilt Rome achieved a remarkable unity of style and effect.

Our walk through the neighborhood of the Campo dei Fiori presents us with many of the physical changes that were brought about by the Catholic Church's decision to make Rome the embodiment of its earthly wealth and power. Situated across the Tiber from the Vatican, this area was an important point of access between the Vatican and the Capitoline Hill, which made this a natural site for much of the

Church's reconstruction efforts. The result is special, however, in that it did not become a sterile Renaissance example of city planning; there remain streets and other hints of an older Rome. This neighborhood's appeal lies not only in its history but in its sharp contrasts. Here Renaissance Rome is at its secular best, and next to it the less refined images of the medieval city are still alive. The sensation of experiencing the change in the city's profile is heightened by the inhabitants and by the life of this neighborhood, which is also one of sharp contrasts: here dwell both some of the city's poorest and wealthiest citizens.

At first glance, it is difficult to sense the much older personality of this area, which was then the western end of the Roman Empire's Campus Martius. Little remains intact, but there are enough hints to tickle the imagination with impressions of the influence and richness of ancient Roman culture. The best description of the early period was written in the seventh century B.C. by a Greek geographer, Strabo, who was one of the first of the numberless foreigners who, taken in by Rome's personality and beauty, have felt compelled to share it with others.

> Superior to all is the Campus Martius. The greatness of the plain itself is wonderful, all open for horses and chariot racing and for the great multitudes who take exercise in ball games; in the circus and in gymnastics. The ground is covered with grass, green all year round, surrounded by buildings and hills that reach to the river's edge; it presents a scenic effect from which it is difficult to tear oneself away.

Vitigis the Goth unwittingly initiated the decline of the Campus Martius as it was described by Strabo when he cut off Rome's water supply by destroying the aqueducts in 537. This act not only killed the verdant fields but forced the dwindling population of Rome to move from the hills to the edge of the Tiber, a part of the city that had never before been residential. Slowly the Campus Martius's few buildings went to ruin, and any portable fragments of columns or stone were recycled as decorative or structural objects in nearby homes. This lack of water marked the beginning of a long struggle that helped shape the history of medieval Rome and changed the face of the city. The glory of ancient Rome became a sentimental memory as the city turned into the huddle of huts, tenements, and battlements that Pope Martin V described to his biographer.

In 1429, Poggio Bracciolini, one of Pope Martin's secretaries, found a lost manuscript in the library of the monastery of Monte Cassino. The manuscript, called *De Acquis* and written by Fontinius, was a handbook to the aqueducts, mountains, and waters of imperial Rome. This handbook became an important tool for Rome's revival—a revival that will appear more dramatic as we walk through the streets of this neighborhood.

We begin our walk in the middle of Ponte Sisto, the bridge that spans the Tiber from the Lungotevere dei Tebaldi to the Piazza Trilussa. Stand in the middle of the bridge and enjoy the view; it is one of Rome's most dramatic. Here you can see the curve of the river; the dome of St. Peter's; to the left, as you face St. Peter's, the dense and colorful quarter of Trastevere edging up to the Gianicolo covered with large, elegant villas and green parks; and on the right bank, the palazzi of Renaissance Rome.

Before he was elected pope, Sixtus IV lived near the Campo dei Fiori. He must have been greatly inconvenienced on his trips to the Vatican, because he vowed that if elected pope he would rebuild the Pons Janiculensi, the bridge that had been destroyed by a flood in 792. The new bridge would provide more direct access to the other side of the river and ease congestion on the Ponte S. Angelo, then the only route from this part of town to St. Peter's. (In 1450, congestion on the Ponte S. Angelo caused the death of more than two hundred pilgrims.) When Pope Sixtus IV laid the foundation stone for the bridge in April 1473 its completion was given the highest priority in preparation for the Jubilee of 1475. The pope was also interested in providing a convenient link with Trastevere, which was then a depressed section of town, and in time the bridge did, in fact, attract new settlements to that community and helped tie it to the growing business center across the river.

The area bordering the river has changed completely in this century. Embankments were built, as were the wide streets along both sides of the river, which provide a direct route between the northern and southern ends of the city. Before this construction humble dwellings stood all the way down to the river's edge, and there were also huge fortified walls that protected the gardens and homes of the rich. The contrast between what we see today and what existed a century ago is best seen in etchings and paintings at the Museum of Rome on the Piazza S. Pantaleo.

The Tiber itself has taken on a very different role in the life of the city. In the late nineteenth century terrible floods plagued Rome year after year—floods so bad that one etching depicts people visiting the Pantheon in a boat. The Tiber was used as a means of transportation and for power to churn the wheat mills on barges. Now there are but a few houseboats, and transportation is possible only on short stretches of the river. Today the Tiber functions primarily as a point of reference—one is more likely to be aware of the bridges than the river flowing beneath them.

In 1878 when the embankments were being constructed, a fountain was moved across the river to the Piazza Trilussa on the Trastevere side of the bridge. The story of this fountain begins with the fact that it spewed fresh water, which literally gave Rome the possibility of renewed grandeur. In 1611, Pope Paul V repaired an ancient aqueduct that had been built by Trajan to carry water to Rome from a group of springs thirty miles northwest of the city. To display this new source of water he commissioned Giovanni Fontana to design an elegant fountain to be incorporated in the wall of a building between Via Giulia and the Ponte Sisto. The building, a hospice for beggars, had been erected by Fontana's brother. In the late nineteenth century, plans for the Tiber embankment called for the demolition of both the fountain and the building; this brought great protest as the fountain had become one of the most popular in Rome. Despite the agitation it was pulled down in August 1879, but it was saved from oblivion some years later when, stone by stone, it was rebuilt on the Piazza Trilussa, where we see it now at the end of the bridge.

For those who have seen photographs or etchings of the fountain in its original setting the current placement seems a great improvement, surrounded as it is by trees and open space. A single classical archway with water flowing from the top of the arch into a huge basin, this fountain is reminiscent of the Fontana Paolina on the Gianicolo Hill, which was also erected to celebrate the arrival of the water known as Acqua Paola, after the pope who repaired the aqueduct. As the original inscription above the arch states, Paul V is responsible for bringing water to the other side of the river. Another inscription under the arch commemorates the fountain's relocation.

The fountains of Rome were not mere decorations; they were a primary source of water for many centuries. And, in this case, the fountain was also meant to be used for bathing by the pilgrims and beggars who lived in the vicinity. This fountain is now in retirement, so to speak, but on very hot summer days it still attracts a dedicated group of vagabonds who consider the Piazza Trilussa their home.

Keeping the fate of the old bridge in mind, architects were careful to ensure that the Ponte Sisto could withstand the strong currents of the flooding river. This single-lane bridge is composed of four supporting arches and a large round eye in the center that allows water to pass through when the river swells. In 1878, at the same time that the embankments were constructed, the two footpaths supported by corbels were added. Also that year sections of an arch from the ancient bridge were found at the bottom of the river; the remains bore an inscription to Valentinian, emperor of Rome in 365, and undoubtedly the builder of the original Pons Janiculensi. Other treasures, including a bronze statue and some pedestals, were also excavated; they now rest in the Capitoline Museum. The only remnant of an earlier structure is a few large stones that can be seen near the Trastevere embankment when the river is low.

Among the earliest Romans, as with many other peoples, there existed a belief that the erection of a bridge was injurious to the gods of the river because it robbed them of a certain number of victims who would otherwise have drowned. With this in mind, a most important duty of the bridge-builder was to pacify Father Tiber with expiatory sacrifices in the form of living human beings and dummies made of rushes. For much the same reason it was unlawful to use nails or other metals in any part of the bridge's woodwork. It was also unlawful to build these first bridges in stone since a more temporary structure was deemed less offensive than a solid piece of masonry. This sacrificial tradition seems to have been a burden to the early Christian Church: St. Calipius, St. Saba, and St. Symphorosa were all thrown into the Tiber from the Pons Janiculensi. Many things have changed over the centuries, and now, instead of this vision of a fierce river god, there is an inscription at the beginning of the bridge near the Lungotevere dei Tebaldi that reads: "You who pass, invoke the divine bounty so that Sixtus IV, excellent Pontifex Maximus may be healthy and for long be preserved. You then, to whom this request is made, whoever you are, be healthy, too."

Walk past the inscription, across the Lungotevere dei Tebaldi and toward the shop Handles on the corner of Via Giulia and Via dei Pettinari. On the corner to your right is one of the few arcaded buildings in Rome, styled after so many in northern Italian cities. The Piazza Trilussa fountain would have been located in the same spot as the children's clothing store, Il Paloncino Rosso (The Red Balloon). If you have to take a present home to a child, you might browse through this small shop that sells expensive but beautifully designed clothes. Handles, across the street, is also worthy of special attention. They have a huge selection of door handles made of almost any material, almost to emphasize that only the Italians could have turned the design of such objects into a fine art.

If you stand with Handles to your left you will be at the beginning of Via dei Pettinari, named for the combmakers or wool-combers who once lived and worked on this street. Nothing remains of these artisans; now jewelers and watchmakers occupy the small shops on the ground floor. This change probably took place in the eighteenth century when the state office for stamping gold and silver was established just a few blocks away. The right-hand side of the street is dotted with the kind of signs that are such a trademark of Rome's center-city streets—signs of ownership, law enforcement, and religious fervor. Here, such signs are more noticeable because they are not upstaged by dramatic architecture or obscured by hanging laundry.

At Via dei Pettinari 39–40 is an *edicola*, an image, of

the Virgin Mary. This is a rather simple example of popular displays of religious fervor, which are often associated with particular events—a tragedy, a feast day, a miracle. Such images are seen all over the city with the Virgin and Child a favorite theme. Their manifestations range from simple photographic images protected by a glass box to great pieces of art almost always accompanied by a candleholder and some flowers. As with most of these *edicole* the story of this one is untold and now long forgotten.

Embedded in the wall of no. 56, a few yards to your right, is a very common street sign that often causes confusion among tourists. It reads: *"Per ordine espresso di monsig. ill. mo. rev. do. presidente delle strade si proibisce espressamente a qualqunque persona di gettare immondizie e fare mondezzaro in questa strada sotto pene di scudi diece ed altre pene ad arbitrio di sua sig.ria. ill.ma. in conformita dell edito emnato il p.o. marzo MDCCXXXXI."* This merely states that it is illegal to throw trash in the street and that a fine is imposed. The fact that this is so carefully engraved in marble is part of what makes walking the streets of Rome such a unique and marvelous visual experience.

Ten feet past no. 56 is a sign that marks the dedication, in 1944, of this building to the Madonna of Divine Love for saving Rome from the destruction that befell other Italian cities during World War II. Just around the corner stood one of the few buildings destroyed by Allied bombing.

On the left-hand side of the street are two buildings of architectural interest. The first, no. 79–80, is a small fifteenth-century house with a loggia on the top story. This house's exterior was once completely covered with paintings in the decorative style so popular during the century in which it was built. Few traces remain, but right after a summer storm, when the wall is wet and the light is bright, you may be able to discern what little pigmentation is left. The other building is the palazzo on the corner of Via dei Pettinari and Via Capo di Ferro, no. 81–87. This is the Palazzo Salmoni Albertischi, which belonged to a family known in Rome since the twelfth century. This building, in the style of Renaissance Roman palazzi, has two large portals, both of which bear an inscription that identifies this as the family's home. The portals are decorated with motifs from the family's insignia—lions' heads and the knot of Solomon. These same symbols are also seen as decorations on the overhanging cornice at the top of the building. As the knot of Solomon is usually considered a Jewish symbol some observers have speculated about the family's religious affiliations. But this isn't one of Rome's many puzzles. For centuries, and certainly during the sixteenth century when this house was built, the Jewish population of Rome was congregated in a small section of the city. Although this section, the Jewish Ghetto, is only a few blocks away its boundaries were always well defined. So the family almost certainly wasn't Jewish. (Also to be remembered is the degree to which Christianity incorporated into its designs the traditions and symbols of the Old Testament. Another example of this cross-fertilization is in the history of the piazza and church immediately to the right.)

The Piazza Trinità dei Pellegrini is a landmark that dates from the golden age of the Catholic Church, when hundreds of thousands of pilgrims came from all parts of the world to celebrate the Jubilee year. This celebration originated in the ancient Jewish Jubilee and gradually became one of the most popular events in the Catholic Church's calendar. Proclaimed by Pope Boniface VIII in 1300 this tradition of celebrating every twenty-five years has continued uninterrupted to the present day, except for the nineteenth century when because of political tensions in Europe there was only one. The idea of a pilgrimage to Rome seems to have existed even before the first Jubilee: the Jesuit scholar Thurston tells of a man 107 years old whom Pope Boniface questioned after seeing him carried into St. Peter's Basilica in January 1300. "I remembered," the old man said, "that at the beginning of the last century my father, who was a laborer, came to Rome and dwelt here as long as his means lasted in order to gain the indulgence. He bade me not to forget to come at the beginning of the next century, if I should live so long, which he did not think I should do." As this pilgrimage became institutionalized, thousands of people have continued to descend upon Rome.

Though pilgrims are still very much a part of the Roman scene today, patterns, style, and even the ways of manifesting religious devotion have changed. Earning a plenary indulgence, which is the difference between purgatory and heaven for the pious Catholic, is certainly not what it used to be. Buses and cabs make the journey to the five basilicas a rather simple task, and this is not to mention the availability of water, hotels, and paved streets. I imagine that there are few cases these days of the weary but determined pilgrim for whom this trip to Rome is the only journey he will make outside the town or village of his birth. Pilgrims arrive with their sneakers and practical dress like all other tourists; only during the weeks before and after Easter, when the main streets to the Vatican suddenly become obstacle courses, is one particularly aware of the pilgrims. This sudden influx of foreigners is always a surprise, yet it is more predictable than the weather. They soon become part of the huge tourist crowd though they come to Rome as Petrarch did "in a spirit of fervor because I wished to put an end to the sinfulness of my life, which overwhelmed me with shame" and whose visit held a higher importance than a mere "poet's curiosity."

Back in the days when pilgrims were Rome's only tourists the Piazza Trinità dei Pellegrini, where we are now, was as important as the Via Condotti is today. Here a church with an attached hospice was built for the Jubilee of 1550 by S. Filippo Neri, a remarkable man, perhaps the most appealing figure among the saints of the Counter-Reformation and dear to this day as the patron saint of Rome. The hospice was for centuries one of the city's greatest centers of hospitality, receiving and nourishing for a period of three to seven days pilgrims of "pious intent" who traveled more than sixty miles. An example of the traffic on this piazza is a statistic from 1675: that year the hospice accommodated 582,760 pilgrims. During Holy Week it was the site of the ritual public washing of feet when princes and cardinals washed the feet of the pilgrims. This custom endured into the nineteenth century and Augustus Hare, who witnessed it, was shocked by the fact that "here the washing is a reality, the feet not having been prepared beforehand."

To the left of the church, in what is now a shop, is the old refectory of the hospice, within which is a series of memorials. Above the door is a bust of S. Filippo Neri in a setting designed by Cosimo Fanzago. This bust and most of the others in the room are plaster casts of the original bronze sculptures. The tablet on the wall is in memory of the poet Goffredo Mameli, who was brought to the hospice to die after he was mortally wounded in the defense of Rome in 1849. (The hospice had been turned into a hospital for the Garibaldi forces.) All this came to an end during World War II when, in 1940, one of the few bombs to fall on Rome fell here and destroyed the building as well as a small oratory that stood in the middle of the piazza. In its place rose an apartment complex and garage, one of the few examples of postwar architecture you will see during this walk.

Except during August, Rome's traffic and parking problems are a constant intrusion on one's ability to enjoy calmly and leisurely the sights of the city. You have no doubt already had to squeeze up against a wall to avoid a speeding car or two on the narrow Via dei Pettinari. Here in the piazza you will have to maneuver through the parked cars to see the front of the church. Although this church, SS. Trinità dei Pellegrini, was built between 1587 and 1597 from a design by Martino Longhi the Elder, the façade was not executed until 1723. Designed by Francesco de Sanctis, the façade is a skillful variant on Carlo Fontana's S. Marcello on the Via del Corso. It is based upon the principle of a curved façade as first introduced by Borromini and Cortona in the 1630s but is reinterpreted here in a simpler fashion. Instead of the double-S curve or the play of convex against straight or concave, this front is planned on a single, steady curve. During the seventeenth and eighteenth centuries this principle of baroque architecture, with its many variations, was probably more frequently imitated than any other in Rome. The expressive, oversized statues of the four evangelists by Bernardino Ludovisi are also worthy of attention.

The bar in any Roman neighborhood is an institution. Bars do a thriving business on practically every corner and each has its attraction—it makes the best coffee or ice cream, it is a gathering place for friends, or it has the right atmosphere. The one on this piazza is a good example of the truly neighborhood bar that has nothing going for it but the fact that it is where the people who live and work on this street congregate to pass the time. Certainly it is the best place to get any information about apartments, people, directions, and local history.

At this point we turn to the Via Capo di Ferro, which borders the Palazzo Salmoni Alberteschi and intersects with Via dei Pettinari. As you stand facing the church you should turn right and go straight. At the very beginning of the street is another example of the inexhaustible curiosities of Rome. For six months I walked this path daily without noticing the four Ionic columns embedded in the wall of the house to your right. How these Roman columns found a place in the walls of a thirteenth-century house is not known for certain. They may have been a small section of the miles of porticoes built during the empire. They may also be an example of the widespread vandalism of the Middle Ages. In any case the columns were undoubtedly bricked in after 1475. At that time Pope Sixtus IV acted on the warning of King Ferrante of Naples that it was impossible to keep order in a city that provided dark hiding places for rebels and thieves. Sixtus decreed an end to open porticoes in Rome. The few that exist today are on a small number of free-standing medieval houses or have been incorporated into nineteenth- and twentieth-century architecture. This house lost its medieval character when it was completely remodeled in the eighteenth century.

Via Capo di Ferro is named for an old Roman family that was distinguished as early as the 1100s. Throughout the late Middle Ages and well into the sixteenth century they controlled this part of the city and in the name of their successors, the Spada family, they have left two different examples of Renaissance architecture. The family's name literally means "chief of the sword"; in time it changed to Spada, the more common word for sword. No. 7, to your left, the Palazzetto Spada, is a stately and classical example of early sixteenth-century architecture. This *palazzetto*, "small palace," is attributed to both Peruzzi and Vignola, two of the greatest architects in Rome at that time. Debate over attribution aside, one look at the elegant façade leaves little doubt, even among the least sophisticated observer, that its conception was the vision of a master. In addition to the harmony of its arched shop doors on the ground floor and the classical lines of the *piano nobile* with windows separated by Ionic pilasters, its appeal lies in its scale—more human and livable than the grand palazzi that often dazzle by sheer volume.

Just beyond the Palazzetto Spada, to your right, is the Vicolo della Madonnella, a little street that ends in one of the undistinguished but nevertheless charming courts that are so characteristic of medieval vestiges. In the court you may see many typical Roman sights—alley cats sleeping under the shade of a parked car, a window lined with potted geraniums, a wooden cart from the market parked by a small doorway, and, yes, garbage.

Return to the Via Capo di Ferro. There are a couple of things to note before we reach the second and most famous palazzo of the Spada family. The house at no. 10, to your left, is a relatively new addition to the block. Until the beginning of the seventeenth century this was the site of a street called Arcaccio after an arch built as part of its promenade. The street connected the end of Via Giulia to the Via Capo di Ferro. While a small segment of that street still exists off the Via Giulia, both the arch and this entrance to the street disappeared when a building was erected in the 1600s to connect the two Spada family palaces. Also to the left, no. 12, is a house built in the fifteenth century that was once adorned with a picturesque monochrome design; to make room for that, the proportion of window to wall varies from the norm.

Just another ten steps on the Via Capo di Ferro brings us to a by-now-familiar expanse in the road called a piazza. Here we have the Piazza Capo di Ferro, dominated on the left by the fanciful Palazzo Spada. This building's architecture is full of unrestrained, childlike touches. One view is more captivating than the next, and all of it stimulates our artistic sensibility.

The piazza was designed around 1635 by Francesco Borromini, a good friend of Cardinal Bernardino Spada's brother. His intention was to destroy or hide some of the hovels that could be seen from the palace and to ensure the cardinal's privacy. After the demolition work the famous architect built a new wall with battlements and blind windows to keep the neighbors from seeing who was entering and leaving the palazzo.

An ancient sarcophagus-turned-fountain in the Piazza Capo di Ferro

(Only recently have a few of these windows been opened.) These details turned the piazza into a sort of private courtyard, virtually an extension of the palazzo. Borromini built a niche beneath the sundial and belvedere to hold a fountain of Venus standing on a shell with water flowing from her breasts. That statue has long since been replaced by the less romantic, but still beautiful configuration of a lion's head spurting water into a sarcophagus, also decorated with lions' heads.

Above a stonework base rises the façade of the palazzo. On the *piano nobile* the windows alternate with statues representing figures from Roman history: Trajan, Pompey, Fabio Maximus, Romulus, Nema, Marcellus, Caesar, and Augustus. Above that floor the windows are surrounded by stucco tondos and garlands. The boxed inscriptions refer to the figures in the niches below. This stucco decoration, so popular in the later days of the Renaissance, is seen here at its best. All, or nearly all, of this work is by Giulio Mazzoni, who was commissioned by the Papal Apostolic Camera in 1550 during the reign of Pope Julius III.

A document dating from the first half of the sixteenth century suggests that the palace may originally have been intended as the French Embassy. In 1555 the building became the property of Cardinal Girolamo Capo di Ferro; he may have received it (along with the Villa Giulia, now the Etruscan Museum) as compensation for the large sums of money he donated to the Vatican for the construction of this palace. When he died in 1559 the palace was inherited by the Mignanelli family who in turn sold it to Cardinal Bernardino Spada in 1632. As soon as he purchased the palace Cardinal Spada had it adapted to his own needs. He employed Borromini, whose design is seen not only in the piazza but also in the wing that houses the Galleria Spada, the great staircase, and the garden that extends to the Via Giulia.

Walk through the grand portal, and don't be intimidated by the guards with machine guns. Since 1927 this palace has been the headquarters of the Council of State. If approached, explain (or gesture) that you are here to look at the building and its courtyards.

The main courtyard surrounds us with the world of Greek mythology, which had such a strong influence on the Romans who are depicted on the façade. This courtyard, too, was decorated by Giulio Mazzoni. There are still a few traces of very faded frescoes in the panels between the top-story windows, but the walls covered with exquisite stucco decoration are the highlight here. Around the court, amidst the acanthus and struggling fauns, are the images of the sea demigod Triton, the son of Poseidon; Amphitrite, with his conch-shell trumpet; and centaurs, the half-man half-horse descendants of Ixion, who dwelt in the mountains of Thessaly. The niches are filled with images of the most important Olympian deities: Hercules, Mars, Venus, Juno, Jupiter, Pluto, Proserpine, Minerva, Mercury, Amphitrite, and Neptune. Every time I stand here my head is filled with fragments of the marvelous tales spun around each of these gods—tales which, by the way, almost every Italian knows by heart.

On the wall opposite the entrance, between the second-floor windows, nude male figures hold shields bearing the coats of arms of Pope Julius III and the king of France. This can be construed as reinforcing the theory that this palace, begun under Pope Julius's reign, was intended as the French Embassy, or it can be assumed to refer to Cardinal Capo di Ferro himself, who was the pope's treasurer and served as the Apostolic Delegate to France.

Facing these coats of arms turn to your left, where a large window on the ground floor gives a view of the library with its beautiful painted globe. Beyond that is Borromini's most famous contribution to the palace: an apparently long arcaded gallery at the end of which is a statue on a pedestal. Although the gallery was originally meant to be seen from this courtyard, it is better to find the custodian and actually walk through it. (He sits in the entrance to the museum, through the courtyard and to your left. For a small tip he will gladly open the door.) Approach, or watch someone else approach, the statue. You will realize that it is an optical illusion created by progressively diminishing columns and arches. Even the floor changes dimensions. In reality the gallery is but ten meters long while the seemingly life-size statue is but a foot tall. Borromini's creation is truly extraordinary! Built in 1663 it replaced a false perspective painted on the wall in 1644. Such *trompe l'oeil* were popular throughout Italy at the time, another example being the Scala Santa at the Vatican. This one, however, also served a very specific function, that of extending the axis of the side court, which was restricted by the surrounding buildings.

The museum in this palazzo is known as the Galleria Spada, and it is certainly worth a visit if it is open. The collection fills only four rooms, but it is probably the most important group of baroque paintings in any public gallery in Rome. The museum also reflects the singular breadth of Cardinal Bernardino Spada's aesthetic taste, as it consists primarily of works he acquired while papal legate to Bologna and has not essentially changed since 1661. Of the many small family collections in Rome this is the only one to survive in its original setting. The state rooms of this palace hold further marvels but written permission is usually required to see them. For an appointment write to the Ufficio Intendenza, Palazzo Spada, Piazza Capo di Ferro 13, 00186 Roma. You might try to get in without an appointment. A little charm and persuasion sometimes works.

If you do gain access to the state rooms you will see in the great throne room the statue of Pompey Byron describes in "Childe Harold":

And thou, dread statue! Yet existent in
The austerest form of naked majesty,
Thou who beheldest 'mid the assassins din,
At thy bathed base the bloody Caesar lie,

Folding his robe in dying dignity
And offering to thine altar from the queen
of Gods and men, great Nemisis! did he die
and thou, too, perish, Pompey? have ye been
Victors of countless kings, or puppets of a scene?

It was at the foot of this statue, which stands eleven
feet high and is among the first representations of the
male nude, that Caesar is thought to have fallen to
death. Actually, there is no real proof to support this
generally accepted notion except that the statue was
found near the Teatro di Pompeo, not far from the
Roman Curia. Of greater interest is the story of its discovery.

The Pompey statue was found in the cellar of a private home on Via dei Leutari. The statue was positioned with the wall of the neighboring house passing
over the neck, and the owner of that house claimed
the entire statue on the grounds that the head was
more important than the body. When the matter went
to court the judges, remembering the verdict of Solomon, decided that the head should be detached from
the torso and each party given the portion found on
his property. This decision so offended Cardinal Capo
di Ferro's aesthetic sensibility that, with the help of
Pope Julius III, he was able to obtain a stay of execu-
tion. Pope Julius promptly ended the debate by paying
each of the rivaling parties a fee for the sculpture. He
then presented it as a gift to the cardinal who ensured
its preservation and safety here in the palazzo. More recently, after the proclamation of the republic by the
French, the statue's integrity was again threatened. At
that time it was transported to the Colosseum to lend a
heightened sense of reality to a performance of Vol-
taire's *Brutus*. Later, when the statue wouldn't fit into
the carriage that was to transport it, the right arm was
severed.

The state rooms of the palace hold other attractions.
In the throne room, where we see the statue of Pompey, the walls are covered with frivolous *trompe l'oeil*
paintings. This room was decorated in the middle of
the seventeenth century for Cardinal Spada by two Bolognese artists, Agostino Mitelli and Angelo Michele
Colonna. Giulio Mazzoni, who did so much on the exterior of the palace, also added his touch to another series of rooms; these are notable for their high-relief

stucco decoration and their superb gilded ceilings. They are the closest imitation in Italy to the Galerie François I at Fontainebleau and were no doubt inspired by Cardinal Capo di Ferro's admiration for the work of Rosso and Primaticcio, which he saw during his visits to France.

A final point of interest is the Meridian Gallery. Here is another example of *trompe l'oeil* this time executed by Domenichino's pupil, G. B. Ruggeri. It is an image of the celestial sphere projected onto a barrel vault that documents the time differences between Rome and other cities of the then-known world. There are also other exotic forms of scientific decoration: a nocturnal disc, which is used to tell time by the night's stars; and tables referring to the positions of the planets. Along the side walls of this room are ten reliefs from second-century Rome that are of great artistic importance. Their fine detail has been preserved because they were discovered lying face down on the floor of the Church of S. Agnese Fuori le Mura. Two of the slabs—the images of Endymion and Perseus—were moved to the Capitoline Museum and replaced by casts. The other depictions include Pasiphaë and Daedalus, Amphion and Zethus, Bellerophon watering Pegasus, wounded Adonis, Ulysses and Diomede robbing the temple of Minerva, Paris saluting his wife before leaving for Sparta, the death of Opheltes, and Paris on Mount Ida.

As you leave the Palazzo Spada turn to your left through the piazza and make an immediate right. (If the shapes of the chimneys in Italy have not yet captured your eye, look back at the Palazzo Spada for a view of them against the sky.) Next, within a few feet, you will be standing before the unusual sight of a solitary oak tree rising from the cobbled street. It marks the adjoining Piazza della Quercia, "of the oak," and memorializes the cult of the Madonna of the Oak Tree. Tucked in the corner, to the right as you face the tree, is the Church of S. Maria della Quercia, which was built by the Confraternity of Butchers, a profession in Rome dominated by men from Viterbo who, with their families, brought this cult to Rome.

In 1523 the Confraternity of Butchers bought this site, which housed the medieval church of S. Nicolo. The foundation stones for the existing church were

laid in 1727 by Pope Benedict XIII, and it was consecrated in 1738. The façade was designed by Filippo Raguzzini, an architect whose design for the Piazza di S.
Ignazio is one of the most ingenious and lively examples of baroque architecture in Rome. The Church of
S. Maria della Quercia also has elements of this design,
but on a smaller scale. To fully appreciate them one
has to look at the façade from different perspectives.
First, stand back as far as possible so you can see the
flowing convex curves. As you move forward to the
first step of the church's entrance the soft curves disap-
pear and are replaced by the strong vertical lines usually associated with the linear architecture of the Gothic
period. Though a minor work, this church certainly
depicts the complexity of form and a sense of the dramatic that is essential to the precepts of baroque architecture.

The church is generally closed, with the exception
of one Sunday service and the celebration of the annual feast of the Confraternity. If you wish to visit the
church, which has an elaborate eighteenth-century organ gallery, ring the door of the building to the right
as you face the church.

The restaurant to the left of the church, the Trattoria
della Quercia, is a neighborhood landmark. It has
been here for decades and was probably established in
affiliation with the Confraternity next door, which
guaranteed fresh meat. As with many restaurants that
have been around for a while this one has a rather
spotty reputation. During the 1960s writers raved
about its lasagna; in the 1970s it became a student
hangout because of its low prices; and in the 1980s the
quality fell to match the prices. It remains, nevertheless, a convenient neighborhood institution, and even
the picky gourmand living in the vicinity occasionally
grabs a bite here, appreciating the clientele if not the
cuisine.

Via dei Balestrari 1, across from the Church of S. Maria della Quercia, is the Palazzo Ossoli. Built in 1527 it
is attributed to Rome's "ghost" architect. "Ghost" because there are three buildings of this period whose
authorship is unknown—Peruzzi? Vignola? Sangallo
the Younger? In a city whose architectural history is so
well documented it is amusing to think about this
clearly talented architect, master of the style of his

time, quietly going about his life's work and leaving to posterity a building of such careful design and harmony that it demands acknowledgment but offers none. Lacking a name for attribution and all the luster that goes with it, the work itself is all that we are left.

Proceed, *sempre diritto*, straight ahead—a typical Roman phrase that you will hear whenever you ask directions. Even if what you are asking about is on the other end of town you will be told to go *sempre diritto*.

The Via dei Balestrari is named for the makers of crossbows who were replaced, when the crossbow was superseded by the harquebus, by the makers of the new weaponry. The harquebus was a portable firearm that had a matchlock operated by a trigger; it was supported for firing by a hook. If you lived in Rome during the Renaissance and needed a crossbow or harquebus, this is where you would shop. As you walk down the street you won't see anything so sinister being built now. Instead the street is a wonderful mixture of the new and the old—the Erboristeria, which sells herbal potions and cosmetics; a local dressmaker; and an old-style wine shop.

This street holds little of interest, but a few of the buildings can be singled out. To your left, at the beginning of the street, is a large building of the 1700s with medallion windows belonging to the Confraternity of Butchers. Only in the last century has this organization been located near a major market. When they first came to this neighborhood the meat market was at the foot of the Capitoline Hill; later it moved to the neighborhood of Testaccio, a few miles downriver from here.

Across the way, at no. 15, is a recently restored house used by a religious order associated with the nearby church of S. Lorenzo in Damaso. That church's coat of arms hangs on the corner of this building at the intersection of Via dei Balestrari and Vicolo del Giglio. No. 8 is a building of the 1600s with stone encasements around the windows and door. Here the local dressmaker sets up shop on the street during warm weather. The house at no. 42–43 with its shrine to the Virgin also belongs to the Church of S. Lorenzo in Damaso and is used by the Archconfraternity of the Immaculate Conception.

At the end of the street, where it intersects with Via dei Giubbonari, is a large marble plaque that commemorates one of the earliest efforts by the Vatican to clean up and organize the streets of the city: "Earth of Marcius which until a short time ago was ugly and drowned in squalid mud, and full of diseases, now under the reign of Sixtus IV, you have been liberated of this undignified aspect and everything appears admirable in the same spot. These dignified changes are due to Sixtus, giver of health. Oh how Rome is indebted to his reign!" It continues with the names of the builders of the street, Battista Arcioni and Ludevico Margani, and the date, 1483.

This inscription hints at the philosophy that motivated the popes' urban plans during the Renaissance. They wanted to make Rome the first city in Europe, the *caput orbit*, a city owing its existence and splendor exclusively to the papacy. In this regard Sixtus probably achieved more than any of his predecessors. The street was paved and widened for aesthetic reasons, but this effort proved a crucial ingredient in his attempt to fuse the many settled areas of Rome into a single city, a city whose arteries centered on the Vatican. Sixtus was also concerned with the problems of hygiene and went so far as to arrange the regular sweeping of this newly paved street, which was known at the time as the Via Flora.

Turn left onto Via dei Giubbonari and then immediately to the right along one end of the Campo dei Fiori. Go past the local movie theater and fresh pasta shop, and you will find yourself in the Piazza del Biscione. Though the name of this piazza no doubt refers to the snake that figured on the coat of arms of the Orsini family (who were responsible for initiating the settlement of this section of town in the twelfth century), its history goes back to the Roman republic. On this piazza stood the temple that, at the height of his success, Pompey dedicated to Venus Victrix. It stood alongside the first permanent theater built in Rome. This temple/theater complex was created for a very pragmatic reason. During the republican period a great prejudice existed against the construction of a stone theater because it was associated with the luxurious habits of the decadent Greeks. In 55 B.C., in order to bypass the senate's anxieties, Pompey built this first stone theater with a temple to Venus Victrix in the top of the auditorium. It was constructed in such a way that the stone steps and seats formed the access to the temple and they were thus made to appear an essential part of the temple and not the theater. In any case it was an impressive structure—150 meters in diameter with a stage 95 meters long and a seating capacity of up to thirteen thousand people. Although it is said to have been inspired by a Greek theater on the island of Mitylene it was not an exact replica; its semicircular form differed from the Greek archetype that was either a complete circle or, in later times, at least more than half a circle.

Pliny, the great chronicler of the Roman republic, tells us that Nero had the theater completely gilded, both inside and out, in a single day. One of Nero's many fits of extravagance, this was part of his preparations for the arrival of King Tiridates of Armenia. Pliny also describes the great slaughter of beasts that celebrated the theater's opening. This kind of extravagance and bloodshed continued for most of the theater's life. During the reign of Augustus it was used for spectacles and fights between wild beasts and gladiators in which no fewer than five hundred lions and twenty elephants were killed.

Aside from the temple and the theater, there was another magnificent architectural display: the Hectostylon, or Hall of One Hundred Columns. Standing at the back of the stage, this building was supported by several lines of numerous columns forming a great portico; the center was planted with avenues of sycamore trees and decorated with fountains and rows of marble and gilded bronze statues. It was here that the Roman Curia assembled. It was also here that Brutus administered his form of justice to Caesar on the fatal Ides of March.

Little is known of the vicissitudes of the Teatro di Pompeo after its restoration by Theodoric in 510 and before the twelfth century. In 1150 the Orsini family built a large towered fortress known as the Arpacata within the ruins of the theater. Centuries later this tower became famous for its clock, which initiated a fad for clocks all over Rome. Under Pope Eugene IV, who began the reconstruction of medieval Rome in the fifteenth century, the Venetian Cardinal Condulmer built a palazzo overlooking the Campo dei Fiori on the ruins of the theater and the fortress. In 1677, when the palazzo became the property of the Pio di Carpi family, it was again remodeled and took on the appearance of the building we see to our right as we stand facing the interior of the piazza.

The building must have enjoyed a wide reputation for elegance in the fifteenth and sixteenth centuries because a number of important dignitaries were hosted here: Caterina Sforza in 1477; the ambassador to the king of France in 1485; a retinue of distinguished visitors from Spain in 1486; and, in 1492, Giovanni de' Medici, who later became Pope Leo X. During the sack of Rome in 1527 the man who was in effect governor of the city chose to make this his home. Today the building, known as the Palazzo Pio, seems to have lost its heritage, but its history is certainly greater than the façade seems to admit.

In 1864, during the renovation of the courtyard (which is not noteworthy), a large bronze statue of Hercules was excavated. This find, along with that of the statue of Pompey, has led to speculation that there is a treasure buried here. The construction of Rome's subway certainly proved that this is still true for most of the city, but given Pliny's description of Pompey's theater and the condition of the two sculptures already found, one can almost feel an especially visceral struggle here between the mundane present and a nobler past.

Ruins of the theater can be seen in the basement of several houses in the area. The best way to visit the vaults and arches of the theater is over lunch or dinner at two restaurants: Da Pancrazio, at Via del Biscione 93, or Costanza, at Piazza del Paradiso 65. Both restaurants occupy the cellars of this 2,000-year-old structure, but at Da Pancrazio you must ask for a table downstairs.

In the far right corner of the Piazza del Biscione is a small archway blocked by a gate. This passage leads to the semicircular Via di Grotta Pina whose outline follows that of the auditorium of the ancient Teatro di Pompeo. In the 1930s and 1940s an elderly man sat near this corner under a tattered awning at a table with pens, ink, and a few sheets of notepaper; he was the local letter-writer who composed letters of complaint, lyrical love poems, or any other missives needed by the illiterate. At night he stored the equipment of his trade in this archway.

Immediately to the left is one of the rare Roman houses that still bears traces of its painted façade. In recent years different shopkeepers have occupied this site, but the insignia tells us that it was once either the local horse stable or a shop that sold horsemeat.

If you turn left on Via del Biscione you will see the once-famous Albergo Sole, said to be the oldest hotel in Rome. Burckhart, Pope Alexander VI's secretary, noted that the French ambassador had stayed there in 1489. Before its restoration in 1869 the entrance was built like a fortress and the courtyard was decorated with a fountain and a sarcophagus. Today it is hardly an elegant or exclusive establishment, but it maintains a reputation as the cheapest hotel in town.

The junk shops and peddlers that set out their wares during the weekdays are probably much like those that cluttered this street in the fifteenth century. One big difference is the lack of elegant (and not so elegant) courtesans strolling, shopping, and flirting on their way to the Campo dei Fiori. At the end of the fifteenth century a powerful and beautiful courtesan, La Grechetta (the Little Greek), lived on this street and one day a jealous duel over her favors turned into a major riot. During the fight a Frenchman killed a member of the prestigious Sanguigni family—who, in revenge, set fire to La Grechetta's home. The fighting grew to such proportions—nearly 2,000 people—that it moved to the Campo dei Fiori, adding yet another dimension to the chronicle of events on this street and the piazza.

Retrace your steps to the Piazza del Biscione and into the Campo dei Fiori. Whether you are here in the morning, afternoon, or evening this long rectangular space will always be filled with activity and local color. In the morning except Sunday, it becomes the largest outdoor produce market in the historic center. In the afternoon it is often a favorite forum for local demonstrations, primarily feminist and Communist, and in the evening it becomes a casual hangout. Beside all this activity are the warm stucco façades of multilevel buildings whose roofs cut a busy network of textures against the sky.

The market day begins about six o'clock in the morning when the men roll in their carts laden with boards, sawhorses, poles, and awnings. (These are hidden away for the evening in warehouses occupying the ground floor of buildings in the surrounding area.) As soon as the stalls are set up the women arrive with crates of the previous day's fruits and vegetables. It is never a one-man operation, but almost always a family endeavor. While the installation takes place another member of the family is at the wholesale market buying the day's produce and delivering it before the market starts hopping at 9:00 or 9:30. Fresh, seasonal produce is an absolute requirement. Only "rich man's row," the aisle on the far right, which caters primarily to the foreigners in the neighborhood and the new expensive boutique restaurants, supplies artichokes in the summer and peaches during the winter. Few of the Italian ladies who make daily trips to the market would consider such unseasonal purchases.

Between the stalls and the shops on the piazza one's entire shopping list can be filled. In front of the movie theater are the fishmongers, who have an especially abundant selection on Tuesdays and Thursdays. To the left of the movie theater is the fresh pasta shop, which makes a delicious tortelloni with spinach and ricotta. The far aisle is devoted to displays of tongues, hearts, kidneys, and less gruesome cuts of meat that hang on hooks above the marble counters. Ruggeri sells canned goods, cheeses, and salamis in the shop on the corner of Via dei Balestrari and the "Campo," as it is colloquially known.

While the temporary stalls in the middle of the piazza disband around 1:30, the shops in the buildings reopen in the afternoon. So if you are not here in the morning you can still appreciate some of the flavor of the market, though not its full vitality. Past Ruggeri's and down the length of the Campo is the *confetti*, or candy, shop. The most popular item in this store is the candy-coated almonds (*confetti*) that are an integral part of family celebrations. Blue and pink *confetti* are given as party favors at a baptism; at weddings the individually wrapped and decorated pouches of white almonds take precedence even over the cake. A few doors down is the wine shop where you can sip at the bar and investigate the selection of wines.

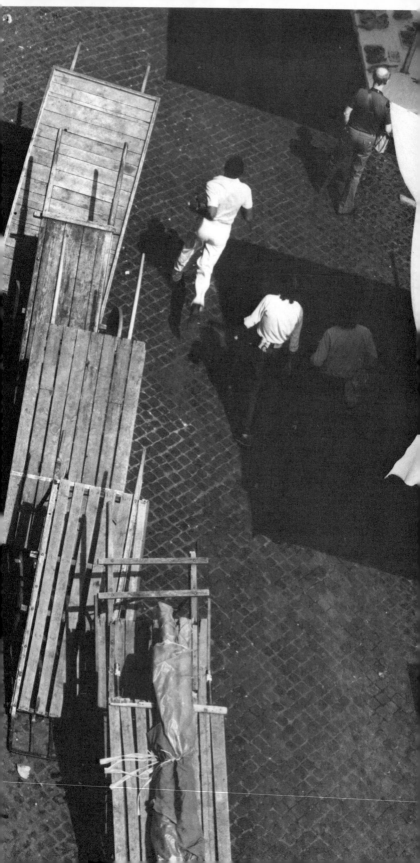

As you round the corner of the piazza you will see a bread store through whose window you can get a peek at the ovens inside. The man who sells olives in the morning in front of this store counts inflation by the number of people walking out with huge packages. Inflation or not, it is one of the market's biggest attractions, especially for the *pizza bianca*. This flat bread covered with olive oil and salt is a Roman specialty that you should definitely sample while you're here.

Past the clothing and sundries shops, along the other length of the piazza, is the pork shop where every part of the pig is sold in all its many forms and reincarnations. Carefully displayed in beds of laurel are endless varieties of sausages made in countless combinations of grind and spice, salamis from all over Italy, prosciutto, and much more. This shopkeeper's eye for display is always catching, especially at Christmas when the portals are draped with laurel branches and lined with pigs' heads.

Campo dei Fiori means "field of flowers" and elicits an image of a huge flower market. There are only four stalls selling flowers, but the sumptuousness of their selection mitigates their small number. The name of the place, however, is much older than the market, which has been here only since 1869. Before the twelfth century this was indeed a huge field extending down to the river banks. "Flowers," however, probably comes not from the real thing but from Flora, Pompey's lover at the time he built the Theater and the Temple of Venus Victrix.

Not much is known about what went on in this area between the sixth century, when the theater fell into ruin, and the twelfth century, when the Orsini family built their fortress. During the fifteenth century other construction began; by mid-century the area assumed such a degree of importance and desirability that the most powerful Roman families vied with one another to buy up the barren land. Toward the end of the fifteenth century, with the help of the papacy—which paved roads into the Campo, built bridges, and ensured a constant supply of water and pilgrims—the piazza became not only the most popular spot in the

Carts on the Campo dei Fiori

area, but, after Pope Sixtus IV's constructions, the very center of the city. At that time economic activity shifted from the foot of the Capitoline Hill to the Campo, and this area boomed with artisans' workshops, business establishments, and hotels. This upswing was reinforced by the transfer to this area of the horse and grain market, which came to be held here every Saturday and Monday until the beginning of the nineteenth century.

While this was a busy center of life in the city, it also became a place of death when at the turn of the sixteenth century it was selected as the stage for public executions. If executions were as popular then as they have been in more recent times this aspect of the Campo's personality may have only added to its diverse spectacles. The most important of these executions occurred in 1600, and the statue in the middle of the piazza stands as a memorial to it. This statue, of Giordano Bruno, was boldly erected in 1889 as a testament to freedom of speech.

Born in 1550, Giordano Bruno committed the heresy of being an ardent advocate of the Copernican system of the universe (Copernicus died seven years before Bruno's birth). This belief, of course, was that the sun, not the earth, was the center of the universe and that the planets revolved in their orbit about the sun. To Bruno's contemporaries the Copernican system aroused serious objections. Some thought it naïve and irresponsible; others deemed it an outmoded Pythagorean notion, an absurd form of sun worship. The Vatican considered it heresy. Bruno also strongly opposed the philosophy of Aristotle and offended many Catholic scholars by setting forth views of his own that strongly tended toward pantheism, the doctrine holding that the natural universe, taken or conceived as a whole, is God. Bruno visited France, England, and Germany, and in each of these countries the uncompromising expression of his opinions excited only hostility. It was in Venice that he first fell into the hands of his ecclesiastical enemies. After six years' imprisonment there he was brought to Rome to be burned to death on the corner of the piazza where Via dei Giubbonari and Via Balestrari meet. Surprisingly enough, Giordano Bruno's solemn stance in the middle of the Campo is one of the few reminders in this city of the Inquisition, a period of several centuries in the Church's history when there was a very thin line between rational thought and heresy. A magazine of political satire, *Il Male*, places wreaths at the foot of this statue to call attention to contemporary examples of blows against the doctrine of free speech.

The Campo was also the meeting place of the cultural bourgeoisie, ambassadors, cardinals, noblemen, businessmen, artisans, and foreigners. All Papal Bulls, court sentences, marriage banns, and citizen complaints were posted here. By the mid-1500s almost every house on the piazza had a public bar or dining facility, and there were numerous hotels. These were run primarily by Germans who did such a good job that Pope Pius II is quoted as saying "it's best not to find others" to do it. On the corner near the entrance to Via del Pellegrino, Antonio Blado opened the first printing press in Rome in the first part of the sixteenth century. Bufalini's map, the first perspective view of Rome, was printed here, as were numerous volumes in Greek. Blado's bread-and-butter work, however, consisted of pamphlets for great feasts, such as the tournament of 1565 held in the Belvedere Courtyard; public notices; statements of miracles; and information on natural phenomena.

We leave the Piazza Campo dei Fiori by the intersection of Via del Pellegrino, at the far end opposite from where we entered. As you face the bread store turn right and walk into the connecting Piazza della Cancelleria. Dominating the piazza is one of the most important palazzi in Rome, the Palazzo della Cancelleria. This building's reputation is based not only on the simple, awesome beauty of its structure, but also on the design itself, which marked a clean break from fifteenth-century Roman architectural traditions. Here, for the first time, are the basic elements that have come to be associated with the design of Roman palazzi. The body of this palazzo, an immense quadrangle of travertine, reintroduced the luxurious scale and materials of the ancient Romans. The base is of incised stonework, and above that, the façade is offset by a series of classical pilasters that create a pattern of symmetry and a rhythm of wide and narrow bays. The windows, arched and set in rectangular frames, became a popular architectural detail after the construction of this palace, as did the arcaded courtyard in the center of the building. While most architectural historians consider this the best example of early Renaissance architecture in Rome, not all are in agreement with the attribution sometimes made to Bramante, who arrived in Rome after the inscription date of 1495 engraved on the façade, which marks the date the palazzo was finished.

The palazzo is also a monument to papal nepotism; it was built by Cardinal Riario, nephew of Pope Sixtus IV, with money he won in an evening of gambling with another papal nephew, Franceschetto Cibo, whose uncle later became Pope Innocent VIII. Following a plot by the Riario family to assassinate him, Pope Leo X (1513–1521) confiscated the property and installed the Papal Chancellery in the palazzo, hence the name Cancelleria. This is the Vatican office that deals with the correspondence of the papal hierarchy. While it still functions as that, and is today under the jurisdiction of the Vatican and not Italy, this palazzo has been an important site for events in Italy's civil history. In 1798–1799 it was the seat of the Tribune of the Roman republic; in 1810, of the imperial court; and in 1848, of the republican parliament, which was summoned here by Pope Pius IX. In July of that year an angry mob of citizens burst into the council chambers and demanded an instant declaration of war against Austria, thus making Rome one of the centers of the nationalist movement. The papacy's neutrality on this issue led to the beginning of a serious rift between the Church and the state. Tensions grew in Rome—which since the fifth century had been ruled by the papacy—until Pellegrino Rossi, the pope's minister, was assassinated at the foot of the palazzo's grand staircase. That act transformed tensions into outright hostility, one of whose manifestations was the establishment of two Roman aristocracies: the "white" civil aristocracy and the "black," allied to the Vatican. The Church's position following the establishment of the republic of Italy was not resolved until the 1920s when, with the signing of the Lateran Treaty, the Vatican's realm of jurisdiction was clearly circumscribed. Today the palazzo no longer tugs on the emotional cords of the anticlerics and few people have qualms about coming here for the chamber concerts played in the Hall of One

Hundred Days, so named because it was painted by Vasari in little more than three months.

Walk into the courtyard; it is one of the most beautiful works of the Renaissance in Rome—a city whose landscape is dominated by the baroque architecture produced a hundred years later. A model of perfection and simplicity, the courtyard stands free of all decorative details besides the elegant architectural lines and Cardinal Riario's rose motifs, which are visible in the spandrels of the arches, on the corner pillars, and as the central theme of the pavement. The forty-four Doric columns of granite supporting the portico are said to have been plundered from the ruins of Pompey's Hecatostylon. They may also, however, have come from the barracks of the Green Squadron, whose site is hinted at in the original name of the church attached to this palazzo, S. Lorenzo in Prasino (St. Lawrence Prasino in leek green). Of the four squadrons of charioteers that used the Campus Martius during the days of the empire—Red, White, Blue, and Green—the Green were favored by the Romans and their barracks were undoubtedly sumptuous, befitting the quarters of popular heroes who amassed fortunes in gifts and prizes from their admirers.

As you leave the courtyard turn left to see the church now named S. Lorenzo in Damaso. Founded by Pope Damascus I, it was conceded to a chapter of the canons, which are said to be one of the most ancient establishments of the sort in Rome. Later it became the titular church of Cardinal Riario and was positioned within a courtyard of the palazzo he built for himself. Because of its placement the space inside the church is nearly square with a double elliptical groined vault. It is also decorated with some interesting works of art and tombs, among them that of the poet Anibale Caro. For more details about the interior of the church listen to the tape-recorded description provided inside, just through the doors designed by Vignola.

Returning to the Campo dei Fiori we pass the Via del Pellegrino, to the right at the juncture of the two piazzas. Named after a route used by the pilgrims in the fifteenth century to get from their hotels near the Campo to the Vatican, the Via del Pellegrino is one of the few medieval streets to retain its original name. Later, at the end of the seventeenth century, the city required all jewelers to live and work there. Though no longer the "gold ghetto," it preserves part of that heritage in the few jewelry shops along its path. Continue walking past this street to the bread store on the Campo.

If you stand on the corner of the Piazza Campo dei Fiori and the Via dei Cappellari you will be opposite a building whose reputation as an inn at the beginning of the sixteenth century was no doubt enhanced by that of its owner, Vanozza Cattanei, the mistress of Pope Alexander VI and mother of his children, Lucrezia and Cesare Borgia. Her crest, which includes the emblem of the infamous Borgia pope, can be seen if you take a few steps straight ahead onto the Vicolo del Gallo to no. 13. Vanozza's relationship with the pope was no secret at the time, as he adopted her children and even made Cesare a cardinal. Nevertheless, adding his family emblem to her shield was considered audacious. Vanozza waited ten years after the pope's death before she hung this crest on the front of her hotel.

Turn right onto Via dei Cappellari, "Street of the Hatmakers." The hatmakers are gone, but little else has changed on this street, which is perhaps one of the most characteristic to have survived from the 1500s. This narrow street, its aging façades festooned with laundry, is still trafficked with wooden carts used to transport produce from the ground-floor storage areas to the market. These visual images of another time are further reinforced by the working-class character of the inhabitants and the real poverty. Here, for a block, we step into an area that recalls medieval Rome, and the contrast between this street and the high-Renaissance elegance of the nearby Via Monserrato, Piazza Farnese, and Via Giulia is striking.

As you begin down the street notice the stucco *edicola* from the eighteenth century on the corner to your left. The image is always flanked with either plastic or fresh flowers left by one of the seemingly innumerable old ladies in black who live here. No. 127–130 is a house owned by the Vatican. Until 1937, when Gnoli, a Roman historian, wrote about it, frescoes could still be seen on its façade. The building at no. 61–62 was also once decorated with geometric designs. This sixteenth-century fashion for decorating houses with architectonic motifs or scenes from mythology and the Old Testament began in Venice, became fashionable in Florence, and finally took hold in Rome, where as many as two hundred façades were painted. It became such a fad that it was often cited as one of the elements that differentiated Rome from other Italian cities during the Renaissance. Polidoro da Caravaggio and Maturino da Firenze, two of the most important artists of this style, distinguished themselves by painting houses with such energy and fecundity that Vasari wrote, "Rome, laughing, became drunk with their efforts."

The arch over the street, called Arco dei Cappellari, was built in the seventeenth century. Under it, at no. 29–30, a marble plaque states that Pietro Trapessi, the boy who recited his verses in the Piazza S. Andrea della Valle and became the famous poet Metastasio (a Hellenized form of his family name), was born here in 1698.

Just to the right of the arch a passageway terminates with a picture from the fifteenth century known as the Crucifixion of the Hatmakers. The picture depicts Christ on the cross with the Virgin Mary, Mary Magdalene, and other worshipers on their knees; it is an object of veneration on September 14, the occasion of the feast of the Exaltation of the Cross. Directly across the street is a courtyard whose walls and small-grated windows are said to be relics of the Corte Savello, one of Rome's grim medieval prisons. The prison was placed under the jurisdiction of the Savelli family, who, in the thirteenth century, were given the title of Hereditary Marshals of the Conclave. With a guard of five hundred men and some sort of criminal court the Savelli Marshal's function was to control, among other things, the courtesans from whom he exacted a tax (in addition to license fees) that added a nice sum to the papal coffers. The prison, which extended to Via Monserrato, was closed by Pope Innocent X for its unsanitary conditions and was replaced by a new one on Via Giulia.

In about ten yards we come to an intersection. On the right, the Vicolo del Bollo is named for the office that stamped hallmarks on gold and silver. This office was established here in the eighteenth century for the convenience of the jewelers on the neighboring Via

Rustic antique shops

del Pellegrino. Straight ahead, rows of rustic antique furniture shops line the remainder of Via dei Cappellari where a bargain can be found if you are interested, but it takes some patience and a good eye.

Turn left onto Via Montoro, whose name was taken from the palazzo immediately to your right. This street functions as a bridge between the older medieval quarter of this neighborhood and the more elegant creations of the sixteenth through the eighteenth centuries. The Palazzo Montoro, a building that extends the length of nineteen windows, was built in the mid-eighteenth century by a noble family from Umbria who came to Rome as part of the Savelli Court. The family did well for themselves in the city. One of their daughters married into the famous Sienese banking family, the Chigis, and added that family's name and insignia to their own. You can see the Chigi insignia, an oak and a star, decorating the building. Later a son married the last member of one of Rome's oldest families, Maria Verginia Patrizi, and assumed her family name. As the longevity of a family name is very important to an aristocratic society, this young Chigi Montoro saved the day for the Patrizis.

When we reach the intersection of Via Montoro and Via Monserrato we enter a section of the neighborhood and the city distinguished for its refined beauty. Via Monserrato is lined with palazzi built between the late sixteenth century and the eighteenth. From the corner take note of the house at no. 105, the Palazzo Giangiacomo, and its beautiful portal with columns whose capitals are female heads, and no. 111–112, the house belonging to the Confraternity of S. Caterina da Siena. It is a replica of the saint's birthplace in Siena.

From the sixteenth century until recent times this section of Rome was known as the *quartiere degli stranieri*, "quarter of the foreigners," because so many people of foreign nationality or from other regions of what is now Italy lived here. On one end of the street is the Venerable English College, established in 1362 and said to be the oldest English institution abroad, and to our right is the Church of S. Maria in Monserrato, the national church of Spain. This church is dedicated to the celebrated Black Virgin, whose miraculous appearance in the mountains outside Barcelona made her one of the most loved of Spanish idols. The two Borgia popes, Calixtus III and Alexander VI, are buried here.

Pope Calixtus III suffered from the reputation of his nephew, Pope Alexander, who was considered capable of any crime. Just as some people would like to attribute every monumental work in Rome to Michelangelo, so, too, crime was popularly associated with the Borgia name in the fifteenth century. Both popes were originally buried in the vaults of St. Peter, but when Julius II, a great enemy of the Borgias, was elected, their bodies were promptly exhumed and turned over to the Spanish Church here on Via Monserrato. The gesture was tantamount to transferring their remains to Spain, and it was more than three centuries before the soothing nature of time could allow the acknowledgment of their positions as leaders of the Church. A proper monument was finally built for them in 1881.

S. Maria in Monserrato was built on the site of a house bought by Pope Innocent VI (1352–1362) as a hospice for Catalan pilgrims. Work on the present structure was begun in 1518 by Antonio Sangallo the Younger but was not finished because of the political problems between Rome and Spain, which lasted more than a century.

Turn right onto Via Monserrato. Pass the church and on your left you will see a small street called the Via della Barchetta, named after a boat service that operated between this point on the Tiber banks and Trastevere back in the days when only two or three bridges spanned the river. Across from the beginning of this street, at no. 34, is the Palazzo Capponi. Walk into the courtyard. There, a large amorphous space is divided by a fountain portal into a small paved area and a large garden beyond. In the garden court one finds a woodworking shop, a garage, and a small, one-story building, a storage shed that has been converted into an architect's office. The garden is filled with plants and a few benches. At the far end is an ivy-covered wall, all that remains of a building from the 1500s. Signs of its age are seen in the travertine windows, the shades of antique chiaroscuro frescoes, and the niches with statues. This is a very tranquil spot; the sounds of water dripping in the fountain, the saws humming in the background, and the palm trees swaying in the wind are a pleasant contrast to the city streets.

Return to the street. At no. 17, to your left, is a house whose renovation in 1870 caused enough of an uproar that its owner had the following motto inscribed over the door: *"Trahit sua quemque voluptas,"* meaning that everyone has his own taste and that in finding his the owner had done what pleased him. What "pleased him" was removing the frescoes, antique travertine windows, cornices, and the ancient family crest of the previous owners.

The Palazzo Pocci, later Pallavicini, at no. 25, was built by a family who came to Rome from Cremona. The family included two cardinals and a city magistrate, and all are buried in the family chapel at S. Maria in Monserrato. Carlo Maderno designed the main entrance, the windows of the façade, and the main staircase of this residence. The balcony above the entrance was added in the eighteenth century. Also in the eigh-

A garden courtyard on Via Monserrato

teenth century the palazzo became the home of the
Carmelite Order, and they built a church to S. Teresa
just to the right of the entrance. A watercolor by Achilli
Pinelli shows the façade of this palazzo and that clearly
includes a church, but when the Carmelites moved to
S. Maria della Vittoria (one of the "must" churches in
Rome, if only to see the erotic sculpture of S. Teresa by
Bernini), all traces of the church were removed.

Across the street from the Palazzo Pocci, on the corner of Piazza Ricci, is the charming, ancient Church of
S. Giovanni in Ayno, which has been converted into a
private residence. The church dates back to 1186. In
the fourteenth century it was described as a basilica
with an entrance porch similar to other early Christian
churches such as S. Cecilia and S. Maria in Cosmedin.
In the fifteenth century, however, it was given this deli-
cate Renaissance face-lift. Some signs of its medieval
origins remain in the corbeled cornice and the saw-
toothed decorative design.

On the far end of the square is the palazzo that gives
the piazza its name. Built in the 1500s by Nanni di Baccio Bigio, it boasts probably the best example of the
frescoed façades that were once so much a part of the
city's color. The palazzo was once entirely covered by
the monochromatic paintings of Polidoro da Caravaggio and Maturino da Firenze, but time has taken its
toll, especially in the last forty years. Photographs tak-
en by Alinari show that these frescoes were still prominent during the 1940s; their recent destruction is
blamed entirely on auto pollution. At the end of the
nineteenth century Luigi Fontana restored these paintings and added the family crest on the third floor and
the scenes on the fourth. With a sharp eye and some
imagination you can decipher these historical and
mythical studies: the Tiber, the she-wolf with Romulus
and Remus, Faustolo with his wife, Romulus with a
plough marking the position for the walls of Rome
while men around him dig the foundations for the
new city, and the rape of the Sabines.

Polidoro and Maturino were quite a pair during the
early days of the sixteenth century. Vasari in the *Lives
of the Artists* says of them:

> They began to study the antiquities of Rome, and copied
> the ancient marbles until they both alike acquired the an-

tique style, and the one was so like the other that, as their minds were moved by the same will, so their hands expressed the same knowledge. Of what great use they have been to the art of painting may be seen by the number of foreign artists who continually study their works; for all artists in Rome copy the pictures of Polidoro and Maturino more than all the other modern paintings. . . . But if I were to name all their works, I should have to make a whole book of the doings of these two men, for there is no house or palace or vineyard where there are not works by Polidoro and Maturino.

Walk through the principal gate into the courtyard, which also bears signs of ancient frescoes. You can see embedded in the wall a marble column that reaches to the first floor. There is speculation that it is only one of many such columns that once formed a loggia. There are also ancient marble fragments; a funeral vase; and a sculpture of the Marchesa Campana seated with a pillow at her feet, which was given to the Ricci family by the unknown sculptor in payment for a debt.

A member of the Ricci family still keeps an apartment in this palazzo, which otherwise has been divided into numerous dwellings. Not too long ago, when he decided to have the main salon painted, workmen found under the wallpaper a beautifully preserved painted frieze with figures of seated women. The painter is unknown but the style is mannerist, of the period between 1570 and 1590. This kind of story, incredible as it may seem, is frequently heard in Rome.

The restaurant on this piazza is especially popular among a crowd of young professionals. While the specialties change with the season there is always a chocolate cake for dessert, and it's one of the few in Rome that is spared a dousing of liquor. In the summer this is an inviting spot; you can sit under a large umbrella and admire the decoration of the Palazzo Ricci or the marble busts in the second-floor windows of the palazzo on Via Monserrato.

Return to Via Monserrato, and turn left. About twenty feet to your right is the Palazzo Corsetti, at no. 20. Walk into the high passageway that slopes to the courtyard and you will find a true gem: a small courtyard rich with classical and pastoral references. The arches, the outside staircase, the columns, the stone,

and stucco are reminiscent of the most elegant sixteenth-century courtyards. The marble fragments and
plaques recall the glory of classical Rome while behind
the gate the plants, orange trees, and birds recall the
countryside. This courtyard's clutter of associations
combines the most delightful of possibilities for this
city space somewhere between the street and the
house.

The courtyard and the Palazzo Corsetti were built by
Monsignor Podocatori, the doctor to Pope Clement VII
and rector of the University of Padova, one of the oldest universities in Europe. Across the street are two
other palazzi built during the sixteenth century by families connected to the Vatican.

Via Monserrato ends in a rather desolate piazza, a
converging point for several important streets: Via dei
Banchi Vecchi, Via del Pellegrino, and Via Monserrato.
The restaurant to the left on Largo Moretta may be in
the same place as that which gave the piazza its name
in the seventeenth century. The customers of that long
ago restaurant were taken with the owners' daughter,
an exotic mulatto child. Nicknamed "La Moretta," she
soon gave her name to the street and the piazza. At
that time a pharmacy, once famous for its antique
vases and a bronze mortar made by Cellini, also
took the name.

The Largo Moretta is synonymous with an important
juncture in the street map of old Rome called the Chiavica de Santa Lucia. At this point the Cloaca di Ponte,
one of the ancient Roman sewers, flowed into the Tiber. These *cloacas,* "sewers," were incredible feats of
engineering. The drains flushed not only the sewage
of the city but all the water from a large number of
fresh-water springs and, also, all of the water that con-
stantly poured into Rome from the aqueducts. As a result of this draining system places like the Forum and
the Campus Martius, originally mere marshes, became
dry, habitable land. What's more, this was not just a
system of narrow pipes; Pliny describes Agrippa, when
minister of public works in 33 B.C., as inspecting the
cloaca by boat.

Cellini's autobiography mentions this spot on several occasions. He was obviously friendly with the pharmacy's owners, as the mortar was a gift to them, and
he lived in the immediate area for a while. (A street is

named for him off the Via dei Banchi Vecchi.) Both the pharmacy and the Chiavica were the setting for one of his violent adventures.

> In the meantime my enemies had proceeded slowly towards Chiavica, as the place was called, and had arrived at the crossing of several roads, going in different directions, but the street in which Pompeo's house stood was the one which leads straight to the Campo dei Fiori. Some business or other made him enter the apothecary's shop which stood at the corner of Chiavica, and there he stayed a while transacting it. I had just been told that he had boasted of an insult which he fancied he had put upon me, but be that as it may, it was to his misfortune; for precisely when I came up to the corner, he was leaving the shop, and his bravi had opened their ranks and received him in their midst. I drew a little dagger with a sharpened edge, and breaking the line of his defenders, laid my hands upon his breast so quickly and coolly, that none of them were able to prevent me. Then I aimed to strike him in the face, but fright made him turn his head round; and I stabbed him beneath the ear. I only gave him two blows, for he fell stone cold at the second. I had not meant to kill him, but as the saying goes, knocks are not dealt by measure. With my left hand I plucked back the dagger, and with my right hand drew my sword to defend my life. However, all those bravi ran up to the corpse and took no action against me, so I went back alone through Strada Giulia considering how best to put myself in safety.

During the sixteenth century Rome witnessed a huge upsurge of construction as popes, cardinals, and other nobles tried to outdo each other in the building of homes along grandiose classical lines. The house to your right, between Via Monserrato and Via del Pellegrino, is one of the vestiges of an earlier Rome—not a palazzo but an elegant human-scale townhouse. For centuries it was known as the "house of the treasurer" after its owner, Pietro Paolo Francesci, the first person to be appointed to supervise the coinage of money. The capitals on the top-floor loggia, facing the piazza, are similar to others on buildings of the late fifteenth century, and, in keeping with the fad of the time, there are still traces of frescoes on the façade (depicting Cloelia crossing the Tiber). An equally dramatic fresco could have been painted about an event that took

place within the walls of this house: in 1462 the Austrian emperor Fredrick III came to Rome to ask for the
hand of Elenora di Portogallo, a guest in the Della
Zecca residence. Until 1870, when it was moved to the
German Hospice of S. Maria dell'Anima, the crest of
the Austrian emperor with its overreaching motto—
Austriae est imperare orbi universo—hung on this
house and overlooked the group of streets that epito-
mized the rebirth of Rome as the center of the Christian world.

Across the way, at the beginning of Via del Pellegrino, near no. 145, is another emblem that adds poi-
gnancy to the fates of great nations. Here, standing in
the wall of the local grocery store, is a carved boundary stone from the reign of Claudius in A.D. 49. This
stone was one of the many that marked the boundary
between the city and the country, which by Roman
law was redefined according to the size of the empire.
This particular stone indicates the enlargement of the
city at the time of the conquest of Britain.

Walk through the Largo Moretta toward the dilapidated church and the Tiber. Despite the images con-
jured by Cellini, by the ancient Roman *cloaca*, or by
the bordering Vicolo del Malpasso (Street of the
Wrong Step—a warning against all the courtesans who
once lived here), this is one of the least picturesque piazzas in the center of Rome. Essays advocating its restoration periodically appear in Rome's papers and
many architects have designed their solution to this
forty-year-old problem created when the war aborted
Mussolini's plan to build a wide avenue here to connect the Mazzini Bridge to the Corso Vittorio Emanuele II. Even the church on the far corner, dedicated to
Rome's patron saint, S. Filippo Neri (or the Pipo
Buono as he is endearingly referred to), stands in
semiwrecked abandon. Its architectural credentials,
built in 1728 by Raguzzini on the orders of Pope Benedict XIII, have not been enough to rescue it from ruin.

The Largo Moretta and the church open onto Via
Giulia. At this point we find ourselves about halfway
down the famous one-kilometer stretch of road created by Pope Julius II. This street was to be another
monumental entrance to the Vatican (from the Ponte

The boundary stone on Via del Pellegrino

Sisto), and Bramante was hired to design a magnificent gate and to construct a new, huge court of justice on the end closest to the Vatican. Both these projects were abandoned for lack of funds, but the foundation stones for the court of justice can be seen along the walls of the Hotel Cardinale (a few blocks down); they have been nicknamed the pillows of Via Giulia. What Pope Julius did accomplish was the alignment and paving of the street. All protruding porches and stairways obstructing the thoroughfare were removed, and to this day this road's course is one of the few straight lines on the map of the center-city.

As you stand at the intersection with Via Giulia look to your right. A block away is a large building with guards at the entrance; this is what replaced the Corte Savello jails on the Via dei Cappellari. This forbidding structure, built in 1655 by Antonio del Grande and known as the Carcere Nuovo, "new prison," was considered for centuries a model of prison design. Now the building is used as offices by the police.

Directly across the street is a public high school, the Liceo Galileo, and its parking lot. Though this building is new the site has been associated with education since 1670. At that time one of the earliest educational institutions in Rome, the Collegio Ghislieri, built its boarding school here. Primarily it served the sons of noble families in the Papal Court; the descendants of the founder, Ghislieri; and the descendants of Ghelmino Crotti who contributed to the foundation—but every year one boy was selected for admission from the Roman populace. As many of Rome's wealthiest citizens were educated here, this school played an important role in the life of the city until 1928 when it was closed for financial reasons.

Turn left onto Via Giulia and enjoy a full view of this street, which is framed by the arched bridge at the far end. This is undoubtedly one of the most attractive streets in the city and certainly, since the sixteenth century, one of the most fashionable. It could be a set design for an Italian Renaissance play and often seems so during the spring and summer when circus and music festivals add their spectacles. These festivals are a very recent revival of the street entertainments popular in the seventeenth and eighteenth centuries that kept the torches of Via Giulia burning late into the night. Attracted to both its beauty and street life, artists also came to live and work here. Sangallo built himself a huge palazzo, now the Palazzo Sachetti, and Cellini, Pier Luigi da Palestrina, Raphael, and many others helped create a tradition of art now long associated with this street's name. Today that tradition lives on in the structures that continue to excite the eye and in the antique trade that in the last thirty years has occupied the ground-floor shops.

Our walk down the Via Giulia leads us toward the bridge and past enough palazzi, churches, and shops to give the full flavor of this street's ambiance. To your left, past the simple house of the 1600s at no. 146–147, is another entrance to the Palazzo Ricci, whose painted façade we admired from Via Monserrato. If the gate on the Piazza Ricci is closed, this entrance is almost always open.

On the other side of the street, next to the school, is the Neapolitan Church of S. Spirito. While this church is hardly representative of the grandeur of the kingdom of Naples at the time it was built in the mid-seventeenth century, it is the "pantheon" for the last sovereigns of the kingdom who died in exile waiting to be restored to their throne. The design itself doesn't even hint of the grand tradition of church building fostered in Naples. An effort has, however, been made recently to assign its authorship correctly. For centuries guidebooks stated that the design was that of a certain Cosimo Fansage, a misspelling of Cosimo Fanzago, one of the maestros of the Neapolitan baroque, and therefore, certainly not the author.

A dozen yards to your right, before the intersection, look above the wall and you will see the small but beautifully proportioned cupola of the Church of S. Eligio degli Orefici. Turn right onto Via di S. Eligio for a closer look at this church, which is an architectural gem. S. Eligio, a goldsmith, became the patron saint of jewelers, who made up a wealthy community in Rome at the turn of the sixteenth century. They commissioned Raphael to design their church in the form of a Greek cross surmounted by a cupola, reproducing, on a small scale, the lines of St. Peter's. The work was completed by Baldassare Peruzzi.

The church deserves attention in its own right, but it is also an example of the type of design of what has come to be referred to as the "golden period" of the Renaissance when Bramante, Michelangelo, and Raphael were all working in Rome. This church confirmed Raphael, a man who considered himself above all a painter, as one of the best architects of his time. Although the church is rarely open there is a custodian at no. 9 on the short stretch of Via di S. Eligio parallel to the Tiber. Even if you don't wish to see the simple interior of the church, turn the bend to have a full view of the small but charming seventeenth- and eighteenth-century houses that flank it. Also climb the stairs at the corner, which lead to the sidewalk along the Lungotevere, for a better view of the cupola.

Return to Via Giulia, turn right, and in just a few steps, No. 16, on the right-hand side of the street, is the Palazzo Varese, built by Carlo Maderno in 1617 for a Milanese monsignor. The cornice, richly decorated with flying eagles and towered castles, is another fine example of this architectural detail. Inside the courtyard is a four-story loggia with two stories of arcaded openings and two with flat entablatures, all of the Tuscan order. Across the street from this palazzo, at no. 151, is the only nineteenth-century palazzo on Via Giulia, which, despite its recent age, blends in well with the architecture on the rest of the street. The inscription on this building, which is known as the Palazzo degli Stabilimento Spagnoli, tells us that it was built by Queen Elizabeth II of Spain for the poor, the pilgrims, and the sick. Attached to the Spanish Church of S. Maria di Monserrato, this building enclosed a courtyard containing tombs of Spanish clergy, among which is the one of Monsignor Pietro Foix de Montoya that was designed by Bernini.

Next, on the left, is the Church of S. Caterina da Siena, often referred to as the last baroque work in Rome. Originally built under Leo X for the Sienese colony in the city, which had a defense tower in this area along the banks of the Tiber, it was rebuilt in 1766–1770 by Paolo Posi. The firmly curved concave design on the façade was built at a time when the baroque was superseded by flatter, more classical lines. Note the coat of arms of the city of Siena over the door and above that the two medallions of the she-wolf and twins, symbols of the city of Rome.

Next to the church, at no. 163, is the Palazzo Cisterna, built in the sixteenth century by the sculptor Guglielmo della Porta as his home and studio. At the beginning of this century, it was the home of the painter Eugenio Cisterna. No. 167 is another sixteenth-century palazzo; it was restored in 1928 by Lord Rennel Rodd, author of *Rome of the Renaissance and Today* and then the British ambassador to Rome.

We have already passed several antique shops, but there are many more along this street, among them some of the best dealers in Rome. For the last two centuries Via dei Coronari and Via del Babuino have been known as the centers of the antique trade. Only since 1950, when dealers looking for cheap, desirable space bought out the mechanics and garage-owners who occupied the ground-floor shops of the palazzi, did the Via Giulia also acquire this reputation. Originally, these ground-floor spaces were used as stables. When horses were replaced by cars in this century, the noble families sought new ways to earn income to maintain their palazzi, and the spaces were rented out or sold to people involved in the automobile business. Now, only a motorcycle repair shop farther down the road hangs on as a reminder of this short period in Via Giulia's history.

As we approach the arch over Via Giulia, another great palazzo with large falcon heads suspended from the corner pilasters rises to the right at no. 1. This is the Palazzo Falconieri, now the seat of the Hungarian Academy of Art. In the early nineteenth century it was the home of Cardinal Fesch, Napoleon's uncle and one of the greatest collectors of Italian art. When Orazio Falconieri bought this palace from Pietro Farnese in 1638 it had a frontage of seven windows. In 1645, Falconieri bought the adjacent palace and commissioned Borromini to remodel the whole complex. In this instance the great architect's work on this façade is not characterized by his usual overwhelming individuality—lots of movement and perspective, as in the Palazzo Spada or my favorite work, the Church of S. Ivo. His most interesting contribution here is the belvedere on top of the south wing, which can be seen from the river's edge or the Gianicolo (the best point in town from which to admire the entire cityscape). This belvedere, with its concave corners and herms of the two-headed Janus, isolates the palazzo on the skyline and stands in clear contrast to the nearby loggia on the Palazzo Farnese, which was designed by yet another of Rome's great architects, Giacomo della Porta.

Just beyond the palace is the rather macabre Church of S. Maria dell'Orazione e Morte, whose façade is adorned by skulls and a sculpture of a winged skeleton pointing to a scroll on which is written "me today, thee tomorrow." This image became the famous "wizened hag of Strada Giulia" in one of Belli's poems. The church itself is considered the finest example of the architecture of Ferdinando Fuga, one of the masters of the late baroque who incorporated into his designs elements from the three founding fathers—Bernini, Borromini, and Cortona. The church was built between 1732 and 1737 and is a rare example of a single, cohesive style. The macabre symbols, such as the winged heads on the tops of the pediments, are in reference to the confraternity established here whose job it was to provide a Christian burial for all abandoned bodies and all those unable to afford a proper burial. This group was similar to the Confraternity of Sacconi Rossi on the Tiber Island, which occupied itself with the burial of bodies drowned in the Tiber.

At one time there were underground burial chambers connected to this church extending to the Tiber. All but one of these were destroyed in 1886 during the construction of the river embankment. The vaults and walls of these chambers were covered with bones and skulls displaying such fantasy that they became mere decorative elements. In the only remaining chamber, for example, there is a candelabra created out of vertebrae and other small bones; in a niche a skeleton hangs much like a Halloween display representing not our present image of horror, but the popular decorative tastes of the seventeenth century. In fact, this church, along with the Capuchin Church of S. Maria della Concezione on the Via Veneto (which today is a more extensive representation of this macabre baroque style—and easier to get into), was for centuries one of the important tourist sites in Rome. This fact is illustrated by the numerous engravings and lithographs of the burial chambers that were sold to make money for the confraternity. Gregorovius's conclusion to this fascination is that it transformed fears of death into playful familiarity.

At this point in our walk down the Via Giulia we stroll under the bridge that spans the street. This bridge is Via Giulia's mark of distinction, now almost a souvenir of Rome because of the paintings Roesler Franz did of it in the last century. This arch is the only structural trace of Michelangelo's grand scheme to connect the main family house of the Farnese with yet another of their possessions, the Farnesina, across the river in Trastevere.

Just beyond the bridge, to your left, is the back gate to the Palazzo Farnese. I will discuss the story of this palace when we reach the main entrance at the end of our walk. For now, enjoy the sight of the green garden, a luxury in this crowded neighborhood. Admire, as well, the elegant three-bay loggia facing the river that was built by Giacomo della Porta.

You have probably already heard the sound of trickling water that flows from the combined wall-fountain and horse-trough a dozen yards away on your right. This is the Mascherone fountain, named after the colossal marble face of Roman origin that spews a steady stream of water. It is not a favorite among Romans except perhaps when, at the end of the nineteenth century, during a period of three days on the occasion of a feast, it sent out a stream of wine rather than water. Its importance on the Roman street scene is that of being one of three puzzling ancient faces; the other two are the Bocca della Verità (Mouth of Truth) at S. Maria Cosmedin and the large face with a moustache in the little square near S. Sabina on the Aventine Hill.

The Mascherone fountain was built in 1570 by the Farnese family who crowned the piece with their emblem of a lily. Completed before there was any water flowing to this section of Rome it was hoped that the Acqua Virgine would reach this far. However, the Acqua Virgine made it only to the Campo dei Fiori, and this fountain, as well as the two on the Piazza Farnese, stood empty until Pope Paul V, in 1613, piped the Acqua Paola across Ponte Sisto to the left banks. At one time this fountain stood on the landing for the *traghetto* "ferry," to Porta Settimiana.

Turn left onto Via del Mascherone, which is directly across from the fountain. To the right, at no. 63, is a house with two plaques mounted in the wall. One was posted in 1926 by the city government; it informs us

The streets of historic Rome with ornamental design

that the celebrated intellectual Francesco Cancellieri (1751–1826) lived here. The other, mounted in 1930, is a memorial to the German poet William Frederick Waiblinger, who died here in 1830. The entrance hall of this house has a touching inscription: "I belong to Francesco Cancellieri, may I, a small and not illustrious house, be always frequented by faithful friends."

Next door is the Church of SS. Giovanni e Petronio dei Bolognesi. On this site was a medieval church dating back to at least 1186 that was given to the Bolognese community by Pope Gregory XIII in 1581. The present church was built in the last years of the sixteenth century to the design of the Bolognese architect Ottaviano Mascarino.

Having passed the Spanish, the Neapolitan, the Sienese, and now the Bolognese churches, you can understand better why this neighborhood was considered for centuries "of the foreigners." One must remember that only at the end of the nineteenth century was Italy united; until that time each of these cities was part of a separate state. The neighborhood's foreign community currently includes a large number of Americans, British, and French.

As you walk up the Via del Mascherone you can't help but be aware of the vastness and height of the structure to your left, the Palazzo Farnese. It is the largest palazzo in Rome, and its construction involved many of the greatest architects and artists of the sixteenth and seventeenth centuries. The result is a sumptuous monument to the power and wealth achieved by the Farnese family, primarily through the pontificate. As you may have already noticed, it was the elite of the Church, and not the merchants and politicians (as in Florence), who were responsible for the domestic architecture of Renaissance and baroque Rome.

As this palazzo should be appreciated from the piazza in front, walk there and rest near one of the two huge vases of gray Egyptian granite that have been turned into fountains. Known as the Farnese bathtubs, these were brought here by Alessandro Farnese from the Baths of Caracalla by way of the Piazza S. Marco. Here, next to the soothing sound of the water and in the middle of one of the most impressive piazzas in Rome, you can read the story of this palazzo, a story that tells a lot about the Renaissance in this city.

A whole chapter could easily be devoted to the history—architectural, artistic, and social—of this palace that was so grandly conceived by Alessandro Farnese. The Farnese name derives from a castle near Lake Bolsano and appears rarely in the chronicles of Roman history until Alessandro's time. One of the first stories set the tone for spunk and drama: Alessandro was imprisoned for forging a paper as a student in the Collegium de Parco Majori during the reign of Innocent VIII. Cellini refers to Alessandro's escape, with the help of a basket and a rope, from Castel S. Angelo. As with other great stories in history the real force behind Alessandro's rise to power was the face of a beautiful woman, his sister Giulia. The wife of Ursino Orsini and known as Giulia Bella, Alessandro's sister so captivated the Borgia Pope Alexander VI that she replaced Vanozza in his affections. Alessandro Farnese's appointment as cardinal was a direct result of this liaison. Once a prince of the Church, he seems to have rapidly assumed leadership in the hierarchy and, as was the case at that time, concomitantly amassed a huge fortune.

Following the example of his papal patron and namesake, Alessandro Farnese never disguised his affection for his children, Pierluigi and Constanza. His son became duke of Parma, Piacenza, and Nepi, while his daughter carried on her aunt's reputation for beauty and fortune. Even his grandchildren were able to benefit from his position; one was made a cardinal at the age of fourteen and the other was married to Margaret of Austria, the widow of Alessandro de' Medici.

Both as cardinal and later as Pope Paul III, his taste for magnificence (passed to his grandson, Alessandro) left Italy a far more beautiful and interesting country. The inheritance includes not only this example in front of us, but also the Villa Caprarola designed by Vignola and the famous collection of antique sculpture that is now the treasure of the National Museum of Naples, to say nothing of Pope Paul III's artistic influence on the Vatican.

Though Alessandro remained a cardinal for forty years it wasn't until he was made the titular cardinal of S. Eustachio that he called upon Antonio Sangallo to design his new palazzo on land acquired from the monks of S. Maria del Popolo. The construction spread over many years; seventeen years into the project, when Alessandro finally assumed the papal tiara, Vasari says "he felt he should no longer build a cardinal's but a pontiff's palace." Immediately, Alessandro had Sangallo enlarge the building from three to five bays in the court and from eleven to thirteen on the façades. The row of shops on the street were eliminated, and the entrance was enlarged by the addition of a monumental colonnaded vestibule. Ironically, this papal palace was inhabited not by Alessandro Farnese, who moved to the Vatican, but only by his ancestors.

Upon the death of Sangallo, Michelangelo was called in to finish the work. He is generally credited with the top story, the famous cornice, and the central loggia window above the Piazza Farnese entrance. James Ackerman says of this collaboration:

> Michelangelo, though noted for his inability to collaborate with colleagues, showed remarkable skill in harmonizing his own dynamic style with the portions already built by Sangallo. No two architects of the mid-sixteenth century were less congenial than these; it is symptomatic of their relationship that at St. Peter's Michelangelo erased almost every trace of Sangallo's Basilica. Perhaps he would have done the same at the Farnese palace if it had not been so far advanced when he started, but economy must have forced him to keep what was there and even to make use of members that had been carved but not put in place, such as the uppermost façade windows. Consequently the palace has a Sangallesque personality throughout. Michelangelo enhanced and gave vigor to his personality and at essential points rescues it from dull propriety; in doing so he created Sangallo's masterpiece.

Michelangelo did have one scheme that, if it had been completed, would have left his distinctive mark on this introspective palace: the single arch, which we saw over Via Giulia, is all that remains of his plan to connect the garden of this palace with that of the Farnesina. His intention was to create a vista and access that spanned the courtyard, the garden of the Farnese Palace, the Via Giulia, the river, all the way to the other garden. When Michelangelo died Giacomo della Porta completed the palazzo with a loggia on the riverfront and left the bridge unfinished. An inscription assigns the final year of work to 1589.

Besides its rich architecture the Farnese palace became the recipient of the rarest and best collections ever formed by a private individual even before its completion. The collection may have begun in the early days of construction when Sangallo discovered the barracks and stables of the Red Squadron of Charioteers, which dated back to the heyday of the Campus Martius. These walls, together with a beautiful mosaic pavement in black and white, representing feats of horsemanship, are still in the cellars of the right wing. The collection comprised works of statuary, pictures, books, manuscripts, *objets de vertu*, and curiosities. Many of the statues came from Cardinal Alessandro's excavations throughout Rome but especially from those in the Baths of Caracalla, which brought him a great reputation as a savior of antiquity. Notwithstanding his will, which declares "that none of my heirs and successors shall dare to sell or give away, or transfer to other places, or pawn any of the objects of art and curiosity which exist at the moment in my collection," Pope Pius VI did manage to ship the entire collection to Naples to assuage the Bourbon dynasty. It is this collection that now distinguishes the National Museum of Naples.

The collection and the love of art from which it stems dictated the design and decor of many of the rooms, which unfortunately are now closed to the public. If you can, catch a fleeting glimpse of the vestibule leading to the courtyard while the gate opens to what is now the French Embassy. It is one of the most beautiful features of the palace—a quadruple row of columns and semicolumns holding a stuccoed ceiling.

The windows to the left of the center balcony, including both the *piano nobile* and the row of windows above, look onto one room—the Salon d'Hercule, named after the gigantic statue of Hercules standing in that room. The original statue, now in Naples, was found in 1540 at the Baths of Caracalla and is signed by Glycon of Athens. It was the pride of the Farnese collection, and the room that was designed around it more than matched its size.

The other room worthy of mention is the Carracci Gallery, which is used on state occasions as the French

Embassy's dining room. There the themes of the loves of gods and goddesses from Ovid's *Metamorphosis* are spread across the walls in a colorful praise of pagan voluptuousness. This work, done between 1597 and 1604, had a tremendous influence on subsequent decorative painting in Rome. It is also believed to have led to Carracci's death; disappointed at the fee he received he took to drink and died at the age of forty-nine.

During the pontificate of Clement VII, Cardinal Farnese's (Alessandro's grandson) records show that he had 306 people living in the palace, including family and servants. Both the palace's reputation and its magnificence attracted famous dignitaries. In 1635, Cardinal Richelieu stayed here, attracted by the library, which at the time was considered the best in Italy; and in 1655, Queen Christina of Sweden made this her home. But the opulence of the Farnese family was never again matched. During the late seventeenth century this served as a residence for the French ambassador to the Holy See. Through marriage it was inherited by the Bourbon kings of Naples, who lived here in utmost seclusion after their exile in 1861. The French classic historian Jerome Carcopino tells a story about flocks of chickens kept on the attic terraces during this time of decline for the Bourbon dynasty. Since the union of Italy in 1871 the palace has been the home of the French Embassy under a remarkable arrangement that must have been negotiated during the French occupation of Rome. The palace was exchanged for the Hotel Galiffet in Paris (hardly a match), for a rent of one lira payable every ninety-nine years. Thus the French now have an exclusive right to one of the most magnificent palazzi in all of Italy.

Today this monumental palace still induces the awe and thrill that it was intended to—maybe more awe than ever. Pope Martin V, who started the ball rolling with his dismay and concern over the sight of Rome in the early fifteenth century, would probably be both surprised and thrilled at the efforts of his successors. Here in the neighborhood around the Campo dei Fiori, the Vatican certainly accomplished what it set out to do—make Rome the queen of all cities.

Walk

4

A Village Within the City: The Island and Southern Trastevere

Away from the heart of imperial Rome and never a
part of any of the grand Renaissance, baroque, or
twentieth-century city plans, the island on the Tiber
and the southern end of Trastevere retain a character
all their own. Here we find no great ruins of antiquity,
no elegant palazzi, no monumental piazze. Instead, we
have a very introverted neighborhood more reminiscent of a village than a capital city. It is a quarter of
small houses, family businesses, community institutions, and quiet streets. Yet behind this façade is a
quarter with an historical and artistic heritage as captivating as any in Rome's historic center. Discovering
this neighborhood has the added pleasure of real adventure because the area is so unassuming and so
many of its treasures are not readily visible. Even if
you are not "treasure" hunting there are few pastimes
in Rome more enjoyable than walking down the back
streets of Trastevere absorbing the unique charm of its
medieval and Renaissance architecture.

Our walk begins on the Ponte Fabricio, which joins
the left bank of the Tiber along the Lungotevere de'
Cenci to the small but prominent island in the Tiber.
This graceful, double-arched bridge with its narrow
cobbled passage was built in 62 B.C. by Consul L. Fabricius. It is the oldest bridge in Rome. To most Romans it is known as the bridge *de Quatro Capi*, of
"four heads," alluding to the two herms on the parapet
of the four-headed Janus, the Roman deity who guards
over gates, doors, and all beginnings—in this case, the
once primary entrance to the center of the city.

Stand on the bridge for a while to examine the scen-
ery. It is said that while crossing this bridge to the island Gregorovius decided to write his great work on
the Middle Ages. Ahead is a profile of the island with
its jumble of buildings framed by the green of oak,
palm, and cyprus trees and the hills beyond. To the
right is the Ponte Garibaldi, Trastevere's primary access route. On the left, in the foreground, is the appropriately named Ponte Rotto, "broken bridge," and

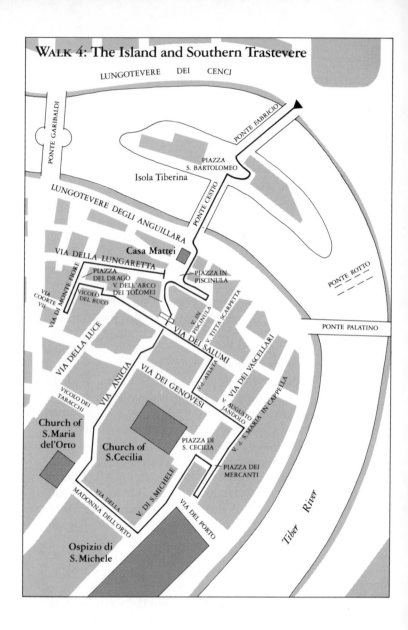

LUNGOTEVERE DEI CENCI

PONTE GARIBALDI

PONTE FABRICIO

PIAZZA
S. BARTOLOMEO

Isola Tiberina

PONTE CESTIO

LUNGOTEVERE DEGLI ANGUILLARA

PONTE ROTTO

Casa Mattei

VIA DELLA LUNGARETTA

PIAZZA
DEL DRAGO

PIAZZA IN
PISCINULA

V. DELL'ARCO
DEI TOLOMEI

VICOLO
DEL BUCO

VIA
COORTE
VII

VIA DI MONTE FIORE

PONTE PALATINO

V. IN
PISCINULA

V. TITTA SCARPETTA

VIA DEI SALUMI

VIA DELLA LUCE

V. ATLETA

VIA ANICIA

VIA DEI GENOVESI

VIA DEI VASCELLARI

VICOLO DEI
TABACCHI

V. AUGUSTO
JANDOLO

V. d. S. MARIA IN CAPPELLA

**Church of
S.Maria
del'Orto**

**Church of
S.Cecilia**

PIAZZA DI
S. CECILIA

PIAZZA DEI
MERCANTI

V. DI S. MICHELE

VIA DELLA
MADONNA DELL'ORTO

VIA DEL PORTO

Tiber River

**Ospizio di
S. Michele**

behind, its newer replacement, the Ponte Palatino. Below is the famous muddy water of the Tiber.

In these waters Tiberinus, king of the Etruscans, drowned, giving the ancient Romans an unexpectedly easy victory as well as a name for their river, which makes three dramatic curves as it possessively winds its way around and through the city. The river springs from the same mountain ridge that feeds the Arno—Monte Coronaro, northeast of Florence. The Tiber then flows for 210 miles through the Tuscan, Umbrian, and Lazio countryside. Twenty-two miles from this point it empties into the sea at the port town of Ostia.

The Tiber's reputation as a great river is questionable when we see it today hidden by the massive travertine embankment, untraveled, tame, and murky. It does, however, hold many cherished memories. In days past it was trafficked by international vessels. Navigable for seagoing vessels as far as Rome, it also supported a busy river business into Italy's interior; for example, most of the materials used in the construction of the Cathedral in Orvieto were carried upstream on barges. The Tiber also carried the elegant splendors of imperial courts and floating pageantries. Pope Gregory XI made his triumphal return to Rome from Avignon in 1377 by way of the Tiber, not one of the city's gates, as did emperor Frederick III in 1452, Pope Sixtus IV in 1483, and Pope Alexander VI, coming from Spain in 1492 to assume the papacy. In 1464, Pope Pius II navigated the upper reaches of the river on his way to Ancona to command his fleet against the Turks. As late as 1848 the port of Ripetta was the embarkation point for the Papal Grenadiers in the campaign against the Austrians. Also at one time the pontiffs visited the Basilica of S. Paolo in splendid galleys, and it was the custom of many nobles to hold lavish boat parties along the river within the city walls. Before all the bridges were built, *traghettos*, ferries, carried passengers back and forth across the river.

These days the river shows a touch of life courtesy of the rowing clubs that hold occasional regattas and the few social clubs who have boathouses anchored upriver. Recently there has been an effort by a group called the Friends of the Tiber to resurrect the river's reputation. During the summer months they encourage festivals along the quay below the embankment and run a boat service between the Ponte Garibaldi and the ruins of Ostia.

Personified by the ancient Romans as a majestic old man crowned with laurel, holding a cornucopia, and supported by the she-wolf and Romulus and Remus, the Tiber nourished the fledgling city for centuries. Before the aqueducts were built this was Rome's only source of water. Again, after the sixth century, when the aqueducts were destroyed by the Goths, and until

The Ponte Fabricio and the island in the Tiber

they were finally repaired in the late fifteenth century, the whole topography of the city changed as the population moved to be near the river. During this period a fascination, not unlike the contemporary Roman craze for mineral water, arose for the taste and healing powers of the Tiber's water. When Pope Clement VII went to Marseilles in 1533 to marry his niece, Catherine de' Medici, to the Duke of Orleans (later Henry II), he took with him, on the advice of his physician, enough water from the Tiber to last until his return. Today it is so polluted no physician would advise you even to wash your hands in it.

The same murky yellow waters are described by Virgil: ". . . through which the Tiber flowed pleasantly, with rapid eddies and yellow from the quantities of sand, to burst forth into the sea." His allusion to the rapid stream is a reminder of yet another important trait of this river. Before the river was harnessed in 1900, Rome was devastated by major floods three or four times a century—the Corso under more than two meters of water; churches and houses on the ancient

Campus Martius flooded; the Trastevere fields inundated; and the crops destroyed.

The island is perhaps one of the most traditional sites in Rome. According to legend it came into being when the Tarquins were expelled in 509 B.C. The Roman senate confiscated their land, which later became the Campus Martius, and, to ensure their victory, cut down the crops and threw them into the Tiber. As the river was low the stalks of corn landed on the sandbank and soil gathered around them. In time there formed a solid piece of land that become a lasting symbol of the Roman victory over the Tarquins.

The next important event took place in the third century B.C. when Rome was hit by a terrible plague. In response to an oracle of the Sibylline Books the Roman senate sent ambassadors to Epidaurus in Greece to bring back a statue of Aesculapius, the god of healing. They returned with the statue, and as the ship berthed on the river a serpent slithered overboard and took refuge on the island. This was interpreted by the Roman people as a sign that the god himself had come to them. To commemorate this event they built a temple on the island to Aesculapius, and in remembrance of the ship that carried the snake (or, perhaps, because the island is shaped like one) the island itself was encased in marble and travertine to look like a ship with an obelisk as the mainmast.

Three temples were eventually built by the ancient Romans. The Temple of Aesculapius was the first, erected on the tip to your left as you face the island. It was adorned with paintings brought from Greece, and on the threshold of the cella was inscribed Antiochus the Great's recipe for curing snakebite. According to Ovid the Temple of Faunus (the god of fields and shepherds) was to your right, on the end of the island that divides the Tiber into two streams. The Temple of Jupiter, the father of gods and men, adjoined that of Aesculapius and was erected by Lucius Furius Purpureo, a Roman consul, in fulfillment of a vow made during the Gallic wars. In that temple a statue of Caesar was erected; it is said that the face turned from west to east during the reign of Vespasian. As Georgina Masson says, "sacred statues that move are no new thing in Italy." The obelisk was erected at the height of the empire, after the reign of Augustus, who introduced them to Rome. These Egyptian symbols of the sun's rays are but another example of the Romans' engineering prowess. Pliny tells us that huge vessels had to be constructed specifically for their transport and then they were installed with the aid of massive wooden scaffolding, special pulleys, and the labor of thousands of men.

Straight ahead is the square medieval tower with a small marble head embedded in the brick, perhaps in memory of Matilda Canossa, who gave it the name Torre della Contessa. In 1087 she drove the antipope factions off the island and later gave protection to both Pope Victor III and Pope Urban II.

Walk to the end of the bridge. To your left is the Church of S. Giovanni Calibata, built in 1640 on the site of an earlier church to St. John the Baptist. The baroque façade was designed in 1711 by the architect Romano Carapecchia. The church is named after a recluse of the fifth century, a member of a rich noble family in Constantinople who secretly left his home to become a monk. He earned his place on the Catholic Church's Mount Olympus when, after six years, he returned disguised as a beggar and lived in a hut near his family's mansion. Only upon his deathbed did he disclose his identity to his mother. The fact that the remains of this man, brought to Rome after his death, were venerated for centuries is an interesting insight on medieval religious fervor.

Since 1584 the church has been a part of the hospital that belongs to the Order of the Fatebenefrattelli, which covers the entire right side of the island. The hospital, along with the pharmacy on the corner, derives its eccentric name from a sign on an almsbox in the church with the exhortation "*Fate Bene, Frattelli*," "Do good, brothers." Established by a brother of the Order of St. John of God, who arrived in Rome with Don John of Austria after the victory of Lepanto in 1571, the hospital has carried on the tradition started with the Temple of Aesculapius. Today it is one of the most popular obstetrics hospitals in Rome and certainly a distinctive location to have as one's birthplace.

A few steps ahead, on your left, is the picturesque Piazza S. Bartolomeo. In the center rises a pillar surrounded with the statues of St. Bartholomew, St. Paulinus of Nola, St. Francis, and St. John of God. This pillar was commissioned at the expense of Pope Pius IX to commemorate the opening of the Vatican Council in 1869. Here once stood the obelisk, the only one in Rome of unknown origin, whose fragments are now in the ducal palace of Urbino.

The church with a medieval porch at the end of the piazza is now dedicated to St. Bartholomew in another example of the medieval passion for the saints' relics. Originally founded at the end of the tenth century by Emperor Otto III, it was consecrated to his friend St. Adalbert, who had been killed by the Prussians in 998. When the church received the body of St. Bartholomew, poor St. Adalbert was upstaged by this apostle's dedicated following. Despite later claims that the body was actually that of St. Paulinus of Nola, the church retains its association with St. Bartholomew.

Walk through the piazza to the church, which has gone through numerous restorations and remodeling after flood damages. The bell tower dates back to 1118, as do many of the marble fragments embedded in the walls of the portico. This medieval portico has also survived a seventeenth-century restoration during which a new façade was added. The modern sculpture, in rather sharp contrast to its surroundings, is the work of one of the brothers now residing in the attached monastery. Inside we have the typical basilica style with the nave and aisles divided by red granite columns, which are said to be relics from the Temple of Aesculapius. On the whole, however, the impression is that of a much later church including frescoes by Carraccci in three of the side chapels (the second to the right and the third and second to the left). A special feature is a small carved marble well-head of the twelfth century set in the chancel steps. An inscription in Latin states that "One here sees the saints arranged in a circle around the mouth of the well," and another, now illegible, concluded, "Let him who is thirsty come to the fountain to draw from the spring of health-giving draught." In the past people came from all over to drink the miraculous water. The dream cure of the ancient Romans, akin to the Greek practice of drugging or hypnotizing, was thus replaced in time by the Christian faith in the healing power of the water from this well. This island's healing tradition was reinforced further by a legend that said that Henry II's court jester,

Rahere, had a vision here that led to the founding of the Hospital of St. Bartholomew in London.

Other important highlights are the prophyry urn, under the high altar, which contains the disputed saint's body, and the shrine of St. Paulinus of Nola at the end of the right aisle. For exact details about the church you should listen to the recording on the machine near the entrance.

Return to the piazza with its busy traffic of pregnant women and young parents with infants piling in and out of cars. In the evenings, as the sun sets behind the Gianicolo and reflects its rich light against the ocher tones of these buildings, this becomes one of the most unforgettable spots in Rome. To the left, as you face the church, is the Oratory of the Sacconi Rossi. This was a confraternity whose mission was to provide Christian burials for all bodies drowned in the Tiber. A subterranean cemetery, not easily accessible, contains a curious design made of human bones—these designs are similar to those in the Church of S. Maria dell'Orazione e Morte on Via Giulia and the Capuchin church on the Via Veneto. (Go to the Capuchin church if you want to see an example of this macabre baroque decor.)

Near the beginning of the bridge that connects the island to the Trastevere mainland, on the right toward the hospital, is a staircase that leads to the river's edge. When you reach the bottom, turn left and walk under the bridge toward the Ponte Rotto and the office of the river police, who, along with the monks and patients of the hospital, comprise the bulk of the island's residents. From here there is a fine view of the Ponte Rotto, which was built in 179 B.C. by M. Aemilius Lepidus. Because of its slanting position across the river and the pressure of the flooding waters against its side piers this bridge was carried away four times—in 180, in 1230, in 1557, and in 1598. After the last disaster it was never repaired, and only one arch now stands in the middle of the curving stream. At the end of the island, against the base of the buildings on the Ponte Fabricio side, you can still see a fragment of the old Roman travertine wall that represents the prow of a ship; carved on it is the familiar symbol of the Aesculapius serpent. From here you also have a good view of the structure of the Ponte Fabricio.

The serpent of Aesculapius

In days past the barges of millers and fishermen surrounded the banks of the island. For whatever reason, this was considered the best place along the Tiber to fish—a fact attested to by the ancient fish markets nearby at the Portico d'Ottavia and the Piazza in Piscinula. It is an opinion that must still hold true because a few brazen fishermen are always on the Ponte Palatino. The floating river mills are said to be the clever invention of Belisarius following the destruction of the aqueducts; before that they were located on the Gianicolo Hill. They remained here on the Tiber until the last century and were a colorful addition to the setting around the island, as well as being the city's source of ground wheat.

Retrace your path back up the stairs to the Ponte Cestio. This bridge was originally built in the first century B.C. but has been restored many times. It takes us to Trastevere, that part of town "across the river," a boundary that is more than merely physical. The residents of Trastevere consider themselves descendants of the purest Roman stock: Horatius, Scaevola, and other early patriots who defended the republic against the assaults of Lars Porsena and the exiled Tarquins. While this pure lineage is far from true, the Trasteverini have through the centuries maintained a self-sustaining community isolated from the rest of the city. That isolation has given the people a character all their own as well as their own dialect, immortalized in the nineteenth century by the poet Gioacchino Belli. The Trasteverini's sense of independence was only encouraged by the Romans on the left bank, who looked upon them as uncivilized neighbors. Augustus Hare's description of the Trasteverini—"more hasty, passionate, and revengeful as they are a stronger and more vigorous race"—would probably have satisfied the citizens on both sides of the Tiber. Since World War II the differences have become less apparent, especially now that Trastevere has become a chic place to live and a favorite part of town in which to dine. No longer will you meet a Trasteverino who has never gone to Rome or vice versa. Still, no other quarter in the city preserves its identity so strongly, and it is not just the dialect or the people, but also the ambiance that is responsible.

The first bridge connecting Trastevere to Rome was probably built by King Ancus Martius, who was motivated by reasons of both commerce and defense. Ancus was the legendary founder of Ostia, at the Tiber's mouth, where lay the salt-beds that formed the basis of a prosperous trade with all of central Italy. To protect this trade Rome needed to control both sides of the Tiber. In addition, the hill beyond Trastevere became an important military outpost against the frequent attacks of the Etruscans. The land near the river was farmed, and here the legendary farmer Cincinnatus has his field of four *ingera*.

During the empire the sailors for the imperial fleet, largely drawn from the Adriatic, were settled in Trastevere in what became known as the city of the Ravennatti. When Hadrian's harbor of Portus eclipsed the older port of Ostia commercial agents from many lands filtered into this community of "pure Roman stock," including the first Jewish settlement in Rome. A maritime trade mingled with such small industries as leather workers and tanners, potters, carpenters, fishermen, and the millers from the barges on the river. For centuries the high seas molded the character of this neighborhood, and while the port is gone, its memory continues in the street names and the institutions.

Cross the busy Lungotevere degli Anguillara at the traffic light and take note of the picturesque medieval house in front of you with its small, walled garden, cross-mullioned windows, and tower. Walk a few yards to your left till you see a staircase on the right; this leads to the sunken Piazza in Piscinula. Here we plunge right into the quiet atmosphere of the southern end of Trastevere, which contrasts sharply with the busier and more familiar northern section. This is a neighborhood of old-world charm, narrow streets, and unobtrusive institutions. While a bit dated we can still share Roderick Hudson's experience of Trastevere as described by Henry James.

> He was particularly fond of this part of Rome, though he could hardly have expressed the sinister charm of it. As you pass from the dusty swarming purlieus of the ghetto you emerge into a region of empty, soundless, grass-grown lanes and alleys, where the shabby houses seem mouldering away in disuse and yet your footsteps bring figures of startling Roman type to the doorways. There are few monuments here, but not a part of Rome seemed more oppressively historic, more weighted with ponderous past, more blighted with the melancholy of things that had their day.

The name Piazza in Piscinula and its topography indicate that this may once have been the site of one of Rome's famous baths. As this area has never been excavated, we see instead two important relics of the Middle Ages. The first of these is a house part of which we saw crossing the Lungotevere, the Casa Mattei. This block of handsome masonry still shows traces of its twelfth-century origins, but there are also details from later centuries, including some of the fancies of its owner/restorer in the 1930s. At that time it was rescued from years of abuse as a cheap inn, appropriately called the Spendthrift. Even if far from authentic, the details—the windows, fragments of Roman marble, iron bars and rings to harness horses, *edicola* to the Virgin Mary, and the egg and billet moldings—create a captivating and suggestive building. Certainly it is a wonderful introduction to this neighborhood, where the medieval is most insistent.

For several centuries, until the fifteenth century, the Matteis were one of the most powerful families in Trastevere. As was the case with most of this quarter's baronial families, their history was one of intrigue, murder, and arrogance. The Matteis, however, went too far, and in a rare example of democratic power were forced by the community to flee across the river after an appalling series of murders that culminated in a homicidal brawl during a family wedding. Settling on the edge of the Jewish Ghetto they saw their fortunes turn around, and they established themselves among the Roman nobility, eventually becoming masters of three grand palazzi near the Turtle Fountain. One of their members even became one of the great collectors of Roman antiquities, which led to quips by the Roman nobility that the Matteis' move to Rome obviously saved them from the bad influences of Trastevere's environment. It must be added that part of their wealth was acquired from taxes they levied as keepers of the Ghetto gates.

Across the piazza, next to the local bar, is the other medieval building, the Church of S. Benedetto in Piscinula. It is famous as the smallest Romanesque church in Rome, and it has an equally minute campanile housing the oldest bell in the city. This church, built in the eleventh century, rests on the site of the house where St. Benedict lived as a boy. Here he pursued his studies before leaving for Subiaco where, at the age of thirteen, he founded a monastic order. Within a century this order covered Europe from Italy to Britain. The façade of this church dates from the seventeenth century, but if you wish to see the older interior, ring the bell of the convent door, which is to your right as you face the church. Inside is an atrium with ancient Roman columns, a vaulted ceiling, and a particularly interesting cosmatesque, or inlaid tile, pavement of unusual arabesque patterns in dark green serpentine marble. This is said to be the cell where St. Benedict lived. The main part of the church also has ancient columns dividing its small nave and aisles. On the altar is an early fifteenth-century Venetian Madonna and Child and, on the walls, fragments of ancient frescoes.

For a good view of the campanile, walk fifteen feet down Via in Piscinula. (As you exit the church this street enters the piazza a few yards to the right.) From here you can clearly see the brick structure intersected with terra-cotta moldings. On the right-hand corner of the intersection is an ancient marble fragment of a tiger, and further down, at no. 37, is a small fifteenth-century house. On the left-hand side of the street is a large iron *edicola* to the Virgin and a small marble plaque with a fish, indicating that there was once a fish market on the square.

Return to Piazza in Piscinula. A look at some of the other buildings and shops shows us that even this part of Trastevere is slowly being gentrified—the fancy gift shop and the semicolon name-sign indicating the entrance to a Brazilian restaurant. We also have a nucleus of typical businesses. Next to the church is the local snack bar, Il Punto, with a sign showing that it also serves as a *tabacchi*, or "cigarette shop." This means more than is immediately apparent; aside from the sandwiches, light snacks, coffee, and liquors, they sell all state-controlled items—cigarettes, matches, legal sheets with government stamps printed on them, postage stamps, and salt. Fresh milk is also bought at this bar. Next door is a restaurant. At one time *ristorante* meant that it was more elegant and expensive than a *trattoria* or an *osteria*, but in Italy's big cities these distinctions no longer mean anything. As with many of the restaurants in Trastevere this one specializes in fish. The Macelleria, no. 48, is a meat store, but, as the sign says, it sells only lamb and chicken. The Alimentari is the dry goods store; on the wall next to the entrance are little metal plates from the government announcing that the store is allowed to sell seed oil, wine vinegar, margarine, processed milk, cheese, and butter. Other items are also sold but you can be sure that even this store won't provide one-stop shopping. Across the way is the Torrefazione Filipetti, which roasts its own coffee and sells a variety of gourmet items.

As you may have guessed, specialization is the system here in Rome. There are a few supermarkets, but they tend to be on the outskirts of the city along with their modern counterparts, the suburbs. In the center of the city the compulsory morning *cappuccino* is followed by a daily visit to a number of stores and to the open market for fresh fruits and vegetables. The pretext for this daily event is the need for fresh food, but in fact it is social. These grocers are usually the friendliest people in the neighborhood, and in addition to the items on a shopping list come the intimacies that draw people's lives together.

Turn left by the Alimentari onto Via dell'Arco dei Tolomei, which is filled with the details that make this neighborhood so charming. The steep incline is, no doubt, another one of those *montes* created by the accumulation of dirt over an unexcavated archeological site. In the air is the aroma of baking bread; a sign on the narrow door of no. 24B announces that at 6:00 A.M., Raphael, the baker, leaves with baskets of his produce so please don't block his entrance. To your right, leading to a wooden door at no. 9, is an outside staircase. This typical medieval entrance is decorated with fragments of carved marble and looks like it may well lead to a small enclosed garden, a typical part of medieval house plans. The house itself is painted that burnt orange that dresses so much of Rome, and one of its windows has been blocked up to make room for another of this city's many shrines to the Virgin and Child.

Ahead is one of those buildings whose structure spans centuries of architectural styles, from the medieval to the baroque. The history associated with it is equally interesting. In ancient times this was the site of the estate of the Anici family, a wealthy clan who in the sixth century produced Pope Gregory the Great, the first pope of the Middle Ages in Rome. The original medieval structure with its tower and arch was built by the Tolomei family of Siena, who claimed to be descendants of the Ptolemies of Egypt and came to Italy with Charlemagne. Today it is a Jewish orphanage, one of the few reminders of the community that had originally established itself in southern Trastevere during the time of Augustus.

The street curves and is soon engulfed by a dark massive stone arch, the Arco dei Tolomei. In the far left corner is a rare and practical reminder of the city's past, an open urinal. These public conveniences are known as *Vespasiani* after the Roman emperor Vespasian (from whom the statue of Caesar on the island turned in disgust). Vespasian made a considerable income during his reign from the sale of the contents of the city's urinals, which, one writer says, were used for fulling woolen cloth and also may have been, as in China in the 1930s, sold to farmers for fertilizer. While not many of these once numerous items are left in the city, a few more private versions along the two streets bordering the river are the cause of mild blasphemy when the congested traffic comes to a complete halt and a driver jumps out of his car for a quick stop.

We leave the Arco dei Tolomei and head straight along the Via Anicia, a more open area filled with the institutions that are also a feature of this neighborhood. To your left is a local school; farther down are the high walls of a convent. To the right, amidst the anonymous buildings, a couple of restorers' studios catch the eye with their variety of eclectic inventories. At the end of the block, on the corner of Via dei Genovesi, is a captivating view of the medieval campanile and Romanesque apse of the Church of S. Cecilia behind the bare convent wall. In July this otherwise lifeless street is festooned with arches of multicolored lights decorating the parade of *Noantri*, "We others," which is the Trasteverini's festival. For an entire month they celebrate their heritage with a mixture of religious, cultural, and commercial fanfare that ends with an explosion of fireworks on top of the Gianicolo Hill.

Halfway down the next bock, to your right at no. 12, is a plaque that identifies the Confraternity of S. Giovanni Battista dei Genovesi. Ring the button on the lower left-hand corner for the *guardiano*. He will open the door to the most beautiful fifteenth-century cloister in Rome. This is one of those hidden spots in Rome that gives this already well-endowed city such a

special place in the heart of all romantics. The cloister and its adjoining convent were built in 1481 for the colony of sailors from Genova who resided near the river's port. Conceived by Meliaduce Cicala, Pope Sixtus IV's treasurer, it was dedicated to St. John the Baptist, protector of the city and port of Genova. The lush garden is circumscribed by stately octagonal columns supporting a double loggia designed by Baccio Pontelli, one of the pre-Bramante architects of the early Renaissance in Rome. In the center, surrounded by orange trees and fragrant jasmine, is a well framed by two marble columns. Within this protected space Antonio Lanza in 1588 planted Rome's first palm tree.

The church attached to the cloister is usually closed. Inside, the simple design of a nave without a transept has been completely restored, meaning, as it usually does in Italy, that it was altered during the last century. It is interesting to note that the money to pay for this work came from Rome's Genovese community, who still have a strong attachment to their ancestral home. Among the few remains of the ancient church are the fine tomb of the founder, Meliaduce Cicala, which is an example of the work done in the shops of Mino da Fiesole and Bregno. The principal tabernacle is from the eighteenth century, as are the altarpiece and other objects in the sacristy. An inscription on the wall commemorates the birth in this hospice of the baritone Antonio Cotogni, 1831–1914.

Back on Via Anicia, to your right as you exit, you pass the Vicolo dei Tabacchi. This name, odd for a street, comes from the tobacco factory around the corner that was founded in 1863 by Pope Pius IX. The factory was part of his plan to industrialize Rome, which, unlike other Italian cities, never developed a vigorous manufacturing economy. The factory was also an effort directed specifically at the population of Trastevere, who never enjoyed the economic prosperity of their neighbors across the Tiber. Past this street, at no. 11, is an example of more contemporary planning measures—a recreation center for the unemployed and the retired.

Follow this seemingly lifeless street for another block until you reach (on the right) the Church of S.

The Arco dei Tolomei

Maria dell'Orto, with its curious series of obelisks across the top. The church harks back to the days when this part of Trastevere and beyond was a large field cultivated by truck farmers who supplied the city with fruits and vegetables. Built under the auspices of the Corporation of Fruit Growers, the church is a tribute to the economic and social power of guilds in fifteenth-century Rome. These guilds were at once trade organizations, social networks, and religious sodalities with origins dating back to the empire. However, it wasn't until the fifteenth century that they became an integral part of the city's social fabric. Essentially they were local organizations that, aside from setting strict requirements for the exercise of their particular craft, served important welfare functions, such as financing the dowries of poverty-stricken members, paying for members' funerals, and funding orphanages and hospitals. On the whole they were autonomous organizations but ultimate control was held by the Vatican.

S. Maria dell'Orto and the attached hospital included among its patrons a large cross-section of the population of Trastevere: the delicatessen workers, the shoemakers, the millers, the merchants and brokers of the court of Ripa, the pastamakers, the grape growers, the chicken sellers, the fruit sellers, and the lemon growers. The church was dedicated to a Madonna who was painted on the wall of one of the gardens. In the sixteenth century the reputation of this "Madonna of the Gardens" spread beyond the confines of Trastevere to, of all places, Japan. The story is told that on the occasion of Rome's first Japanese visitors, a group of recently converted Catholics coming to pay their respects to Pope Gregory XIII, the Vatican organized a trip for them down the Tiber to Ostia. It was a splendid flotilla meant to impress and entertain the guests, but halfway the journey was interrupted by a terrible storm. Only when the captain, a Trasteverino, invoked the Madonna dell'Orto did the storm subside, leaving on these tourists a lasting impression of the miraculous powers of this virgin.

The construction of the church began in 1419; until its completion in 1579 a number of Rome's architects were involved. Guidetto Guidetti is generally credited with the body of the church; Vignola, with the façade. Other names associated with various stages of the church's construction are Raphael and Francesco da Volterra. The obelisks, which are such a distinguishing mark of the church, were probably added in 1762. The interior is only open for Sunday morning services, but it is worth a special trip to see the opulence of its decor. Between the vestry and the altar is an area covered with stucco work of the Neapolitan-Roman school, and in it is a splendidly carved wooden turkey donated in the eighteenth century by the chicken sellers' guild to commemorate the arrival of the first turkey from America. The sumptuous baroque decor includes frescoes by di Taddeo, Frederico Zuccari, Giovanni Baglioni, Corrado Giaquinto, and, on the main altar, Giacomo della Porta. The vault is wrapped in the stucco and gilt work of the eighteenth century. On the back wall is an impressive organ. When you enter on a Sunday morning you join a congregation still associated—either as descendants or current members of the same trades—with the guilds that made this church. Those once-important institutions are now nothing more than religious sodalities, but here at S. Maria dell'Orto their rituals continue as they have for centuries.

To the right of the church is an attached building with a lone tree standing in the courtyard. This was the hospital and pharmacy associated with the church; they were built in 1739 by Valvassare, the confraternity's architect at the time. Today sections of it have been taken over by the tobacco factory and the rest has become dwelling units.

Note the *edicola* in the wall across from the church to your left. This is reminiscent of the original shrine in the 1400s that initiated the Trasteverini's following for the Madonna dell'Orto.

We continue our walk on the Via della Madonna dell'Orto, straight ahead from the entrance to the church. To your left is a large institutional building covered with Communist party graffiti, Trastevere being one of the party's strongholds in Rome. The building is a high school named after Italy's first queen, Regina Margherita, who inaugurated it herself in March 1888. In Italy children start specializing in the ninth grade; they may choose a classical college preparatory course, a scientific and technical one, or a trade school. This one is a professional trade school.

To your right behind the wall is a military unit encamped in one of the gardens, which until the turn of the century still produced fruits and vegetables. This military camp is suggestive of days in ancient Rome when troops camped in the fields on this side of the river to defend the city from the threat of the Etruscans. Here also was the sacred grove of the goddess Furina, where Gaius Sempronius Gracchus was killed in 123 B.C. after the failure of his reforms: protected by his friends, Gracchus had escaped from the Aventine and crossed the Tiber at the Pons Subblicius with his servant Philocrates. When they failed to find a horse to continue their escape Philocrates killed his master and then himself. The senate, in the meantime, had issued a proclamation stating that anyone who brought them the head of Gracchus would receive its weight in gold. Septimulenus, when he found the bodies, cut off Gracchus's head and filled it with lead. He walked into Rome with the head on the top of his spear and was paid the promised reward.

Beyond, on the left and looming directly in front of us, is the Ospizio di S. Michele. This immense complex occupies 27,000 square meters and encompasses several buildings around courtyards and two churches. Its construction spans a period of 150 years, from 1672 to the beginning of the nineteenth century. Originally founded by Cardinal Odescalchi, nephew of Innocent XI, this was a refuge for vagabond children. Here they were properly housed and taught a trade. Later a variety of papal assistance programs were added for the aged poor, juvenile delinquents, lone women, and mendicants.

Out of this institution's provisions to train their charges in the industrial arts rose the city's most important craft schools and workshops in tapestry, typography, bookbinding, weaving, etching, woodcarving, sculpting, welding, tailoring, etc. Among the alumni were etchers Pietro Mercuri and Luigi Colamatta and sculptor Ercole Rose.

On the whole the complex is purely functional with little if any architectural character, even though Carlo Fontana worked on the design. To him is attributed the first prototype of a juvenile correctional facility that for a long time was the basis, both in concept and design, for all such facilities in Europe. Ferdinando Fuga also worked on this complex, unifying its long façade near the river's edge.

This institution, once central to the city's social welfare and artisan endeavors, was slowly dismantled at the beginning of this century and dispersed among various government bodies. For decades it stood abandoned; since 1970 it has been in the process of being restored, in a rather fitting transition, for use by the Ministry of Cultural Affairs and Restoration.

Turn left at the end of the street onto Via di S. Michele. Immediately to your right in a building of the Ospizio di S. Michele is the entrance to ICCROM, the International Center for the Study and Preservation of Cultural Property, an institute started in the 1960s after the disastrous flooding in Florence. Since then ICCROM has contributed greatly to the preservation of art works in Italy and throughout the world. Continue down the street for a block to Piazza di S. Cecilia. Here we return to a more residential section of the neighborhood.

Set behind a large iron gate, to your left as you enter the piazza, is the dramatic entrance to the Church of S. Cecilia. The church stands behind a garden courtyard adorned with a magnificent classical vase in its center. As we walk through the gate we step into centuries of history, most of them documented by works of art. We also step into the equivalent of the neighborhood's park, filled with the season's blooming flowers and the gentle sound of the water flowing down the vase's brilliant white body. A bench offers some rest in pleasant surroundings and some time to read about the life of St. Cecilia.

Stories of the saints' lives were once the basis of the earliest guidebooks to Rome, written for the pilgrims whose visit to this capital of Christianity was intended solely as a religious experience. The details of St. Cecilia's life seem appropriate here because of the important inspiration she has been to Western art: in poetry from Chaucer to Dryden and Pope; in art from Raphael to Cimabue, Tintoretto, and Rubens; and in music as its patroness. Furthermore, the church is built on the site of her home and naturally evokes the drama of Christianity's struggle in ancient Rome. Ruins from her home can be seen in the basement of church but here, in the *cortile*, the vase suggests the fountain that may once have adorned the peristyle of the Valerii family.

St. Cecilia is said to have lived during the time of Marcus Aurelius and was the daughter of one of Rome's noble families. She was married to Valerian, a member of another illustrious family, but maintained her vow of virginity taken when she became a Christian. She later converted her husband and her brother-in-law. One reason for her association with music probably comes from this story: when her husband returned from being baptized he found her singing hymns of triumph for this event, which was meant to be a surprise to her. But her rejoicing soon ended in a series of tragedies. Valerian and his brother Tiburtius were beheaded for refusing to worship the Roman gods. Cecilia inherited the fortunes of both men, becoming one of the wealthiest women in Rome and the object of great resentment. It wasn't long before the prefect of Rome, Almachius, condemned her to death as well. This decision, we are told, was motivated more out of jealousy for her wealth than fear of her religion.

She was locked in the *sudatorium,* "steam room," of the baths in her own house and kept there for three days with the fires blazing. According to the story in the *Lives of the Saints*, "God sent a cooling shower" and when the door was finally open she was found singing "with a voice of such sweetness" that it was clear she was still very much alive. Fearing the consequences of this story and its association with such a prominent Roman family, Almachius immediately sent one of his guards to behead her. After three blows of an ax, the most allowed by law, she remained alive for three days. During that short time she converted more than four hundred people to Catholicism and bequeathed her palace to the Church for the construction of a chapel. She, "who sang to God in her heart to the sound of musical instruments," is remembered on November 22 with concerts. The Academy of Music in Rome is named after her.

Pope Urban I founded and consecrated a church in her palace. This was rebuilt by Pope Pascal I in 821

The entrance to the Church of S. Cecilia

when, according to an account in the Vatican archives, St. Cecilia appeared in his dreams and revealed her burial site in the catacombs of St. Calixtus. The remains of her body were then transferred to the new church. In 1599 the saint's legend enters the domain of verified history when Cardinal Sfondrato opened the tomb and found her body absolutely intact and dressed in a shimmering golden robe. Led by Pope Clement VIII, all of Rome came to see this miracle, including the sculptor Stefano Maderno, who carefully sketched Cecilia's graceful pose. In celebration of this event the church was restored and a statue of the saint by Stefano Maderno was commissioned.

In the convent adjoining the church a fascinating medieval ritual continues to be maintained. Here the nuns weave the papal pallia, narrow bands of white wool decorated with six black crosses. The pope wears the pallium around his neck over the chasuble. Every year on January 21, the feast of St. Agnes, two lambs are carried to the Church of S. Agnese on the Via Nomentana during the singing of "Agnus Dei" (Lamb of God). The lambs lie on the altar in wicker baskets decorated with blue ribbons and, after the pope has blessed them, are sent here to the convent of the Church of S. Cecilia. They are specially cared for by the nuns until Holy Thursday when they are shorn to make wool for the twelve pallia that are made every year. After the pallia are woven the nuns hand them over to the subdeacons of St. John the Lateran, who hand them to the subdeacons of St. Peter's, who, in turn, hand them to the canons. They are then placed in a golden casket beneath the high altar at St. Peter's, which is built above the traditional tomb of the apostles.

In the early days of the Church the pallium was worn only by the pope; even today only he may wear it on all occasions. This, one of the most ancient of ritual vestments, is older than the papal tiara and far more significant. In fact, during the papal coronation the most solemn moment comes when the new pope is vested with the pallium, a symbol of his role as the shepherd of Christ's flock.

Now look at the exterior details of the church. The bell tower and the portico were built in the twelfth century. This bell tower, to the right as you face the church, stands out amidst the thirty-eight Romanesque campaniles left in Rome as one of the most impressive. The atrium incorporated into the eighteenth-century façade by Fuga has antique marble columns from ancient Roman ruins and a mosaic frieze with medallions of the heads of Cecilia, Valerian, Tiburtius, Urban I, and other saints. Along the walls are several medieval tombs and inscriptions, as well as fragments of crosses and sculpture.

Walk through the portico into the church. This transition is rather shocking, as what we immediately see is not the expected ancient church, but eighteenth-century stylistic details. The ancient marble columns have been encased and a fresco of the *Apotheosis of S. Cecilia* by Sebastiano Conca covers the ceiling. A further restoration in 1822 almost concealed every medieval feature but a more discerning look will show us marvelous examples from this period and others; the church is almost an anthology of Italian art.

To the right of the main door is the fine tomb of Adam Easton, titular cardinal of the church, who died in 1398. The tomb bears the coat of arms of the Plantagenets, members of the English royal house founded by Geoffrey, Count of Anjou. To the left of the door is another tomb by Mino da Fiesole, which is noteworthy for its simplicity and delicacy; buried here is Cardinal Forteguerri who died in 1473. Passing the first chapel on the right enter a narrow passage decorated with landscapes by Pomarancio Paul Brill. This leads into the *sudatorium* where Cecilia survived the first attempt on her life. Lining the walls are fragments of the ancient terra-cotta pipes used to conduct the steam from the boiler. On the wall is Guido Reni's *Marriage and Martyrdom of St. Cecilia*. The next chapel is the Ponziani family chapel with frescoes of the school of Pinturicchio and Antonio da Viterbo. Beyond that is a chapel of relics designed by Vanvitelli, a *Madonna and Child* by Perugino, and a last chapel with an unfortunate example of twentieth-century neo-baroque sculpture.

The apse of the church is decorated with fine Byzantine mosaics from the ninth century. The Savior stands in a golden robe; at his side are Saints Peter, Paul, Cecilia, Valerian, Pascal carrying the model of his church, and Agatha. Also represented are the mystic palm trees and phoenix, symbols of eternity, and beneath that, the four rivers and twelve sheep that represent the apostles walking through the gates of Bethlehem and Jerusalem to the adoration of the lamb. If you are lucky you will see the nuns moving silently like giant white butterflies against this mosaic and, in the tradition of St. Cecilia, hear them singing their prayers in a lovely a cappella that resonates throughout the church.

Above the main altar stands Arnolfo di Cambio's noble canopy dating from 1283, and below that lies Stefano Maderno's inspiring representation of St. Cecilia as he saw her when the coffin was open—lying on her side in a state of peaceful and elegant repose, her robe gracefully molding her body and limbs, and her neck showing the wounds from the three blows. So impressive is the masterpiece of this Lombard sculptor that Gregorovius said, "Hardly a more gracious figure was created by the imagination of Christian art."

The rather stiff Byzantine qualities of the background mosaic stand in pointed contrast to Maderno's work, and both these pieces must be compared to Pietro Cavallini's fresco, which at the end of the thirteenth century forever buried the Byzantine style and paved the way for the Renaissance. This important fresco is in the back of the church in an upper gallery once used by women (a custom brought to Rome by the Eastern Church). This area is now part of the convent and a tour must be arranged. (Go through the door to your right at the end of the church near the entrance to make arrangements.)

Ghiberti wrote of Cavallini, with an enthusiasm we cannot help but share, "This most learned and noble of artists." While only two of his major works exist—the *Last Judgment* here in this church painted about 1293, and his mosaic of the story of the Virgin at S. Maria in Trastevere—one look at this fresco is enough to confirm Cavallini's genius. In the fresco Christ sits enthroned and surrounded by angels with outspread wings dressed in jeweled robes. They are depicted in deep pastel colors in an array of tones and shades that even Missoni has not been able to duplicate. Above this are the apostles and saints painted in grays and blues. This is one of the most beautiful frescoes in Rome and is especially remarkable for its age and for the fact that it is pre-Giotto.

Ask the person at the desk where you pay to see the Cavallini frescoes about a visit to the crypt. There you will see a good imitation of the Byzantine by Giovenale, the sarcophagi of the saints, and some older underground structures including the pavement of a bath house and some republican columns.

Leave the church and courtyard as you entered and return to the Piazza di S. Cecilia. Across from the entrance of the church is another medieval house, the Casa dei Ponzani, whose family chapel we saw in the church. What these houses actually looked like in medieval Rome is hard to visualize because most, like this one, have been heavily restored. This house is an example of several structures fused into a single complex; the raised corner gives us the impression of an ancient tower, and across the façade are signs of an ancient portico constructed to unify the various parts.

Walk toward the house. Along its side is the beginning of the Piazza dei Mercanti, which more than any other part of the neighborhood evokes the spirit of the old port of Ripa Grande. In the past this piazza was busy with the activities of Syrian porters carrying litters, Jewish moneylenders, sailors and bargemen of the Tiber, dockworkers, tradesmen, and brokers. Here corn was unloaded from Sicily and Africa, wine from Chios, marble from Paros and Luna, and all kinds of luxurious merchandise from the East. It was anything but this now quiet and charming space, carefully restored to give a flavor of the medieval and flanked by restaurants.

At the far end of the L-shaped piazza is a small, picturesque medieval house at no. 18. On its exterior staircase there is little distinction between inside and out—it is an entry, a stand for flowerpots, a storage area, an extension of the living room, and a place to hang the laundry. Ten steps farther is the intersection with the Via del Porto and a place from which you get a splendid view of the Aventine Hill. From here we see none of the new constructions, just the high wall covered with vegetation and crowned with churches and bell towers—S. Sabina, S. Alessio, S. Maria del Priorato, and S. Anselmo. At the end of the street once

A restaurant on Piazza dei Mercanti

stood the Tiber's most important port, and in the fourteenth century we would have seen surrounding the port a number of churches and watchtowers. Within the monotonous façade of the Ospizio di S. Michele is the Church of S. Maria della Torre, better known to the users of the port as the Church of the Madonna del Buon Viaggio, Madonna of the Safe Trip. The tower that gave the church its name, of which there is only a trace (not visible to us standing on this street), corresponded with another on the opposite bank of the Tiber. Both were built in the middle of the ninth century and between them a chain was stretched to close the river to traffic and to protect the city against an attack by the Saracens. This pair was but one of a series along the river, some of which can still be seen outside the Porta Portese.

Retrace your steps past the Siena-red "stage-set" house and walk straight ahead to the Vicolo di S. Maria in Cappella. This is one of those typical narrow streets framed by a string of dangling ivy. Its small houses, low dark entrances, small windows, and arched wooden doors preserve the look, if not all the habits, of this ancient quarter. We mustn't forget that in the days when everything was thrown into the gutter, it was a wise precaution to have as few windows as possible looking outward. Instead, attention was directed to the inner courtyard or garden, something that most if not all of these houses have behind their workshops. While this street may look as it did centuries ago, work habits have changed; now we have a carpenter making custom furniture and a movie production house. To the right is a single building combining an old-age home with a public shelter. Here the homeless poor can find refuge from the streets after sundown and a bed for the evening.

At the end of the block to your right is the entrance to the miniature Romanesque Church of S. Maria in Cappella. Here there is no elaborate iron gate and beautiful garden, just a spare desolate square. Still, it has a charm all its own: petite, adorned with a blue and white della Robbiaesque image of the Virgin, and a bell tower said to be the smallest in Rome. This church dates back to 1090 and was one of the many associated with the merchant community of the old port. In the fifteenth century it became the headquarters for the barrelmakers' guild, which controlled one of the most important monopolies in the city, that of wine and transport.

In the seventeenth century Donna Olimpia Pamphili, Pope Innocent X's sister-in-law and the power behind the throne, turned the garden behind this church into a riverside playground. Two hundred years later, in 1860, her descendants displaced the garden with the building that is to your right as you face the church. It was the first old-age home for the poor in Rome and continues as such.

Leaving S. Maria in Cappella we follow Via Augusto Jandolo straight ahead. No. 6, to your left at the end of the block, is the home of *Facchini's* Cooperative, meaning not what in common vocabulary is the word for "coarse" and "vulgar," but rather "porters." Here the unemployed youth of Trastevere find temporary work using their muscles. A few steps beyond this is the intersection with Via dei Vascellari, named for the boatbuilders who for centuries kept up a busy trade in this neighborhood. On the same path, past the inter- section, the street becomes the Via dei Genovesi and suddenly we have a lively section of shops, grocery stores, a bar, and a restaurant.

Turn right at the next street, just beyond no. 33, into the narrow Vicolo dell'Atleta. Here you enter one of the most unique and characteristic streets of the medi- eval city. In the few meters of its length the street curves, divides, and widens; and on its path are a com- bination of elements that create this neighborhood's ambiance. At one point this street is so narrow that the marble post placed on a curve to prevent damage to the building is almost worn through from the carriage marks. Where it widens stands a fine fortified house with loggia, one of the few of its kind left in Rome. This is the most impressive of a series of old houses on this street. Across the way are the simple and unpre- tentious shops of a local furniture restorer and dress- maker, both of whom move their work out onto the street during warm weather. The Blue Inn Piano Bar and Nite Club waves its new awning at the next curve, warning us of the changes slowly making their way into this neighborhood that for so long a time was untouched by the trend now established in northern Trastevere. On this street in 1849 was discovered the Apoxyomenos, a sculpture of an athlete using a stigil, copied from an original by Lysippus. Thus the street's name, Vicolo dell'Atleta, "Street of the Athlete." The Apoxyomenos is on view at the Vatican Museum.

This *vicolo* leads us to the Via dei Salumi, where once sausagemakers had their warehouses for storing salami. This trade is not typically Roman but rather that of people from the mountain regions of Tuscany and the Abruzzi. They, along with the Syrians, Greeks, Jews, and Genovesi, help disprove the Trasteverini's age-old claim of descendence from "pure stock." In this neighborhood, more than elsewhere in Rome, the population fits the more modern criteria for a true Ro- man—that forefathers should be established here no later than 1850. The city's population of 200,000 in 1870 was doubled by 1900, augmented by another million in 1946, and since then by more than 2 mil- lion. Without belaboring the statistics it is clear that most of Rome's citizens are Johnny-come-latelies, hailing from all over Italy, but primarily from the south. While the Trasteverini have helped accommodate this huge insurge, true to their parochial character they have been less willing to share their neighborhood than the Romans across the river. Only in the 1960s, with the help of the expatriate American community, did Trastevere become a fashionable bohemian quarter. The southern end, however, was spared that onslaught except for some scattered artists' studios. Today, no section of Rome is free from the modern real estate boom.

Already, before this and as we enter Via dei Salumi, we see the signs of change. Here it is visible both at the street level with its funky used-clothing store and up above with the green traces of an elegant rooftop terrace. This latter, so seemingly Roman, was introduced to the city by the British in this century. Next to this the less than posh car body shop across the street and the used metal trader a few yards ahead hang on to give a more typical image of Trastevere's business life.

The first intersection to your right is the Via Titta Scarpetta. It was originally named only Scarpetta after a carved marble foot that stood along its path. After the foot was stolen the city government found the street's name, which meant "shoe," unseemly and no longer appropriate. With the cunning resourcefulness often attributed to the Trasteverini, one of its residents remembered Scarpetta Giovambattista, called Titta, who fought for the defense of Malta against the Turks in 1559. Thanks to this vague historical figure a compromise was reached and the residents were able to keep their street name.

To your left is the junior high school, Goffredo Mameli, named for a Genovese compatriot, poet, and soldier who died in combat for the republic in 1849. He wrote several martial hymns and is best remembered for his song "*Fratelli d'Italia*," "Italian Brothers." Across from this, on our right, we pass the Via in Piscinula. On that street lives an older man who every day stacks a wooden handcart full of books and trudges with it across the island and at least another ten blocks to sell his books at the Piazza dei Librai along the Via dei Giubbonari. His efforts are especially impressive given the fact that he is the only one to

keep up the tradition of bookselling on that square, which was named for the Roman booksellers.

Keep walking down Via dei Salumi. At the end of the block occupied by the school we find ourselves once again at the intersection of Via Anicia and Via Arco dei Tolomei. From this perspective we can better admire the remains of an ancient medieval tower at no. 32 and some of the detailing on the ancient Tolomei family residence. Continue another block down Via dei Salumi until you come to the Via della Luce.

The house on the left corner usually has a canary hanging in a cage outside of the second-story window, a sight reminiscent of travels in southern Italy where there is a canary by the entrance to almost every house. This habit comes from the belief that if a curse is put on a house it will fall on the smallest member of the family—in other words, the canary and not the children. This family appears to have the double protection of both the canary and a Madonna over the building's entrance.

We will take a small detour to our right down Via della Luce. Immediately to your left is a Casalinga with its colorful display of household items pouring out onto the street and hanging around the entrance. Here a mother/housewife finds almost anything she may need for her home, ranging from disposable diapers and toys for the children to a garlic press and a broom. It is the one store in every Roman neighborhood with the largest variety of items, almost equivalent to our five-and-dime. Next door is a shop especially important to this neighborhood, which was the last section of town to get gaslights in the nineteenth century and which even today has many apartments that do not have access to the city's gas lines. The shop sells *bombole*, the gas tanks used for cooking and heating.

Across the street, at no. 3A, is one of those unique stores that makes shopping such an adventure in this city. Specializing in stucco, the shop offers a variety of decorative pieces: capitals, columns, moldings, masks, reliefs, and plaques. A glimpse into the front of the shop is like looking at one of Piranesi's collage series or a colorless Joseph Cornell on the theme of Rome.

Across the street is the church of S. Maria della Luce.

The Casalinga on Via della Luce

Both the church and the street take their name from a miracle that took place on March 28, 1730. The story is told that a young unemployed man was about to commit suicide by throwing himself into the Tiber near Ponte Cestio when he saw the image of the Virgin Mary against the peeling paint of an ancient wall. This apparition caused him to forget his anxieties; after a few days he was even able to find a job. Later a blind man recovered his sight thanks to the same virgin, who then became known as St. Mary of the Light. The miraculous image was transferred to this (renamed) church, which was originally built in the twelfth century and named S. Salvatore in Corte. At about the same time the church was rebuilt and only the apse and the campanile survive from the earlier structure. The façade, designed by Gabrieli Valvassari, was never completed.

Retrace your path half a block to the intersection with Via dei Salumi and make a right-hand turn onto the small Vicolo del Buco, which winds its way around the Church of S. Maria della Luce. As you round the curve beyond the restaurant you can admire a small medieval house and the elegantly simple Romanesque apse of S. Maria della Luce. This brings us to the Piazza del Drago. Straight ahead, toward the modern buildings, is the Via di Monte Fiore. Turn left down this street, whose name recalls the period in Trastevere's history when the area was full of flowering gardens, and walk one block.

On the corner to your right is the explanation for the name originally given to the church we just passed—S. Salvatore in Corte. Here in the first century was the Coorte dei Vigili, the ancient Roman fire station for the region of Trastevere. These ruins of a large building partly visible from the street were discovered only in 1866 beneath other construction. If it is open you can see the atrium covered with ancient graffiti and the *impluvium* used to catch rainwater.

Return to the Via di Monte Fiore. At the intersection is a picturesque grouping of medieval houses, one with an outside staircase. It was here in 1656 that the first case of the plague that devastated all of Europe was discovered.

Pass the Piazza del Drago and make a right onto Via della Lungaretta, once an important route for pilgrims between St. Peter's and St. Paul's Outside the Walls. While Pope Julius II is responsible for paving this street we do not find here the examples of papal opulence and control that are so visible in other neighborhoods in the historic center. The houses that line this street continued to be of the same dimensions and type as their predecessors, interrupted occasionally by a compact baronial house and not a palazzo. Even the churches are scattered about the neighborhood and not focused along a particular path.

Today this is a commercial street lined with a bakery shop, a dry cleaner, a restaurant, a shoe repair shop, bars, and a lottery and off-track betting stand. On your right, halfway down the first block, no. 25 is the Open Book Shop, which specializes in new and used English-language books. It caters to the fairly large British and American population here in Rome and the occasional tourist who makes his way to this section of Trastevere. Further down to your left, at no. 161, is an old-fashioned *latteria*, "milk bar," with its black-and-white tiled floors, white marble counter and tabletops, and white tile walls. Not many of these *latteria*— where you can sit and enjoy a drink as well as buy eggs and milk products—are left. In fact this *latteria* is so old-fashioned that it is now stylish. Next to it is yet another charming example of medieval architecture with crenelated design across the front and an outside staircase leading to a side entrance.

As we continue down the next thirty yards of Via della Lungaretta there is one final observation to be made about Roman life from the street—the shutters. If you haven't already noticed them you will see that every window has a pair of shutters that is usually closed. The most common assumption is that Romans love their privacy, but more than that, these shutters are an elaborate means of temperature control. During the summer they are open only in the early morning and again as the sun sets to capture the cool breeze. In the winter (and you can't imagine how cold and damp these old houses get) they are open only when the sun is shining in order to capture some heat and then are bolted tight to keep the wind and rain out. The rules are so stringently observed by all Romans that, whenever one sees a window whose shutters are not conforming to the routine of the others, it is safe to assume that the apartment is inhabited by foreigners.

In the nineteenth century Roesler Franz document-ed in watercolors the street life of Trastevere. There is one painting of a scene on the Via della Lungaretta that shows what a depressed area this was at that time. Large pools of water formed in the street where the cobblestones were missing, and in place of horses and carriages he saw two oxen pulling a cart. Around that were slums and destitution. This was a typical street scene in the Trastevere of pre-1870. While this certain-ly does not describe the street or the neighborhood to-day, there remains a clear image of this neighborhood as having a hardy and simple working-class population that is more suspicious and less extroverted than its neighbors across the river.

The Via della Lungaretta returns us to the Piazza in Piscinula, where our walk ends. The bar in the piazza gives an opportunity to sit back and watch the street scene. Today, they no longer play *morra*—the *micare digitis* of their ancestors that sometimes left the man holding the wrong finger-count dead—but the con-stant gesturing closely resembles that old game. Al-ways there is unrestrained enthusiasm about the coffee, the weather, the soccer scores, one's health, and, most of all, beauty. Their response to beauty is verbalized by the Trasteverini's own poet, Belli:

What a great gift of God beauty is!
You have to put it higher than money:
Because riches won't give you that
and with that you get rich.

A church, a cow, a girl
if they are ugly, you despise them and don't look at
    them:
and God himself, who is a well of wisdom,
the mother he took he wanted beautiful.

No doors are closed to beauty:
Everybody makes sweet eyes about it, and
    everybody
Sees the blame in it after the excuse.

Look at the kittens, my dear friend.
The prettiest are raised: and the ugly one?
The poor ugly ones go to the garbage heap.

Restaurants and Shops

Restaurants

It is hard to find a bad meal in Rome, so don't hesitate to walk into any of the many *trattoria*, *ristorante*, or *osteria* that may catch your eye. Below is a short list of some of my favorites. All restaurants close one day a week so it is wise to call beforehand to make sure they are open.

ELEGANT AND MORE EXPENSIVE (Reservations a Must)

Alberto Chiarla, Piazza San Cosimato 40, tel. 58-86-68. At this elegant seafood restaurant, which serves only dinner, you will be greeted with a glass of sparkling wine. The menu includes fresh oysters, lobster, an assortment of grilled fish, and, of course, pasta. There is no meat dish. (In Trastevere, not far from Walk 4.)

Carmelo alla Rosetta, Via della Rosetta 9, tel. 656-10-02. This restaurant, in a more casual setting, claims to have the freshest fish in town; they, too, serve only fish. Try the risotto made of squid in its own ink. (Near the Pantheon.)

Coriolano, Via Ancona 14, tel. 86-11-22. You will dine in an atmosphere more reminiscent of Switzerland than of Italy but the food is Italian at its best. They also have one of the largest wine cellars in Rome. (A cab ride away in the northern section of town.)

G.B., Via delle Carceri 6, tel. 656-93-36. At this exclusive restaurant you must ring the bell to get in. While a favorite of all elegant Romans, it is especially popular among the French residents and visitors. Here, too, they serve only dinner. (Near Walk 3, off Via Giulia.)

Papa Giovanni, Via dei Sediari 4, tel. 656-53-08. Here they pride themselves on nouvelle Italian cuisine, and their huge cellar is stocked with the best of Italian and French wines. (Near the Piazza Navona.)

Pino e Dino, Piazza di Montevecchio 22, tel. 656-12-19. The two brothers who run this restaurant serve you the best seasonal dishes in a charming setting, which during the summer includes outdoor dining in a quiet piazza. One word of warning, the service is not always what it should be. (Walk 1.)

MODERATE

Buca di Ripetta, Via di Ripetta 36, tel. 678-95-78. Run by a family, this is the kind of restaurant in which you would feel happy to eat all of your meals. (Near the Piazza del Popolo.)

Campana, Vicolo della Campana 18, tel. 65-52-73. This is not the prettiest restaurant in Rome, but it is recognized for its good food at good prices. (Near the beginning of Walk 1.)

Cannovata, Piazza San Giovanni in Laterano 20, tel. 77-50-07. This is a classic Roman restaurant offering very good value. (Across from St. John the Lateran.)

Galeassi, Piazza S. Maria in Trastevere 3, tel. 580-37-75. You can dine outside and watch the endless parade in the piazza, which is situated in the heart of Trastevere. They serve both fresh fish and meat dishes. (Near Walk 4 in northern Trastevere.)

La Tana di Noantri, Via della Paglia 1–3, tel. 580-64-04. Another favorite restaurant in Trastevere, this is always crowded with Romans as well as tourists. The food here is good and reasonably priced. (Near Walk 4 in northern Trastevere.)

Otello alla Concordia, Via della Croce 81, tel. 679-11-78. A good lunch place situated near the Via Condotti and the Spanish Steps shopping area.

Nino, Via Borgognona 11, tel. 67-56-76. Another favorite lunch place near the Spanish Steps, this one is also good for a quiet dinner.

Pier Luigi, Piazza de Ricci 144, tel. 656-13-02. Especially popular among the young professionals and students, this is a friendly restaurant that has tables on the piazza during warm weather. (Walk 3.)

Sora Lella, Via Ponte Quattro Capi 16, tel. 656-99-07. Situated on the island, this Roman restaurant serves the hardy food typical of small neighborhood *trattoria*. (Walk 4.)

Vecchia Roma, Piazza Campitelli 18, tel. 656-46-04. Many of my friends consider this the best restaurant in Rome; certainly you will enjoy a magnificent meal in a pleasant setting. (Walk 2.)

REGIONAL

Ambassiate d'Abruzzo, Via Tacchini 26, tel. 87-82-56. This restaurant has wonderful atmosphere and specializes in the hardy cuisine of the mountainous Abruzzo region. You will be given an assortment of salami to nibble on as you study the menu. (In Parioli, north of the center.)

Colline Emiliane, Via Avignonesi 22, tel. 475-75-38. Specializing in the cuisine of Emilia Romagna, the chef prepares some of the best tortellini and boiled meats I have ever had. You come here not for the decor, but for the excellent food in a friendly atmosphere. (Near Piazza Barberini.)

Il Drappo, Vicolo del Malpasso 9, tel. 65-73-65. Sardinian food is served in a warm intimate setting with draped ceilings and flowers on every table. You will enjoy every bite of your meal, which is carefully prepared by the brother and sister who run this establishment. (Near Walk 3.)

Girarrosto Toscano, Via Campania 29, tel. 49-37-59. Highlighting Florentine cuisine, this is the best place in town for grilled steak. (Near the Via Veneto.)

Piperno, Piazza Monte Cenci 9, tel. 654-60-29. The best of the Roman Jewish restaurants, it specializes in such dishes as fried artichokes, fried mozzarella, and salt cod. It is also pleasantly located and some of its back rooms are the most elegant in town; be sure to ask for a table in the rear if you are not dining on the piazza. (Near Walk 2.)

Taverna Giulia, Vicolo dell'Oro 23, tel. 656-97-68. This is a Genovese restaurant with the best pesto in town. They also have that tasty, creamy walnut sauce used to coat oversized tortellini. (Near Walk 3.)

LESS EXPENSIVE

Fiaschetteria Beltrame, Via della Croce 39 (no phone). At this family-run establishment you sit wherever there is a seat, sharing your table with shopkeepers at lunch and with an artistic crowd at dinner. (Near the Spanish Steps.)

Il Palmiere, Via Chimarra 415 (no phone). This restaurant is a favorite among Roman students and is run by a group of young people including an Arab who adds his touch to the menu. Vegetables are especially good here. (Near Via Nazionale.)

WINE BARS

Enoteca al Parlamento, Via dei Perfetti 15. (Near the beginning of Walk 1.)

Enoteca Mimmio, Via del Boschetto 19. (Off Via Nazionale.)

CAFÉS AND ICE CREAM PARLORS

Alfredo Pica, Via della Seggiola. Go into this small bar for some of the best ice cream in town. (Located off Via Arenula, across from the Ministry of Justice, just a few blocks from Walk 2.)

Alemagna, Via del Corso 181. This is one of the biggest bars in Rome with a busy hot and cold lunch counter. (Near the Spanish Steps shopping area.)

Babington's Tea Room, Piazza di Spagna 23. If you are in the mood for a cup of tea and scones this is the place, but be prepared to pay an exorbitant price. (At the foot of the Spanish Steps.)

Caffè Greco, Via Condotti 86. In the nineteenth century this cafè attracted a crowd of writers, musicians, and artists; today it attracts a very fashionable set. Walk in if only to see its 1860s environment. (Near the Spanish Steps.)

Europeo, Piazza San Lorenzo in Lucina 33. Visit this bar for ice cream and Sicilian pastries. (Off the Via del Corso.)

Bar San Filippo, Via San Filippo 8. Out of the way in the northern Parioli section of town, but if you are a fanatic you will have to give it a try. (North of Piazza Hungaria.)

Giolitti, Via Uffici del Vicario 40. A visit here is a must; it is the most important ice cream parlor in Rome. You can have anything from a variety of chocolate flavors to watermelon with bits of chocolate made to resemble the seeds. (Between the Via del Corso and the Pantheon.)

Mella Stregata, Piazza Pasquale Paoli 1. This bar has the best *cornetto*—cresent-shaped breakfast rolls—in town. For me it was worth a long walk every morning. It is on your way to the Vatican. Their ice cream also has a good reputation. (Near Ponte Vittorio Emanuele II.)

Rosati, Piazza del Popolo 4. This fashionable café has been a favorite of Roman society for several generations. Its liberty-style decor competes with a view of one of the finest baroque piazzas in Rome. (On the Piazza del Popolo.)

Tre Scalini, Piazza Navona 30. Its view of the Bernini fountain and the *tartufo*—a ball of chocolate ice cream with bits of chocolate and a cherry in the middle—makes this a special hangout for both Romans and tourists. (On the Piazza Navona.)

FOR THE BEST CUP OF COFFEE

Sant'Eustachio, Piazza Sant'Eustachio 82. Here you will find the creamiest *cappuccino* in town. Their *granita di caffè*, chips of iced coffee, is also superb. (Near the Pantheon.)

La Tazza d'Oro, Via degli Orfani 84. This bar serves only coffee, and they take their product very seriously. Supposedly they are located here in order to make their brew with the

Acqua Virgine, considered the best of Roman waters. (Near the Pantheon.)

Shops

LEATHER GOODS AND SHOES

Gucci, Via Condotti 8. The most expensive of the designer's products. The Gucci Boutique, Via Borgognona 25, carries similar products at more reasonable prices.

Fendi, Via Borgognona 39. Expensive leather bags and suitcases all marked with the *F* trademark of the Fendi sisters.

Raphael Salto, Via Veneto 149. Men's and women's shoes.

Santini e Dominici, Via Frattina 120. Stylish shoes for the younger set.

Lily of Florence, Via Lombardia 38C. Specializes in narrow, American-size shoes for men and women.

Alexia, Via Nazionale 76. Moderately priced leather bags and accessories.

Pier Caranti, Piazza di Spagna 43. One of the few shops in Rome that carries Bottega Veneto bags.

Tradate, Via del Corso 176. Shoes and boots for men and women.

Sac Joli, Via del Corso 154. Purses and an assortment of belts.

Skin, Via Crispi 41. The best in town for leather jackets, coats, and suits.

Tanino Crisci, Via Borgognona 4. Probably the best-quality handmade shoes in Rome.

Amadeo Perrone, Piazza di Spagna 92. Specializes in gloves.

MEN'S CLOTHING

Giorgio Armani, Via Babuino 102. Needless to say, carries clothes by the designer of the same name.

Carlo Palazzi, Via Borgognona 75. An ancient Roman palazzo turned into one of the most elegant men's shops in town.

Battistoni, Via Condotti 61A. Another expensive and classic men's clothing store in the courtyard of a Renaissance palazzo.

Testa, Via Frattina 104 and Via Borgognona 13. A reasonably priced shop especially noted for its suits and pants.

Roxy, Via Veneto 110. Silk ties at bargain prices.

Borsalino, Via IV Novembre 157B. The best hats—possibly in the world.

WOMEN'S CLOTHING

Missoni, Via Borgognona 38B. The best knitwear in Italy.

Elsy, Via del Corso 106. Good buys in ready-to-wear clothing.

Fiorucci, Via Nazionale 236A. Smart clothes for the trendy set.

Max Mara, Via Frattina 28. One of the best moderately priced but stylish shops.

Vanita, Via Frattina 70. The most luxurious undergarments and nightwear.

Valentino's Boutique, Via Bocca di Leone 15. This famous designer's ready-to-wear shop.

GIFTS AND HOUSEHOLD ITEMS

Bella Copia, Via dei Coronari 8. Handpainted pottery from all over Italy.

Richard Ginori, Via Condotti 87. The best porcelain, china, glass, and crystal.

Bulgari, Via Condotti 10. One of the world's greatest jewelers.

Pratesi, Piazza di Spagna 10. The most elegant and expensive bed linen in the world.

Pineider, Via Due Marcelli 68. Beautiful stationery and desk accessories.

Caesare, Via Barberini 1. Linens, towels, and lingerie, including custom-made terrycloth robes.

DRAWINGS AND PRINTS

Giuseppe Tanca, Via Salita de Crescenzi 10–12. Prints ranging from cheap to expensive.

Galleria Carlo Virgilio, Via della Lupa 9. Nineteenth- and twentieth-century drawings and watercolors.

BOOKS

The Economy Book Center, Piazza di Spagna. A large selection of new and used paperbacks.

The Lion Bookshop, Via del Babuino 181. The largest English-language bookstore, carrying a selection of books on all subjects, including many recent publications.

POSTCARDS

Piazza della Rotonda 69A. This miniscule shop (across from the Pantheon) has the biggest and best selection of new and old postcards and trinkets.

Index

AAA, 7
Accademia dei Lincei, 57
Accademia di S. Cecilia, 13
Accommodations, 7, 10, 16–17
Ackerman, James, 185
Acqua Felice, 101, 111
Acqua Paolo, 138, 181
  fountain for, 71
Acqua Virgine, 181
Airports, 17–18
Albergo della Catena, 97, 105
Albergo dell'Orso, 49–51
Albergo Portoghesi, 47
Albertoni family, 103, 108
Aldobrandini, Cardinal Pietro,
  91
American Embassy, 27
American Express Office, 25
Ameyden, Teodoro, 68
Angelica Library, 44
Anici family, 204
Antique Dealers League, 60, 61
Ara Pacis, 32
Architectural terms, glossary of,
  29
Arch of Constantine, 32, 33
Arch of Septimus Severus, 33
Arch of Titus, 115–16
Arcioni, Battista, 153
Arco dei Cappellari, 165
Arco dei Tolomei, 205
Arco della Pace, 63
Aretino, Pietro, 54
Arpacata, 154
Aurelian Walls, 33
Aventine Hill, 59, 217

Baglioni, Giovanni, 209
Balbus, Cornilius, 109
Ballet, 12
Banking and money, 25
Basilica Julia, 32
Basilica of Neptune, 41
Basilica Thermae, 33
Baths of Caracalla, 12, 33, 183,
  186

Beach, 13
Belli, Gioacchino, 200, 226
Bembo, Pietro, 53, 56
Bernini, Giovanni, 112, 170,
  178, 180
Bigio, Nanni Baccio, 112, 170
Blado, Antonio, 161
Books about Rome, 8–10
Borghese family, 125
Borromini, Francesco, 74, 75,
  143, 145, 146, 147, 148,
  179, 180
Bracciolini, Poggio, 136
Bramante, 62, 78, 162, 176, 178
Brill, Pomarancio Paul, 215
Buses, 17–19, 27

Caetani, Ersilia Lovatelli, 102
Cambio, Arnolfo di, 216
Camilla of Pisa, 54
Campidoglio, 13, 70, 87, 89, 102
Campo dei Fiori, 50–51, 67, 70,
  156–61, 163–64
Campo dei Fiori, neighborhood
  of (walk 3), 3–4, 131–85
Campus Martius, 32, 41, 43, 51,
  135, 163, 172, 194–95
Cancellieri, Francesco, 183
Capitoline Hill, 13, 87, 105, 116,
  160
Capitoline Museums, 14, 96,
  138, 150
Capo di Ferro, Cardinal Giro-
  lamo, 146, 147, 149, 150
Carafa, Cardinal Oliviero, 64,
  81, 83
Caravaggio, Polidoro da, 55, 56,
  165, 170–71
Carcere Mamertinus, 30
Carcere Nuovo, 176
Carcopino, Jerome, 187
Caro, Anibale, 163
Carracci, Agostino, 197
Carracci Gallery, 186–87
Casa dei Ponzani, 217
Casa dei Vallati, 128

Index

Casa di Fiammetta, 53, 54, 55
Casa di Lorenzo Manili, 119–20, 122, 125
Casoni, Felice Antonio, 71
Cassa Mattei, 202
Castel S. Angelo, 32
Catholic Church, 4, 33–34, 35, 37, 41, 102, 134–35, 139, 141, 162
   see also Vatican
Cato the Censor, 31
Cattanei, Vanozza, 164
Cavallini, Pietro, 216, 217
Cellini, Benvenuto, 70, 172–73, 174, 177, 184
Cenci family, 123–25
Chiavica de Santa Lucia, 172–73
Chigi, Agostino, 53, 63, 65, 75
"Childe Harold's Pilgrimage," 90, 148–49
Churches:
   Agonizzanti, 80–81
   Capuchin, 198
   S. Agnese, 214
   S. Agnese Fuori le Mura, 150
   S. Agostino, 53
   S. Andrea della Valle, 104
   S. Angelo in Pescheria, 98–100, 117
   S. Antonio dei Portoghesi, 45
   S. Bagio della Fossa, 67
   S. Bartolomeo, 196–98
   S. Benedetto in Piscinula, 202–3
   S. Caterina da Siena, 178
   S. Caterina dei Funari, 109–10
   S. Cecilia, 205, 211–17
   S. Eligio degli Orefici, 177–78
   S. Filippo Neri, 174
   S. Giorgio della Divina Pietà, 117, 129
   S. Giovanni in Ayno, 170
   S. Giovanni Calibata, 196
   S. Ivo, 179
   St. John the Lateran Basilica, 75
   S. Lorenzo Fuori le Mura, 98
   S. Lorenzo in Damaso, 152, 163
   S. Lorenzo in Prasino, 163
   S. Marcello, 143
   S. Maria della Concezione, 180
   S. Maria della Luce, 223–24
   S. Maria dell'Anima, 66, 174

S. Maria della Pace, 13, 62–66
S. Maria della Quercia, 150–51
S. Maria della Torte, 218
S. Maria della Vittoria, 170
S. Maria dell'Orazione e Morte, 180, 198
S. Maria dell'Orto, 207–9
S. Maria del Pianto, 121–22
S. Maria in Campitelli, 102, 103–4
S. Maria in Cappella, 219
S. Maria in Monserrato, 167–68, 178
S. Maria in Porticu, 103, 106
S. Nicola in Carcare, 89–91, 127
S. Paolo Basilica, 193
St. Peter's Basilica, 60, 75, 89, 136, 141, 167, 214
S. Pietro in Montorio, 125
S. Rocco, 45
S. Spirito, 177
S. Teresa, 170
S. Tommaso, 123–25
SS. Giovanni e Petronio dei Bolognesi, 183
SS. Simone e Guida, 70, 72
SS. Trinita dei Pellegrini, 142, 143
Ciampino airport, 18
Cibo, Franceschetto, 162
Cicala, Meliaduce, 207
Circus Maximus, 30
Circus of Flaminus, 3, 87, 122–23, 126
Clark, Eleanor, 2–3
Cloaca di Ponte, 172, 174
Cloaca Maxima, 30
Cola de Rienzo, 99–100
Collegio Ghislieri, 176
Colonna, Angelo Michele, 149
Colonna family, 71, 73, 95, 123
Colosseum, 32, 94, 149
Column of Marcus Aurelius, 33
Conca, Sebastiano, 215
Concerts, 12–13
Condulmer, Cardinal, 154–55
Confraternity of Butchers, 150, 151, 152
Convent of the Tor de' Spechhi, 105
Corcos, Salomon, 73
Corsini Picture Gallery, 125

Corso Vittorio Emanuele II, 95, 116, 174, 194
Cortegiana (Aretino), 54
Corte Savello, 165
Cortona, Pietro da, 63, 65, 66, 67, 143, 180
Cossa, Pietro, 76–77
Costa and Armanni, 126
Crime, 27–28

D'Annunzio, Gabriele, 112
De Acquis, 136
del Guernico, 58
d'Este, Cardinal Ippolito, 72
Dickens, Charles, 92, 94
Divine Comedy (Dante), 70
Domenichino, 114, 150
Domus Augustiana, 32
Doria Pamphili Gallery, 15
Dress, 8, 28

Easton, Adam, 215
Electrical adaptor, 8
Emergencies, 27
Esposizione Universale (EUR), 37
Exhibition of the Jewish Community of Rome, 126–27

Fabi family, 127
Fabricius, L., 191
Fairs and festivals, 13
Fanzago, Cosimo, 143
Fappa, Giambattista, 67
Fappa, Marcantonio, 67
Farnese family, 181, 183–87
Fesch, Cardinal, 47, 179
Fiammetta Michaelis, 53, 54, 56
Fiesole, Mino da, 215
Filippo, 127
Films, 12
Foncelli, C., 65
Fontana, Carlo, 143, 210–11
Fontana, Giovanni, 137
Fontana, Luigi, 170
Fontana Paolina, 138
Fontinius, 136
Food and drink, 20–23
Foro Boario, 87
Foro Holitorium, 3
Foro Olitorio, 87, 88
Forteguerri, Cardinal, 215
Forum, 89, 116, 172
Forum of Augustus, 32
Francesi, Pietro Paolo, 173

Frangipane family, 45, 46
Franz, Roesler, 181, 226
Fregene, 13
French and Italian Notebook (Dickens), 92
Fuga, Ferdinando, 180, 211, 215

Galleria Borghese, 14
Galleria Spada, 15, 148
Gambirasi, Donato, 67
Gentileschi, Orazio, 66, 91
Ghiberti, Lorenzo, 216
Gianicolo Hill, 138, 200, 205
Giaquinto, Corrado, 209
Gibbs, John, 65
Glossary of architectural terms, 28–29
Gnoli, 164
Goethe, Johann Wolfgang von, 74–75, 93, 94
Goffredo Mameli school, 221
Grande, Antonio del, 176
Gregorovius, 34–35, 117, 118–19, 121, 180, 191, 216
Guidetti, Guido, 109, 208

Hall of One Hundred Days, 162–63
Hare, Augustus, 142, 200
Hawthorne, Nathaniel, 45–46
Hectostylon (Hall of One Hundred Columns), 154, 163
Heemskerck, Martin van, 79
History of Rome, 30–37, 115–18, 133, 192–96
see also individual sites
Hotel reservations, 7, 10, 16–17
Hudson, Roderick, 201

ICCROM, 211
Il Male, 161
Imperia, 53–54
Institute of Roman Studies, 75
International Driving Permit, 7
Italian Consulate, 7
Italian Government Travel Office, 7
Italian Notebooks (Goethe), 74–75

James, Henry, 201
Jewish Ghetto, 141
history of, 115–18
walk 2, 2–3, 85–129

Index

Lancellotti, Cardinal Scipione, 58

Landini,Taddeo, 111

Largo Moretta, 172–74

Leonardo da Vinci airport,17–18

Lepidus, M. Aemilius, 198

Longhi, Martino, 45

Longhi the Elder, Martino, 74, 143

Ludovisi, Bernardino, 143

Luna, Isabella de, 110

Lungotevere de' Cenci, 191

Lungotevere degli Anguillara, 201, 202

Lungotevere dei Tebald, 133, 139

Maderno, Carlo, 58, 111, 168, 178

Maderno, Stefano, 66, 214, 216

Mameli, Goffredo, 143

Manili, Lorenzo, 119–20, 122, 125

Margani, Giovanni, 106–8

Margani, Ludevico, 153

Mascarino, Ottaviano, 183

Mascherone fountain, 181

Masson, Georgina, 195

Mattei family, 110–14, 117, 122, 202

Maturino da Firenze, 55, 56, 165, 170–71

Mausoleum of Augustus, 32

Mazzoni, Giulio, 146, 147, 149–50

Medical emergencies, 27

Medici Venus, 97

Meleagro, 111

Mendelssohn, Moses, 117

Meridian Gallery, 150

Metellus, Quintus, 97

Michelangelo, 109, 178, 181, 185

Mignanelli family, 147

Milesi, Antonio, 56

Mitelli, Agostino, 149

Money and banking, 25

Monte di Pietà, 61

Monte Giordano, 70, 71

Monte Mario, 70

Monte Savello, 94

Moro, Aldo, 110

Museo Nazionale Romano, 14

Museum of Rome, 15, 83, 137

Music, 12–13

Mussolini, Benito, 37, 58, 59, 83, 88, 174

Napoleon, 36, 47, 72, 82, 118, 179

Nardini, Cardinal Stefano, 78

National Gallery of Ancient Art, 15

National Gallery of Modern Art, 15

National Museum of the Villa Giulia, 14–15

Neri, S. Filippo, 74, 142–43, 174

Newspapers, 12

New York Times, The, 72–73

Opera, 12

Oratorio, 74–75

Oratory of the Sacconi Rossi, 198

Orsini family, 68–71, 72, 95, 129, 153, 154, 159

Ospizio di S. Michele, 210–11, 218

Ostia, 13, 193, 200, 201, 208

Palatine Hill, 30, 32

Palazzetto Sassi, 79

Palazzetto Spada, 144–45

Palazzo Albertoni Spinola, 103, 105

Palazzo Altemps, 52

Palazzo Antonio Massimo, 48–49

Palazzo Boncompagni, 73, 76

Palazzo Capizucchi, 104, 105

Palazzo Capponi, 168

Palazzo Cavalletti, 103

Palazzo Cenci, 122–23, 125

Palazzo Chiovenda, 61–62

Palazzo Cisterna, 178–79

Palazzo Corsetti, 171–72

Palazzo Costaguti, 114

Palazzo degli Signori di Marino, 72

Palazzo degli Stabilimento Spagnoli, 178

Palazzo dei Duchi di Bracciano, 71

Palazzo Delfini, 108–9

Palazzo della Cancelleria, 161–63

Palazzo dello S. Spirito, 74

Palazzo di S. Agostino, 44

Palazzo Falconieri, 179–80

Palazzo Farnese, 180, 181, 183–87
Palazzo Flamino Panzio, 105
Palazzo Fonseca, 80
Palazzo Gadi, 55–56, 57
Palazzo Gambirasi, 66–67
Palazzo Giangiacomo, 167
Palazzo Lancellotti, 57, 58
Palazzo Lovatelli, 102
Palazzo Maccarani, 106
Palazzo Mattei Giove, 110, 111–14, 126
Palazzo Montoro, 166
Palazzo Nardini, 77–78, 121
Palazzo of the Conti di Pitigliano, 72
Palazzo Orsini, 95, 129
Palazzo Ossoli, 151–52
Palazzo Pio, 155
Palazzo Pocci (later Pallavicini), 168–70
Palazzo Ricci, 53, 170–71, 177
Palazzo Sachetti, 177
Palazzo Salmoni Albertischi, 140–41, 144
Palazzo Santacroce, 120–21
Palazzo Spada, 145–50, 179
Palazzo Taverna, 71–73
Palazzo Turci, 78, 79
Palazzo Varese, 178
Palazzo Velli, 106
Palazzo Venezia Museum, 15–16
Pantheon, 32, 41
Papal audience, 13–14
Pasquino, 81–83
Passport, 7, 25, 27
Patrizi family, 166–67
Pepin, 34, 133
Perugino, 215
Peruzzi, Baldassare, 62, 66, 71, 95, 116, 144, 151, 177
Piazza Campitelli, 102–5, 108, 120
Piazza Campo dei Fiori, 50–51, 67, 70, 156–61, 163–64
Piazza Capizucchi, 105–6
Piazza Capo di Ferro, 145–50
Piazza Costaguti, 119, 120
Piazza dei Mercanti, 217
Piazza del Biscione, 153–56
    Teatro di Pompeo, 153–55
Piazza del Campidoglio, 109
Piazza del Drago, 224

Piazza del Fico, 67
Piazza della Cancelleria, 161–63
Piazza della Quercia, 150–51
Piazza dell'Orologio, 74
Piazza del Paradiso, 155
Piazza del Popolo, 23
Piazza del Progresso, 122, 126
Piazza di Monte Savallo, 129
Piazza de Montevecchio, 61–62
Piazza di Pasquino, 80–83
Piazza di S. Cecilia, 211, 217
Piazza di S. Ignazio, 151
Piazza di Spagna, 51
Piazza di Tor Sanguigna, 52
Piazza Farnese, 164
Piazza Fiammetta, 52, 54
Piazza Giudea, 116, 117, 121–22
Piazza in Piscinula, 199, 201–4, 226
Piazza Lovatelli, 109
Piazza Margana, 106–8
Piazza Mattei, 115
Piazza Montanara, 59, 93
Piazza Monte di Pietà, 61
Piazza Navona, 52, 83, 116
Piazza Navona area, 13, 23
    walk 1, 2, 39–83
Piazza Ricci, 170
Piazza S. Angelo in Pescheria, 100–101, 120
Piazza S. Bartolomeo, 196–98
Piazza S. Carlo Cairoli, 123
Piazza S. Maria, 23
Piazza S. Maria della Pace, 63–66, 67
Piazza S. Maria del Pianto (Piazza Guidea), 116, 117, 121–22
Piazza S. Pantaleo, 137
Piazza S. Simone, 58–60
Piazza Trilussa, 133, 136, 137, 138
    fountain at, 137–38, 139
Piazza Trinità dei Pellegrini, 61, 141–44
    church and hospice at, 142–43
Piazza Venezia, 120
Pierleoni family, 94–95
Pier Luigi da Palestrina, 177
Pinelli, Achilli, 170
Pio di Carpi family, 155
Piombo, Sebastiano del, 65
Piovano, Vincenzo, 51

Pisano, Guidotto, 91
Platina, 133
Pliny, 98, 154, 155, 172, 196
Podocatori, Monsignor, 172
Pompey, 153–54, 159, 163
Pons Janiculensi, 136, 138–39
Ponte Cestio, 94, 200, 224
Ponte Fabricius, 116, 191, 198
Ponte Garibaldi, 191, 193
Pontelli, Baccio, 207
Ponte Palatino, 192, 199
Ponte Rotto, 191, 198
Ponte S. Angelo, 50, 123, 136
Ponte Sisto, 133, 136, 137, 138, 174–76, 181
Porta, Giacomo della, 91, 102, 103, 104, 111, 117, 122, 179, 180, 181, 185–86, 209
Portichetto de Via della Consolazione, 88–89
Portico di Filippo, 127
Portico d'Ottavia, 3, 32, 87, 97–98, 115, 116, 123, 127, 128, 199
Posi, Paolo, 178
Post office, 24–25
Purpureo, Lucius Furius, 195

Ragionamenti (Aretino), 54
Raguzzini, Filippo, 151, 174
Rainaldi, Carlo, 45
Rainaldi, Girolamo, 103–4
Raphael, 53, 65, 112, 177, 178, 209
Reni, Guido, 125, 215
Restaurants, 20–23, 227–31
Riario, Cardinal, 162, 163
Riario family, 162
Ricci family, 171
Rienzo, Cola di, 70
Rione Campitelli, 101, 105
Rione Parione, 42, 77–83
Rione Ponte, 42, 44–77
Rione S. Eustachio, 42–44
Ripando, Jacopo, 56
Rodd, Lord Rennel, 179
Romana, Francesco, 105
Roman Elegies (Goethe), 93
Rome and a Villa (Clark), 2–3
Romulus and Remus, 30, 170, 193
Rondinini, Francesco Cavalletti, 103
Rossi, Giangiancomo di, 44, 66

Rossi, Pellegrino, 162
Ruggeri, G. B., 150

St. Cecilia, 211–14
St. Ignatius, 108, 109, 110
Salvi, Nicola, 45
Sanctis, Francesco de, 143
Sangallo, Antonio, 184–85
Sangallo the Younger, Antonio da, 65–66, 151, 168, 177
Santacroce family, 120–21, 123
Savelli, Pandolfo, 91
Savelli family, 95, 165
Schor, Cristoforo, 45
Septimius Severus, 98
Sermoneta, Sicciolante da, 66
Servian Wall, 30
Severan Marbles, 122–23, 126
Shopping, 25–26, 231–34
Spada, Virgilio, 74
Spada family, 144–45, 147, 148, 149
Spark, Muriel, 72–73
Stadium of Domitian, 52
Statue of Fiordano Bruno, 160–61
Statue of Hercules, 155
Statue of Pompey, 148–49
Stazione Termini, 18
Strabo, 135
Subway, 19–20
Symon, Arthur, 66
Synagogue on Via Catalana, 126–27

Tassi, Agostino, 58
Taxis, 17, 19
Teatro Apollo, 57
Teatro dell'opera, 12
Teatro di Marcello, 3, 70, 87, 91–92, 93–96, 105, 116, 123, 127, 129
Teatro di Pompeo, 149, 153–55, 159
Teatro di Tor di Nona, 57
Telegraph, 24
Telephones, 24
Tempietto del Carmello, 120
Temple of Aesculapius, 195, 196, 197
Temple of Apollo, 96, 105
Temple of Faunus, 195
Temple of Janus, 96, 105
Temple of Juno Regina, 97, 101

Temple of Jupiter, 195
Temple of Jupiter Capitolinus, 30
Temple of Jupiter Stator, 97
Temple of Mars, 32
Temple of Venus and Roma, 32
Temple of Venus Victrix, 153–54, 159
Theater of Balbus, 109, 110, 125, 126
Thermae of Agrippa, 41
Thermae of Diocletian, 33
Tiber, island on the, 13, 94, 180, 189–226
Tiber River, 41, 46, 51, 68, 70, 87, 115, 117, 123, 134, 135, 136, 137, 180, 191, 192–95, 200
Tipping, 23
Torre della Contessa, 196
Torre della Scimmia, 45–47
Tours, 13
Traffic, 28, 143
Trains, 18
Transportation, 17–20
Trastavere, 70, 94, 115, 136
  southern, and island of Tiber (walk 4), 2, 4, 191–226
Triumphal Arch of Titus, 32
Tulia d'Aragona, 54
Turtle Fountain, 111–12, 202

Vallicelliana Library, 75
Valvassare, Gabrieli, 209, 224
Vanni, Raphael, 66
Vanvitelli, Luigi, 45, 215
Vasari, Giorgio, 163, 165, 170–71
Vatican, 37, 41, 42, 44, 50, 60, 122, 134, 148, 153, 162, 164, 174, 176, 184, 187
Vatican Museums, 14, 47
Via Anicia, 205–9, 223
Via Arco dei Tolomei, 223
Via Augusto Jandolo, 219
Via Babuino, 47
Via Balestrari, 160
Via Caetani, 110–11
Via Capizucchi, 105
Via Capo di Ferro, 140–41, 144–45
  no. 10, 145
  no. 12, 145
Via Catalana, 126

Via degli Acquasparta, 52–53
Via degli Orsini, 73
Via dei Balestrari, 151–53, 157
  no. 8, 152
  no. 15, 152
  no. 42–43, 152
Via dei Banchi Vecchi, 172
Via dei Cappellari, 47, 164–65, 166, 176
  no. 29–30, 165
  no. 61–62, 163
  no. 127–130, 164
Via dei Coronari, 47, 59, 60–61, 179
  no. 30–32, 61
Via dei Delfini, 108–9
Via dei Funari, 109–10, 111–14
  no. 19, 112–14
Via dei Genovesi, 205, 220
Via dei Gigli d'Oro, 49
Via dei Giubbonari, 153, 160
Via dei Greci, Sala Accademia di, 13
Via dei Pettinari, 139–40, 143, 144, 166
  no. 39–40, 139–40
  no. 56, 140
  no. 79–80, 140
Via dei Portoghesi, 41, 42, 43
Via dei Salumi, 220–23, 224
Via dei Soldati, 51–52
Via dei Tre Archi, 55
Via dei Vascellari, 219–20
Via del Babuino, 179
Via del Biscione, 155
Via del Cancello, 48
Via del Collegio Capranica, 60
Via del Corallo, 77
Via del Corso, 143
Via del Curato, 60
Via del Foro Olitario, 87, 88, 91
Via del Foro Pescario, 33, 99
Via del Governo Vecchio, 73, 74, 75–80, 81
  no. 12–13, 76
  no. 14–17, 76
  no. 66, 80
  no. 91, 80
  no. 96, 80
  no. 104, 80
  no. 118, 78, 79
  no. 121, 78, 79
Via della Barchetta, 168
Via della Chiesa Nuova, 77

Index

Via della Conciliazione, Auditorio di, 13
Via della Luce, 223–24
Via della Lungaretta, 224–26
Via della Madonna dell'Orto, 209–10
Via della Maschera d'Oro, 55–58
  no. 7, 56
  no. 9, 56
Via dell'Anima, 66
Via della Pace, 66–67
Via della Palomba, 48
Via dell'Arco dei Tolomei, 204–5
Via dell'Arco della Pace, 62–63, 66
Via della Reginella, 114–15, 127
Via della Scrofa, 41, 42, 43–47
Via della Tribuna di Tor de' Speechi, 105, 106
Via delle Botteghe Oscure, 110
Via delle Coppele, 60
Via dell'Impero, 83
Via dell'Orso, 47–51
Via del Mascherone, 181–87
Via del Pellegrino, 161, 163–64, 173, 174
Via del Portico d'Ottavia, 97–101, 115, 118–20, 121, 127–29
  no. 8–11, 127
  no. 12–15, 127
  no. 25, 127
Via del Porto, 217
Via del Progresso, 122
Via del Teatro di Marcello, 87, 88, 89–96
Via del Tiempo, 127
Via di Grotta Pina, 155
Via di Monte Brianzo, 50
Via di Monte Fiore, 224
Via di Monte Giordano, 67–68, 70, 71, 73, 76
  no. 4–6, 68
  no. 7–9, 68
Via di S. Ambrogio, 127
Via di S. Eligio, 177–78
Via di S. Michele, 211
Via di S. Pantaleo, 83
Via Giulia, 47, 137, 139, 145, 164, 165, 174–81
Via in Piscinula, 203, 221
Via in Publicolis, 120–21

Via Lancellotti, 58
Via Monserrato, 164, 165, 167–70, 171–72, 173, 177
  no. 17, 168
Via Monte Savallo, 129
Via Montoro, 166–67
Via Paganica, 110
Via S. Agostino, 60
Via S. Ambroglio, 115
Via S. Maria Calderari, 125–26
Via S. Maria del Pianto, 121
Via Titta Scarpetta, 221
Via Tribuna di Campitelli, 97, 101–5
Via Zanardelli, 52
Vicolo degli Osti, 66
Vicolo dei Cencei, 116
Vicolo dei Tabacchi, 207
Vicolo del Bollo, 165
Vicolo del Buco, 224
Vicolo del Gallo, 164
Vicolo del Giglio, 152
Vicolo della Madonnella, 145
Vicolo della Pace, 66
Vicolo dell'Atleta, 220
Vicolo dell'Avila, 76
Vicolo dell'Orso, 48
Vicolo del Malpasso, 174
Vicolo del Montaccio, 68
Vicolo di Montevecchio, 61
Vicolo di S. Maria in Cappella, 218–19
Vicolo di S. Simone, 57
Vicolo Monte dei Cenci, 122–25
Vicolo S. Trifone, 55
Vicolo Savelli, 80
Victor Emmanuel, 36
Vignola, Giacomo da, 144, 151, 184, 208
Villa Ada Park, 13
Villa Borghese, 13
Villa Borghese Park, 125
Villa Caprarola, 184
Villa de' Medici, 57
Visa, 7
Viterbo, Antonio da, 215
Vittorio Emanuele III, 37, 58, 79, 83
Volterra, Francesco da, 58, 209

Warning, word of, 27–28
Weather, 7–8

Zuccari, Frederico, 209